Food and Wine Northwest Style

Matching the wonderful foods and wines of the Pacific Northwest

GILDA BARROW-ZIMMAR & CHUCK HILL

SPEED GRAPHICS
Seattle, Washington, USA

Credits:
Front cover photograph by Jim Mears
Food styling by Christy Nordstrom Foodesigns

Original illustrations by Sandy Haight

Other graphics assistance: Colleen Higgins
Editorial assistance: Virginia Buterbaugh
Back cover photograph assisted by Ted Jordan Meredith

Published by Speed Graphics,
17919 2nd Avenue Northwest, Seattle, Washington 98177
(206) 546-8523

Printed in the United States of America
ISBN 0-9617699-3-9

To David and David, Jr.,
Barbara and Andy.
Thanks for your patience, love
and encouragement.

Table of Contents

ॐ

Appetizers, First Courses
& Others

Entrées

Desserts

ॐ

Acknowledgments

A special thank you to our many friends who submitted recipes for use in *Food and Wine Northwest Style*.

Amity Vineyards - Gewürztraminer Garlic Toast
Myron Redford & Vikki Wetle

Anthony's HomePort - Chargrilled Halibut
Executive Chef Sally McArthur

Bethel Heights Vineyard - Halibut Kebabs
Marilyn Webb

Bonair Winery - Hot and Spicy Shrimp
Gail & Shirley Puryear

Cameron Winery - Flank Steak Salsa
John Paul & Teri Wadsworth

Cascade Mountain Cellars - Raspberry Walnut Tart
Juergen & Julia Grieb

Cedarbrook Herb Farm - Tarragon Sour Cream Dip
Dorothy Rogers & Karman McReynolds

Chateau Benoit - Pesto Chèvre Bread
Fred & Mary Benoit

Chateau Gallant - Cherry Marzipan Tart
Dave & Mary Gallant

Chinook Winery - Smoked Salmon Spread
Clay Mackey & Kay Simon

Covey Run Vintners - Stuffed Chicken Breasts
Mary Jane Willard

Elliott's Oyster House - Northwest Crab Feed
Tony Casad & Jon Rowley

The Emerald of Siam - Emerald Butterflies
Ravadi Quinn

Enoteca Restaurant - Pan-Fried Curried Oysters
Chef Leslie Dillon

Facelli Winery - Rabbit Merlot
Lou & Sandy Facelli

Fullers Restaurant at the Seattle Sheraton Hotel & Towers
Phyllo Purses with Wild Mushrooms
Executive Chef Caprial Pence

The Hogue Cellars - Spit-Roasted Leg of Lamb
Shyla Hogue

The Hunt Club at the Sorrento Hotel
Venison Medallions with Garlic Cream
Executive Chef Barbara Figueroa

Latah Creek Wine Cellars - Pork Tenderloin
Mike & Ellena Conway

Le Tastevin - Poached Pears with Raspberry Couli and
Chocolate Sauce, Jacques Boiroux & Emile Ninaud

Lost Mountain Winery - Fisherman's Soup
Romeo Conca

Mercer Ranch Vineyards - Butterflied Leg of Lamb
Don & Linda Mercer

Mont Elise Vineyards - Canard Beaujolais
Elizabeth Tross-Deamer

Montinore Vineyards - Szechwan Pork with Broccoli
Jeff Lamy

Nick's Italian Cafe - Pesto Hazelnut Lasagna
Nick Peirano

Oak Knoll Winery - Stuffed Grape Leaves
Marj Vuylsteke

Pacifica Restaurant - Beef Tournedos with Blue Cheese
and Cabernet Sauce, John & Kristi Jorgensen

Preston Wine Cellars - Chocolate-Merlot Dipped
Strawberries, Cathy Preston-Mouncer

Quilceda Creek Vintners - Grilled New York Steaks
with Parsley Beurre Blanc, Alex & Jeanette Golitzin

Ray's Boathouse - Mixed Nut Tart, Grilled Scallops with
Fresh Herbs, Executive Chef Wayne Ludvigsen

Rose Creek Vineyards - Summer Vichyssoise
Jamie & Susan Martin

Saddle Mountain Winery - Chicken Tarragon
Julie Rose

Ste. Chapelle Vineyards - Wheeler's Supreme Chili
Kathy Symms Mertz

The Shoalwater Restaurant - Grilled Pacific Salmon
with Cranberry Blueberry Mustard, Tony Kischner

Sooke Harbour House - Sautéed Oysters with Lemon
Balm & Nasturtiums, Sinclair Philips

Stewart Vineyards - Mussels Marinara
Susan Killermann

The Stonehedge Inn - Huckleberry Tart
Chef Patrick Edwards

Tyee Wine Cellars - Hazelnut Cookies
Dave & Margy Buchanan

Veritas Vineyards - Veal Marengo
John & Diane Howieson

Woodward Canyon Winery - Grapewood-Grilled
Salmon with Lettuce Sauce, Rick & Darcey Small

Yarrow Bay Grill and Beach Cafe
Corn and Dungeness Crab Chowder
Chef John Kemnitzer

Introduction

Northwest Style

In titling this book *Food and Wine Northwest Style*, we knew that sooner or later we would have to formulate our definition of what Northwest Style really is. Other regional cookbook authors have found it a simple task to assign their regional specialties to a particular category – Louisiana Cajun and Creole or Texas "Tex-Mex" are both styles that readily bring to mind a banquet-full of recipe ideas, along with matching party favors and decorations.

The Northwest culinary style may seem equally simple from an outsider's view, but those who live here have seen a remarkable evolution that has taken our local ingredients to great new heights. No longer are we limited to the "101 ways to cook salmon" style of entertaining. Indeed our population has come from all parts of the United States and from overseas – both Atlantic and Pacific. Influences to our "regional" style of cooking include those from Europe and Asia and everything in-between.

There are, however, ties that bind our region and our residents into one culinary whole. A dedication to fresh local ingredients is perhaps the most basic tenet to which Northwest cooks subscribe. Whether preparing a complicated, imaginative dinner using fresh herbs, meats and vegetables or simply slicing a succulent peach, fresh from the Yakima Valley for an afternoon snack, we revel in the opportunities provided by Mother Nature and our hardworking, dedicated producers.

A willingness to "agree to disagree" may seem a silly way to unify a group of hedonists, but, indeed, the easygoing nature of Northwestern life eventually mellows the most radical "Type A" geographic transplant. In food, we can equally appreciate simple traditional dishes prepared as they have been for centuries (using local products makes them just a bit better!) and new wave combinations of flavors and textures that push the envelope of culinary tradition to extraordinary new dimensions.

So we celebrate the stereotypes hung upon Northwesterners as those with webbed feet who rust instead of tan. Our recipes are truly of Northwest style, created in the Northwest tradition of sharing the best from home and abroad. Whether you enjoy the simplicity of cracked Dungeness crab with a salad and fresh bread or an elegant dinner party with a leg of lamb and a fancy dessert, we've included the recipes you need to join us in our celebration.

Northwest Wine

When the Northwest table is set, it often includes a wine glass. A fierce loyalty to locally produced wines runs through the veins of many residents, while those who have sampled the best from Europe and California cannot help but remark on how well our Northwest bottlings accompany a wide range of foods. This is another factor that is rapidly being discovered by the entire country. Our wines match well with foods – especially foods prepared with care and thought from fresh local ingredients.

The importance of fine wine accompanying fine cuisine is a personal thing. Many of our friends have wine with virtually every evening meal. Finding the right wine to match with a particular food preparation is an enjoyable intellectual challenge that requires not only a keen mind but a keen palate and memory of past enological encounters.

In preparing this book, we have discovered the versatility of wines made in the Northwest and we have marveled at their affinity for all types of foods. Styles are still emerging in this infant region and, like wine itself, the Northwest more and more shows itself as a living entity, growing and evolving with the years.

We feel that Northwest wines are best enjoyed with the native foods – and vice versa. From a steaming bowl of Fisherman's soup (far greater a statement than simple Cioppino!) to grilled Columbia River Salmon to a freshly baked tart highlighting Northwest fruit, one can find no greater reason to open a bottle of local wine and relax in the confidence that the marriage will succeed.

Many articles and books have been written about Northwest cooking and ingredients to show the way for aspiring gourmets both here and abroad to appreciate the bounty of the region. Unfortunately, little homage has been paid to the stemmed glass next to the dinner plate. We want to illuminate this pathway to complete enjoyment by providing the information necessary to match the best in food and wine.

Each recipe in this book is matched with a particular Northwest wine. Sometimes there is latitude in selecting an alternative such as substituting one Chardonnay for another, but many times the particular wine called for is indeed the quintessential foil for the dish prepared. Experimentation in this area is encouraged.

Recipes and Ingredients

Our recipes have come from varied sources with more than half being of our own creation (Gilda's). The suggestions and complete recipes received from winemakers, innkeepers and chefs have been exhaustively tested and their sources queried when things didn't seem quite right. Pride in presenting versatile, durable and delicious preparations was an important factor in the selection process. You can rest assured that each recipe on these pages will turn out well.

There are recipes here that take just seconds to prepare and there are those that require culinary gymnastics worthy of any food professional's best efforts. The best results come from following instructions exactly and using impeccably fresh ingredients.

The freshness of Northwest ingredients is paramount to creating the best quality preparations. Many chefs have chosen to relocate to this area just for the experience and pleasure of utilizing farm fresh produce, local game and the world famous Northwest seafood in their culinary efforts. The same pleasure comes to the home chef who can shop at local farmers' markets and can find the most accommodating grocery stores and specialty food shops.

All of our recipes were created and tested with fresh local ingredients as we cooked through the seasons for an entire year. Take advantage of the calendar and have sautéed oysters in January, Ellensburg lamb in April, and one of our fresh fruit tarts for a delicious summer finale. The changing seasons provide a wealth of creative cooking opportunities.

A Note About Grilling

A Northwest tradition during the warmer months is cooking outdoors on the barbecue. Perhaps it's a symptom of being cooped up during the winter or just a desire for the juicy, smoky flavors that only grilling can provide. We offer many recipes in this book that will keep your grill busy all during the spring, summer and fall, so take advantage of the good weather, whenever it comes around, to enjoy this popular, flavor-enhancing cooking method.

Wine and Food

Once again, we are strong advocates of enjoying local wines with the foods of our region. If you're a Northwesterner, then you have many reasons to rejoice. If you're from outside the area, come and visit! We know you will return home with wonderful memories of fine meals and fine wines.

Northwest Wines with Food

The grape wines that are produced in the Northwest are mostly from varietals that originated in France. Cuttings found their way to California in the 1850s and then were brought north to Oregon and Washington during the 20th century. Some plantings of vitis vinifera (wine grapes as opposed to Concord species) in Eastern Washington date back to the 1930s and 1940s, although most vines currently in production were planted from the late 1960s to the present. Oregon grape growing for winemaking began seriously in 1961 when Richard Sommer of Hillcrest Winery planted vines in the Umpqua Valley. Soon after, David Lett of The Eyrie planted his first vineyard in Yamhill County near the town of Dundee. These small beginnings have led to a successful and well-respected Northwest wine industry producing wines from many grape types.

The following discussion of varietals and their resulting wines should prove useful in categorizing Northwest wines for accompanying selected foods. Further detail is provided with each recipe and each recommended wine.

Cabernet Sauvignon

This is the king of red grapes grown in Washington, Southern Oregon and Idaho, and offers the most full-bodied red wines with great intensity and character. Not coincidentally, it also has the most potential for gaining complexity and elegance with cellaring. The wines are most often rich ruby in color with inky opacity in the most intense bottlings. Aromas of black currants, raspberries, cherries, spice, coffee, chocolate and mint are often detected. In the most intense versions, the palate is sometimes closed-in when young, yielding a pleasant drinking wine only after several years of aging in the cellar.

Cabernet is the quintessential accompaniment to preparations featuring beef, lamb and game. Rich and hearty sauces, heavy with tomato, garlic and spices, often require the strength of a good Cabernet to make a pleasant match. Cabernet is offered occasionally with dessert by those who prefer intense chocolate preparations accompanied by a wine rich in berry flavor with complementing notes of coffee and cocoa.

Chardonnay

This most popular white wine grape continues to have an identity crisis in the hands of many Northwest winemakers. The questions of barrel fermentation, oak aging and malolactic fermentation (the combination of which yields a smooth and toasty wine, rich with vanilla and butterscotch on the palate) are countered by those who ferment in stainless steel, give a short treatment of oak aging and thus produce a fruitier wine with aromas of green apples and toast with crisp acidity on the palate. Some argue that the latter version is more of a "food wine," but if you ask the wine buyer from your favorite restaurant, he or she will tell you that people vastly prefer the smoother, toastier styles. Many winemakers in the Northwest have labored over this dilemma of providing the public with a "correct" wine to accompany food and then not being able to sell it. It seems that a version somewhere between the two is the answer and, indeed, we are seeing wines now that are well-balanced in this fashion.

Chardonnay is the white wine of choice among the "in crowd" and, as mentioned above, most of the "in crowd" prefer the toasty oak and vanilla of a barrel-fermented version. The best of these are "reserve" bottlings that offer powerful oak, powerful fruit, crisp acidity and a powerful price. They not only accompany lighter dishes but will also stand up to light meats and hearty sauces. Less pricey Chardonnays vinted in a not-so-oaky style are very good wines to accompany chicken and many types of seafood. They also can handle pasta with light sauces and work well with cheeses and fruits.

Chenin Blanc

A prolific producer in the vineyard, large crops of Chenin Blanc find their way (along with Riesling) into the bulk wines labeled white table wine and other low-priced proprietary blends. Several winemakers, however, have a fondness for this varietal that keeps it from disappearing forever into a vat of vin ordinaire. Seeking out the best of these is an easy task because they always take the medals at wine competitions both locally and across the country. Properly handled, the wines offer rich fruit aromas of apples and pears, along with a vanilla character that is utterly charming.

Crisp acids, moderated by slight residual sweetness, make the palate of many Chenin Blancs as enjoyable as the aromas.

The wines described previously are excellent accompaniments to appetizers and light meals. Served chilled, they provide relief on summer days and accompany picnic fare as well as any white wine can. The bonus of fruity complexity and a pleasant, lingering finish keeps this wine on the list of the Northwest's best values and undiscovered treasures.

Gamay

The name Gamay Beaujolais has appeared on numerous Northwest bottlings during the past decade and none of them, according to grape experts in the know, were made from the true grape of Beaujolais, Gamay Noir a jus blanc. Only since 1988 has wine been made from this authentic varietal grown in Oregon by Myron Redford of Amity Vineyards. The wine labeled Gamay Beaujolais over the years has been the Gamay clone of Pinot Noir. A delightful wine in its own right, but not the real McCoy.

When it comes to matching food to these wines, it is less critical that a distinction be made. Both are fruity and forward with aromas of ripe berries and spice. They tend to have refreshing acidity on the palate making them ideal partners for light meats, picnic fare and for simple sipping with appetizers.

Gewürztraminer

Much harder to say than to enjoy, Northwest Gewürztraminer continues to hold the attention of some of our region's best winemakers. The wine offers the classic aromas of lychees and spice and an off-dry palate that is easy to sip and works well with many styles of cuisine.

The tendency of the Gewürztraminer grape to develop a soft skin when ripe leads to many wines with a slightly bitter aftertaste. To many this may seem a flaw, but to the food lover it provides just the right component to stand up to a remarkable array of unlikely partners. Asian cuisine, if not too fiery, makes a great match as does smoked fish and lighter meats. Don't overlook this delicious Northwest specialty when seeking an unusual wine with outstanding culinary credentials.

Grenache

Once relegated to blush proprietary wines and a red varietal "that your grandmother will like," the Rhone Valley origins of Grenache have recently stimulated several Northwest wineries to make characterful versions of great style. Though never a hearty, heavy wine like Cabernet, Grenache offers finesse and elegance with intriguing aromas of cherries and spice, along with herbal notes and just enough tannin on the palate to accompany a wide variety of entrées.

If you throw a little Grenache into your seafood stew, you've just made the connection between red wine and fish. Grill some chicken, veal or game and watch this plucky varietal show its earthy origins. A very versatile performer with Northwest specialties, Grenache hasn't won an Oscar yet, but it will soon.

Lemberger

(Also spelled Limberger.) This red grape from northern Europe has attracted more attention in Washington then it ever did in Germany. Washington Lembergers are fresh and fruity with aromas of cherry and vanilla. The palate is balanced and well-structured with moderate acidity and tannin.

Lemberger best accompanies foods from the grill, gaining complexity from the smoky, grilled flavors and balancing the aftertaste with its firm palate. Several versions are crafted by Yakima Valley wineries with some being rich and full-bodied and some light and fruity.

Merlot

Many feel that Washington's Merlot will someday eclipse Cabernet as the red wine star of the Evergreen State. Certainly as a wine that is approachable at an early age, it has already done just that. The ripe plum and cherry aromas of Merlot invite the taster to come hither and enjoy the palate of voluptuous fruit, often edged with just a hint of the vanilla component that comes with oak aging. There is certainly a wide variety of styles produced in the Northwest ranging from lighter, almost Beaujolais-like versions to rich and complex wines truly designed to give the best Cabernets a run for their money. One winery was intending to try "carbonic maceration" (the Beaujolais system of whole berry, closed-fermenter, fermentation) with Merlot, but the demand for Merlot grapes kept the prices too high for that type of experimentation. Unless this varietal somehow loses popularity, it will almost always be made as a full-bodied red wine and priced accordingly.

With food, Merlot makes a nice background to many dishes where Cabernet would dominate the subtle flavors. Velvety and soft, the varietal caresses the palate and marries well with meats and richly sauced dishes. This same feminine quality allows experimentation with poultry and veal – especially on the grill. Absolutely a first-rate wine for times when the barbecue is at center stage.

Müller-Thurgau

A cross of Riesling and Sylvaner, in Germany this grape produces copious quantities of wine sold as Liebfraumilch. In the Northwest, Müller-Thurgau is taken more seriously and several wineries make well-balanced versions with aromas of flowers and herbs and off-dry palates suited to casual sipping or accompanying light foods.

Muscat

Although easier to say, this wine suffers some of the same problems of identity as Gewürztraminer. Dry styles have been tried, late harvest versions have seduced those with a sweet tooth, but it appears that the off-dry style will win out in the end. These delectable and uncomplicated wines, with delightful aromas of oranges and flowers, yield hints of herbs and a palate that carries the floral notes through to the finish.

Muscats are sipping wines that need no food accompaniment to prove their worth, but they marry extremely well with light cheese and fruit presentations as well as with desserts where some of the wine is added to the preparation to encourage harmony.

Pinot Noir

The great red grape of Burgundy has found a home in Oregon. Pinot Noir is, without a doubt, the most elusive of varietals to describe and among the most difficult to grow. Attempts to describe the aromas lead one into uncharted waters of seemingly invalid descrip-

tors. How can wines that are so complex and enjoyable conjure up verbage like barnyardy, chickeny and other uncomplimentary adjectives? The answer, as known to the Pinot cognoscenti, is that it is the whole of the thing, not the dissected parts, that creates such memorable wines. Simply enjoy and revel in the aromas of black cherries, herbs and smoky spice. The smooth palate yields a velvety texture with fruity complexity and a lingering finish.

With fine cuisine, it is argued that there is no better match than Pinot Noir. The elegant complexity of the wine is a superb foil for chicken, veal and game, and is a wonderful partner for pastas, highlighting both tomato-based and cheese sauces. Both heavy and lighter styles are vinted so that you can match your picnic fare with one and your elegant dinner for eight with another more weighty and complex.

Pinot Gris

The wines made from Oregon Pinot Gris are becoming more and more exciting to the palates of those who appreciate fine cuisine with fine wine. At first thought to produce only a pleasant wine to enjoy with simple fare, Pinot Gris has become quite the darling of local chefs and consumers who rave about the potential for exploring the food affinities possible for this scarcely planted varietal. Vinted in various styles with various treatments (barrel fermentation, oak aging, etc.), Pinot Gris can offer fresh fruity aromas of apples and pears or can be intensely toasty with edges of vanilla and butterscotch. Like Chardonnay, this grape continues to be controversial from style to style.

It is widely agreed that Pinot Gris best accompanies food when created with only modest intervention by the winemaker. Oak aging and barrel fermentation tend to take away the very qualities that make this wine a grand accompaniment to salmon and other seafood. Chicken, veal and other avenues of enjoyment are wide open for experimentation by the culinary adventurer.

Riesling

Settle the confusion among your friends once and for all by explaining that Johannisberg Riesling and White Riesling are the same grape. The two names may be used interchangeably in all states except Oregon where wines must be labeled White Riesling or, simply, Riesling. This is the great grape from the German Rhein and Mosel growing regions that produces well in Washington, Oregon and Idaho. The best dry and off-dry styles offer aromas of apples and pears with floral and spicy notes. The palate also emphasizes the fruity aspect of the grape and often leaves a pleasant, fresh fruit aftertaste. Late harvest Riesling wines have more complexity on the nose and the palate with added aromas of honey and peaches. Botrytis-affected wines (those from grapes affected with the "noble rot," botrytis cinerea) have intense honey and apricot aromas and the undefinable, but enticing, aroma of the botrytis itself.

Riesling grown in the Northwest has not been given a fair chance to prove itself as a food wine. The many low-priced versions from Washington created an idea in the mind of consumers that this varietal was too inexpensive to be taken seriously. Recently, at serious food and wine judgings, Riesling showed that it is a valuable addition to the palate of wines to match with Northwest cuisine. Riesling was the hands-down winner at a fresh crab-with-wine tasting, a top contender with raw oysters, and an excellent choice for dozens of other appetizers and entrees. Late harvest Rieslings from the Northwest have proven for years that they are among the world's best dessert wines. Either AS dessert itself, or accompanying fruit tarts and custards, these unctuous and aromatic wines serve to elegantly complete any meal.

Sauvignon Blanc

This relative of Cabernet Sauvignon serves at the opposite end of the culinary spectrum. A white wine with crisp acidity and usually a thin palate, it best accompanies seafood with a light sauce in which the wine has played a role. Aromas of herbs and citrus are common with intense grassiness often toned down by the addition of Semillon. Fumé Blanc, a creation of Sauvignon Blanc with moderate oak aging, offers additional aromatic complexity (vanilla and toast) and a smoother palate with a slight perception of residual sugar when none is present.

As stated above, it is hard to imagine seafood without Sauvignon Blanc. Simple preparations are called for, limiting sauces to light concoctions of butter, wine and herbs. Likewise, simple chicken and veal dishes – especially those with herb flavorings or sauces – are wonderful partners to this varietal. Sauvignon Blanc from the Northwest does not often have the strength to play the contrast game, where matching with rich dishes most often leaves the wine a thin and hapless victim.

Semillon

A partner of Sauvignon Blanc in many Northwest blends, Semillon shares SB's French heritage and also many of the flavors and aromas although moderated and somewhat more refined. Recent experiments with barrel-fermented Semillon have proven that this varietal has a great future if care is taken in the cultivation of the vines. Aromas of melon, pears and herbs are augmented by toast and butter if the wine has seen oak-aging. The palate is generally lighter in acidity than Sauvignon Blanc, making for a wine better suited to light appetizers and casual sipping.

Look for crisp versions of Semillon if you plan to pair the wine with light meats or sauces rich in butter and herbs. Toast and smoky spice aromas in some versions create a great match with grilled fish and fowl.

Siegerrebe

A cross of Gewürztraminer and Madeleine Angevine, Siegerrebe is crafted by Bainbridge Island Winery into a spicy and characterful late harvest wine with a remarkable versatility for accompanying a wide range of desserts.

Zinfandel

Once thought to be too sensitive to harvest-time mold problems and not able to stand up to cold winters, Zinfandel has been successfully cultivated at several vineyard sites in the Northwest. Bottlings from Southern Oregon, the Columbia Gorge area and from Portteus Vineyard in the Yakima Valley have all demonstrated the potential for this variety if planted in a suitable area.

Northwest Zinfandel wines from the above-mentioned vineyard sites are rich and spicy with typical blackberry aromas and full-bodied palates. Oak aging tends to add additional complexity. An excellent foil for grilled meats.

Principles of Matching Food and Wine

The art of matching food and wine is not complicated. Some basic principles are necessary, as is some knowledge of the components that make up the foods we eat and the wines we drink. We are fortunate in the Northwest that well-made wines from this region are excellent companions to a wide range of foods and seem to have evolved to be especially well-matched to local ingredients.

In this book we have matched particular wines with particular dishes. Recipes may have been created to match a particular wine, or wines sampled to find an appropriate selection for an existing recipe. In any case, much of the work has been completed for you. We are certain that each wine will provide great enjoyment with its recommended preparation and vice versa.

We don't mean to encourage lack of participation on the part of the reader. Indeed you will no doubt find that upon preparing a particular dish you may not have the exact wine on hand. Feel free to experiment using the varietal as the starting point for selecting an alternative wine. If a recipe suggests a Sauvignon Blanc by a particular winery, try a Sauvignon Blanc or Fumé Blanc by another vintner. Or try a Semillon, instead. Various articles have been included to aid you in making these minor adjustments.

Several basic rules may help if you would like to work toward independence in wine and food pairing.

Contrast or Complement

This refers to matching foods with wines of opposing textures or flavors (contrast) or matching foods with wines of similar textures or flavors (complement). For example, an oaky, buttery, low acid Chardonnay with a rich, buttery sauce is a complement. Substitute a crisp, austere Sauvignon Blanc and you have a contrast. This basic principal is largely personal preference and, to a certain extent, can be decided by other factors such as flavors present in the food and wine.

Red Wine with Red Meat, White Wine with Fish

Despite the best efforts of many to force the pairing of Cabernet with Dover sole, we find that the most satisfying partnerships DO fall along lines of color. Tannin in hearty red wines tends to cut through the animal fat of red meats. This leaves the mouth cleansed and ready for the next bite. Crisp white wines cut through the fishiness of many seafoods in the same way that lemon squeezed on top helps to enhance the flavor. This rule is not etched in stone. Pinot Noir with fresh salmon or fresh tuna is often an earth-moving experience. Generally stick to lighter, fresh red wines – and to FRESH fish – when matching red wine with fish.

Sweet Wines with Desserts

Desserts are often difficult to match with wines. For fruit-based tarts and simple fruit desserts with light sauces, we find Northwest late harvest Rieslings with their aromas of honey, spice and peaches to be sublime. For other desserts, the choices can be more personal preference. Chocolate desserts have a certain affinity for red wines – dry or sweet – that has to do with complementary tannin compounds present in each. Not everyone enjoys this indulgence of excess and to many it helps to bring on a rousing headache. Sparkling wines are often served with dessert, but most Northwest versions are bone-dry (Brut) and match well only with light preparations of fruit and certain ices or creams.

Fine tuning the pairings of food and wine is a lot of fun. We encourage everyone to experiment and to discover their own likes and dislikes. Those who are handy in the kitchen can tinker with recipes to better match a wine and those who are regular visitors to the wine shop can seek out the perfect partner through extensive tastings. Try our suggestions from some of the Northwest's best vintners first. We're convinced that wines from our region are the best in the world to match up with your good cooking.

Appetizers, First Courses & Others

Dungeness Crab Vol-Au-Vent ~ 18

Corn and Dungeness Crab Chowder ~ 19

Sautéed Oysters with Lemon Balm ~ 20

Shoalwater Bay Oysters with Semillon
Mignonette Sauce ~ 21

Pan-Fried Curried Oysters ~ 22

Waterfront Steamed Clams ~ 23

Petit Salmon Fillets ~ 24

Smoked Salmon Spread ~ 25

Coquilles Saint-Jacques Au Gratin ~ 26

Grilled Scallops with Fresh Herbs ~ 27

Prawns with Orange Riesling Sauce ~ 28

Hot and Spicy Shrimp ~ 29

Savory Lamb Pies ~ 30

German Sausages ~ 31

Smoked Chicken Salad ~ 32

Pork Tenderloin Oriental ~ 33

Escargots à la Oregon Blue ~ 34

Terrine Forestier ~ 35

Pork Terrine
with Apples and Walnuts ~ 36

Pad Thai ~ 37

Nachos Grande ~ 38

Emerald Butterflies ~ 39

Summer Vichyssoise ~ 40

Phyllo Purses
with Wild Mushrooms ~ 41

Tarragon Sour Cream Dip ~ 42

Walla Walla Stuffed Mushrooms ~ 43

Stuffed Grape Leaves ~ 44

Hummus ~ 45

Marinated Chèvre ~ 46

Garlic Pesto Bruschetta ~ 47

Gewürztraminer Garlic Toast ~ 48

Pesto Chèvre Bread ~ 49

Swiss Rye Bread ~ 50

Gourmet Harvest Pizza ~ 51

Walnut Brie in Brioche ~ 52

Dungeness Crab Vol-Au-Vent

Dungeness crab, considered by some the most prestigious member of the crustacean family, is abundant along the Northern shores of Washington and is available fresh during the winter months. In our treatment of this Northwest favorite, rich, freshly cooked crab combines with other delicious ingredients in a buttery puff pastry shell (vol-au-vent in France) to create an elegant first course. We highly recommend **Chateau Ste. Michelle's** vineyard-designated River Ridge Chardonnay with its nuances of tropical fruit and hints of toasty butterscotch that play beautifully off the delicate flavors in the dish. Crisp acidity balances the richness and ultimately leaves one to delight in the harmony and balance of flavors and textures.

4 servings

1 live Dungeness crab (1½ to 2 pounds)

Stock

3 tablespoons vegetable oil
1 garlic clove, smashed
1 shallot, chopped
½ carrot, peeled, coarsely chopped
½ celery stalk, coarsely chopped
1 tablespoon Cognac or other brandy
¼ cup Chateau Ste. Michelle Chardonnay
3 cups water (or to cover)
2 sprigs fresh parsley
2 sprigs fresh thyme
1 bay leaf
4 black peppercorns

2 cups heavy cream
4 tablespoons unsalted butter, divided
½ pound wild mushrooms*, cleaned, thinly
    sliced
1 teaspoon chopped fresh thyme
    Salt and freshly ground black pepper
4 puff pastry shells*, warmed
2 tablespoons toasted pine nuts
    Fresh thyme sprigs

1. Cook crab and clean well. Remove meat and refrigerate until needed. (You should have 4 to 5 ounces of meat.) Reserve shells to prepare stock.
2. For stock: Heat oil in medium Dutch oven over medium heat. Add garlic with shallot. Sauté 2 minutes. Add carrot, celery and reserved shells. Sauté 3 to 4 minutes. Add Cognac with wine. Reduce to glaze. Reduce heat and add remaining ingredients. Simmer 1 hour. Strain through fine-mesh sieve into clean saucepan and reduce to 1 cup. Set aside.
3. Bring cream to boil in heavy medium saucepan over high heat and reduce by half. Stir in reserved stock and reduce by half. Set aside.
4. Melt 2 tablespoons butter in heavy medium skillet over medium heat. Add mushrooms and cook until almost dry, stirring occasionally, about 5 minutes.
5. Stir in cream reduction, thyme and remaining butter. Gently fold in reserved crabmeat. Season with salt and pepper. To serve, place puff pastry shells on warm plates and fill with crab mixture. Sprinkle tops with toasted pine nuts and garnish with fresh thyme sprigs.

* See **Special Ingredients**

Cook's Tip

For those of you "on the go", purchase a cooked crab from your specialty seafood market. Cleaning these tasty critters is usually yours for the asking. Don't forget to bring home the shells for your stock.

Wine Selection
**Chateau Ste. Michelle
River Ridge Chardonnay**

Corn and Dungeness Crab Chowder

John Kemnitzer has a special knack for blending regional ingredients into wonderful culinary creations. As Executive Chef for the **Yarrow Bay Grill and Beach Cafe** in Kirkland, Washington, he serves Northwest cuisine with a focus on organic and naturally raised foods from local suppliers. A tribute to the fine ingredients available in the Northwest is his satisfying Corn and Dungeness Crab Chowder. The dense and varied nature of the chowder makes it a prime candidate for a fine Northwest varietal. Chef Kemnitzer highly recommends a favorite on the restaurant's predominantly Northwest wine list, **Columbia Winery's** Semillon. In the hands of talented winemakers like Master of Wine David Lake, Semillon's crisp and complex character is brought to the forefront – a real winner alongside chef Kemnitzer's tasty chowder.

10 servings

4 tablespoons butter
1 medium onion, diced (about 1 cup)
2 medium celery stalks, diced (about $1/2$ cup)
1 small red bell pepper, stemmed, seeded, deribbed, diced (about $1/2$ cup)
4 cups fresh corn kernels, cut from cob (4 to 5 small ears), juices from cob reserved
3 cups clam juice, bottled or canned
2 bay leaves
2 teaspoons chopped fresh thyme
$1/8$ teaspoon freshly grated nutmeg
$1^{1}/4$ pounds red new potatoes, diced (about 3 cups)
12 ounces Dungeness crabmeat
3 cups heavy cream
2 teaspoons paprika
$3/4$ teaspoon salt
$1/2$ teaspoon black pepper
$1/4$ cup dry sherry
$1/4$ cup oyster crackers, finely ground
3 tablespoons chopped fresh parsley

1. Melt butter in 3 to 4-quart pot over medium heat. Add onion, celery and red bell pepper. Cook until onion turns clear, stirring occasionally, about 5 minutes.
2. Add juices from corn cob, clam juice, bay leaves, thyme and nutmeg. Bring to boil over high heat.
3. Add potatoes with corn kernels. Return to boil. Immediately reduce heat and simmer until potatoes are crunchy-tender, about 10 minutes.
4. Add crabmeat, cream, paprika, salt and pepper. Return to simmer.
5. Add sherry with oyster crackers. Simmer 10 minutes longer. (If chowder is not thick enough, add more ground crackers; if too thick, thin with clam juice or cream.)
6. Remove bay leaves, stir in chopped fresh parsley and serve immediately.

Cook's Tip

Chef Kemnitzer suggests cutting all vegetables corn-kernel size and scraping the corn cobs with the back of your knife to collect all juices.

Wine Selection
Columbia Winery Semillon

Sautéed Oysters
with Lemon Balm and Nasturtium Flower Butter

Sinclair and Fredrica Philip are the proprietors of what many consider to be Vancouver Island's finest restaurant, **Sooke Harbour House**. The Philips take pride in serving only the freshest Northwest ingredients often gathered from their own herb garden and from the waters near the restaurant. Sinclair provides his "palate pleasing first course" using local oysters and flowers fresh from the garden for both a taste treat and a stunning presentation. His recommendation for an accompanying wine style brought to mind **Whittlesey Mark Brut**, a delightful sparkling wine made by Mark Newton. The crisp acidity and fine bubbles bring forth the flavor of the dish and highlight the freshness of the ingredients. Earthy/yeasty nuances beautifully complete the marriage.

Makes 4 servings

  8 tablespoons unsalted butter, chilled, divided
  2 shallots, minced
  2 garlic cloves, minced
 $^1/_2$ cup Fish Stock (see **Basics**) or oyster liquor
 $^1/_2$ cup dry white wine
4 to 6 lemon balm leaves, finely chopped
6 to 8 nasturtium flowers (of varied colors), finely chopped
 12 plump oysters, shucked
    Nasturtium flowers and leaves

1. Melt 2 tablespoons butter in heavy medium saucepan over medium heat.
2. Toss in shallots with garlic. Cook only until slightly softened, about 1 minute.
3. Increase heat to high and pour in fish stock with wine. Bring to boil and reduce to almost syrupy consistency, 3 to 4 minutes. Halfway through reduction, stir in lemon balm leaves.
4. As sauce is reducing, cut 4 tablespoons butter into small pieces.
5. Remove saucepan from heat and whisk in butter, 1 piece at a time, to make velvety sauce. At last minute, toss in nasturtium flowers. Keep sauce warm over very low heat.
6. Heat medium skillet over medium-high heat and swirl in remaining butter.
7. Sauté oysters about 30 seconds per side. (Their frilly edges should just begin to turn golden brown.) To serve, divide sauce between 4 heated appetizer plates. Place 3 oysters on each and garnish with nasturtium flowers and leaves.

Wine Selection
Whittlesey Mark Brut

Shoalwater Bay Oysters *with Semillon Mignonette Sauce*

Shoalwater Bay oysters, harvested from Willapa Bay on the southwest Washington coast, are among the tastiest you'll ever put in your mouth. Ocean waters flow into the bay, with each tide and bring this popular bivalve the microscopic food necessary for survival. Grown by the rack culture method (which keeps them off the bottom), this delicate oyster is the oyster of choice at most restaurants for serving on the half-shell. In our recipe, freshly shucked oysters are enhanced with a simple sauce and a glass of **L'Ecole No 41's** delightfully refreshing Semillon – a classic combination! The wine's bold varietal character and crisp acidity stand up to the brininess of the oyster, while its addition to the sauce serves as a bridge between oyster and wine. The accompaniment of crusty French bread provides a necessary palate cleanser between bites.

4 servings

Semillon Mignonette Sauce

$^3/_4$ cup L' Ecole No 41 Semillon
2   shallots, minced
1   teaspoon crushed black peppercorns

2   dozen Shoalwater Bay oysters
    French bread

1. For sauce: Stir together all ingredients in small bowl until well blended and set aside.
2. Shuck oysters, leaving oyster with liquor in bottom shells. Discard top shells. Serve with Semillon Mignonette Sauce and accompany with French bread.

Wine Selection

L' Ecole No 41 Semillon

Cook's Tip

For shucking oysters, an oyster glove and oyster knife are a necessity.

How to Shuck an Oyster

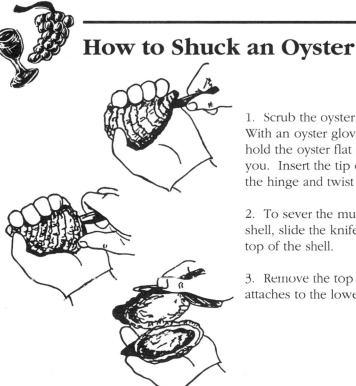

1. Scrub the oyster well under cold, running water. With an oyster glove (on the hand holding the oyster), hold the oyster flat side up, with the narrow end facing you. Insert the tip of the oyster knife into the shell at the hinge and twist to pop open the shell.

2. To sever the muscle that connects the oyster to its shell, slide the knife blade along the underside of the top of the shell.

3. Remove the top shell and sever the muscle that attaches to the lower shell.

Pan-Fried Curried Oysters
with Crème Fraîche and Caviar

For many years, **Enoteca Restaurant and Wine Bar** served Seattle's wine cognoscenti as a place where Northwest food and wine comingled at reasonable prices. A victim of the real estate boom (they lost their lease) and the highly competitive restaurant market in Seattle, Enoteca lives on through chef Leslie Dillon's wonderful Northwest appetizer, Pan-Fried Curried Oysters with Crème Fraîche and Caviar. She highly recommends **Chinook** Chardonnay to accompany this oyster-lovers' delicious first course. The richness of the delightful, barrel-aged wine complements the creamy texture of the oysters and contrasts the aggressive flavors of the curry and caviar.

6 servings

Curried Flour Mixture

$1/2$ cup all-purpose flour
$2^1/2$ teaspoons ground cumin
$2^1/2$ teaspoons curry powder
$2^1/2$ teaspoons paprika
$2^1/2$ teaspoons turmeric
$1/2$ teaspoon kosher salt
$1/4$ teaspoon ground ginger
$1/8$ teaspoon ground cloves
$1/8$ teaspoon ground coriander
$1/8$ teaspoon cayenne pepper

3 tablespoons clarified butter* or vegetable oil
24 small yearling oysters, shucked
6 heaping tablespoons Crème Fraîche (see **Basics**)
6 generous teaspoons caviar (any type or lumpfish roe*)
Lemon wedges
Fresh parsley sprigs or French chives

1. For curried flour mixture: Combine all ingredients in small bowl until well blended and set aside. (Makes about $3/4$ cup.)
2. Heat clarified butter in heavy medium skillet over medium heat.
3. Dredge oysters in curried flour mixture and shake off excess.
4. Pan-fry oysters until well browned (in batches; do not crowd), 2 to 3 minutes per side. Drain well on paper towels. To serve, divide oysters among warm plates and garnish with crème fraîche, caviar, lemon wedges and fresh parsley sprigs.

* See **Special Ingredients**

Cook's Tip

Store leftover curried flour mixture in a spice jar and place in a cool, dark place.

Wine Selection
Chinook Chardonnay

Waterfront Steamed Clams

Bridgeview Vineyard in Cave Junction, Oregon, is one of the state's newest and largest wineries. French-born winemaker Laurent Montelieu crafts familiar Northwest varietals in a style that has won him much praise throughout the region. His success with Pinot Gris has been outstanding and it ranks as one of our favorite food wines. Fresh, flinty aromas and flavors make it the #1 choice for our Waterfront Steamed Clams. In the style of a French Muscadet matching the seafood found at the mouth of the Loire, so does Bridgeview's Pinot Gris provide just the right body, flavor and panache for our informal, regional creation. Pacific Northwest waters are home to over two dozen varieties of clams, so be our guest and experiment with your favorite. We love Japanese littlenecks for this dish, sometimes referred to as Manila clams.

4 servings

Broth

    1 cup Bridgeview Vineyard Pinot Gris
 $^{1}/_{4}$ cup water
    4 tablespoons butter
 $^{1}/_{2}$ celery stalk, thinly sliced
 $^{1}/_{2}$ carrot, peeled, cut julienne
 $^{1}/_{2}$ small red onion, thinly sliced, halved
    5 garlic cloves, slivered
    4 fresh Italian flat-leaf parsley sprigs
    1 bay leaf

    3 dozen littleneck clams, scrubbed,
       degorged of sand (see **Cook's Tip**)
       Salt and freshly ground black pepper
       Melted butter
       Lemon wedges

1. For broth: Bring to boil all ingredients in large pot over high heat. Immediately reduce heat and simmer 5 minutes.
2. Add clams and cover. Increase heat and steam until clams open, 3 to 5 minutes.
3. Discard unopened shells with bay leaf. To serve, divide opened shells among serving bowls. Season broth with salt and pepper. Ladle broth with vegetables over clams. Accompany with melted butter (in small bowls) and lemon wedges.

Cook's Tip

Clams tend to be very sandy. To degorge them of their sand, simply soak them in a solution of 1 part coarse sea salt dissolved in 8 parts water (to cover) at least 1 hour. Rinse well before using.

Wine Selection

**Bridgeview Vineyards
Pinot Gris**

Petit Salmon Fillets *with Sole Mousse and Dill Sauce*

Some of the world's finest salmon come from the waters of the Pacific Northwest. Late in the season, the fall run brings Sockeye from the Straits of Juan de Fuca, Coho from the coast and Chinook from the Columbia River. Savor the season's bounty and enjoy our inspired treatment of this regional specialty, with its mirepoix of contrasting flavors and textures. Accompany with a slightly chilled glass of **The Eyrie Vineyards** richly textured and flavorful Pinot Gris. First planted and nurtured to stardom by Oregon winemaking pioneer David Lett, Pinot Gris offers herbal dimensions that highlight the dill, while its crisp acidity refreshes the palate and cuts beautifully through the richness of the dish.

6 servings

Sole Mousse

8 ounces Dover sole, cut into chunks, chilled
2 large eggs (1 whole, 1 separated), room temperature
Dash nutmeg
1/2 cup heavy cream, chilled
Salt and freshly ground white pepper

Unsalted butter
2 shallots, minced
6 Pacific salmon fillets (about 4 ounces each), preferably King
3 tablespoons chopped fresh dill, divided
Salt and freshly ground white pepper
1 cup The Eyrie Vineyards Pinot Gris
1/2 cup Fish Stock (see **Basics**)
1 cup heavy cream
2 tablespoons unsalted butter
1 tablespoon fresh lemon juice
Dash nutmeg
Fresh dill sprigs

1. For sole mousse: Blend sole, whole egg, egg yolk and nutmeg in bowl of food processor, fitted with steel knife, until smooth, about 40 seconds. With machine running, slowly pour cream through feed tube, scraping down work bowl, as necessary. Transfer mixture to medium bowl and set aside.

2. Using electric mixer, beat egg white in medium bowl to stiff but not dry peaks. Gently fold into sole mixture and season with salt and white pepper. Spoon mixture into piping bag, fitted with 1/2-inch opening and twist to close. Refrigerate until needed.

3. Position rack in lowest third of oven and preheat to 450° F. Butter baking dish, large enough to accommodate fillets. Sprinkle with shallots and set aside.

4. Rinse fillets well and pat dry with paper towels. Arrange in prepared baking dish and sprinkle tops with 1 1/2 tablespoons dill. Season with salt and pepper.

5. Pipe sole mixture atop fillets and pour wine with stock around.

6. Bake fillets until opaque and tops are light golden brown, about 18 minutes. With slotted spatula, transfer to warm plate and tent with foil.

7. Strain fish cooking liquid through fine-mesh sieve into heavy medium saucepan over high heat. Bring to boil and reduce by half.

8. Add cream and reduce by half. Stir in butter, remaining dill, lemon juice and nutmeg. Season with salt and pepper. To serve, briefly reheat fillets (in microwave) and place on warm plates. Surround with sauce and garnish with fresh dill sprigs.

Wine Selection

The Eyrie Vineyards Pinot Gris

Smoked Salmon Spread

In the scenic Yakima Valley, grapegrower Clay Mackey and winemaker Kay Simon produce wonderful food wines at **Chinook Winery**. The absence of residual sweetness in their wines – and the presence of the North-west's trademark crisp acidity – make them ideal partners to a wide variety of Northwest cuisine, especially seafood. Their popular Sauvignon Blanc (blended with 25% Semillon to tone down the herbaceous quality and con-tribute fruitiness) is a lovely complement to the rich, smoky flavors of their Smoked Salmon Spread. Created by Clay's mother, this tasty spread is a great choice for that next spur-of-the-moment appetizer!

Makes about 3 cups

6$^1/_2$ ounces smoked salmon
1 pound fresh cream cheese,
room temperature
3 generous tablespoons mayonnaise or
plain yogurt
Minced fresh dill to taste
Salt and freshly ground black pepper
(optional)
Fresh dill sprigs

Rye crackers

1. Flake salmon into small bowl and set aside. Discard skin with bones.
2. Using electric mixer, soften cream cheese in medium bowl about 2 minutes.
3. Blend in mayonnaise until smooth.
4. Blend in salmon with dill until smooth. Season with salt and pepper, if desired. To serve, transfer mixture to serving dish and garnish with fresh dill sprigs. Accompany with rye crackers.

Cook's Tip

Substitute 2 packages (8 ounces each) Philadel-phia brand cream cheese, if fresh is not available.

Wine Selection
Chinook Sauvignon Blanc

Coquilles Saint-Jacques Au Gratin

The first winemaking efforts of **Silver Lake Winery** in Bothell, Washington, convinced wine lovers that this was a winery to watch. Their superb Chardonnay is a fine match for classical dishes like our Coquilles Saint-Jacques Au Gratin. Focusing on the multifaceted flavor associations of fresh tarragon and the earthy character of wild mushrooms, the dish beautifully complements the aromatic qualities of the wine. Refreshing acidity provides a delicious component contrast to the sweet flavor of the bay scallops and cuts the richness of the cream. Scallops go a long way in this delicious first course!

4 servings

2	tablespoons unsalted butter
¼	pound wild mushrooms*, cleaned, thinly sliced
3	garlic cloves, minced, divided
¼	cup Silver Lake Winery Chardonnay
1	tablespoon Cognac or other brandy
1	teaspoon Madeira
½	pound bay scallops
1	tablespoon chopped fresh tarragon
1	tablespoon chopped fresh parsley
1½	cups heavy cream
1	bay leaf
2	teaspoons Dijon mustard
	Dash nutmeg
	Dash cayenne pepper
3	tablespoons freshly grated Parmesan cheese, divided
	Salt and freshly ground black pepper
½	cup fine dry bread crumbs
	Chilled unsalted butter

1. Position rack in center of oven and preheat to 400° F. Lightly grease 4 large coquille shells and set aside.
2. Melt butter in heavy medium skillet over medium heat. Add mushrooms with 2 garlic cloves. Cook until almost dry, stirring occasionally, about 5 minutes.
3. Stir in wine, Cognac and Madeira. Bring to boil over high heat and reduce to glaze.
4. Add scallops, tarragon and parsley. Sauté 1 minute. With slotted spoon, transfer mixture to warm plate and tent with foil.
5. Add cream with bay leaf to skillet. Bring to boil and reduce by half. Remove bay leaf.
6. Reduce heat and stir in mustard, nutmeg, cayenne pepper and 2 tablespoons Parmesan cheese.
7. Return scallop mixture to skillet and stir well to coat with sauce. Season with salt and pepper.
8. Divide mixture among prepared coquille shells and set aside.
9. Combine bread crumbs, remaining garlic and remaining Parmesan cheese in small bowl. Sprinkle over shells. Dot with butter.
10. Place shells on baking sheet and bake until tops are lightly browned and bubbly, about 15 minutes. Serve immediately.

* See **Special Ingredients**

Wine Selection

Silver Lake Winery Chardonnay

Grilled Scallops *with Fresh Herbs*

Executive Chef Wayne Ludvigsen at **Ray's Boathouse** in Seattle, Washington, does wonderful things with fresh, local seafood. His straightforward approach to scallops lets the sweet and tender nature of the tasty mollusks speak for itself. Punctuated with two of our favorite fresh herbs, oregano and basil, this lovely dish brings to mind Mike Conway's Semillon from **Latah Creek Wine Cellars** in Spokane, Washington. The simple preparation of this tantalizing first course makes a perfect match for the delicious citrus and herb flavors in the wine, while the crisp acidity refreshes the palate with each sip. Chef Ludvigsen invites you to experiment with your favorite herb combinations, and we challenge you to enjoy other delicious wine matchups from the great Northwest!

6 servings

Marinade

- 1 cup olive oil
- 1/3 cup fresh lemon juice
- 1 tablespoon chopped fresh oregano
- 1 tablespoon chopped fresh basil
- 4 garlic cloves, smashed
  - Salt and freshly ground black pepper to taste

- 2 pounds medium sea scallops
  - Lemon wedges
  - Fresh basil sprigs

1. For marinade: Whisk together all ingredients until well blended in nonreactive bowl, large enough to hold scallops with marinade.
2. Add scallops to marinade and toss to coat. Cover and refrigerate 2 hours.
3. Prepare grill with medium-hot coals. Adjust rack 3 to 4 inches from heat and lightly oil.
4. With slotted spoon, remove scallops from marinade and drain well. Reserve marinade for basting.
5. Thread scallops onto 6 sets of double bamboo skewers.
6. Place skewers on grill and cook to desired doneness or 3 to 4 minutes per side, basting occasionally with reserved marinade. To serve, place skewers on warm plates and garnish with lemon wedges and fresh basil sprigs.

Cook's Tip

Double bamboo skewers are great for grilling scallops – they keep the scallops from flipping around when you turn them. Soak the skewers in water about 30 minutes before threading to prevent them from burning on the grill.

Prawns *with Orange Riesling Sauce*

Nestled in the foothills of Oregon's Coast Range northeast of Eugene, **Alpine Vineyards** specializes in making estate-bottled wines. Owner Dan Jepsen, doctor by trade and wine-maker by passion, produces a delightful dry Riesling that captivates the beauty of our shellfish creation like no other wine. Judiciously incorporated into the sauce, the wine is a natural complement to the dish and beautifully highlights the delicate anise-like flavor of chervil. Be creative in your choice of orange – Satsumas, Blood Oranges and Navels are among our favorites. All make great sauce-partners for our Prawns with Orange Riesling Sauce – a dazzling starter for that mid-winter dinner party.

6 servings

Orange Riesling Sauce

  1 cup fresh orange juice (about 3 medium oranges)
  1 cup Alpine Vineyards Dry Riesling
  2 small shallots, chopped
  1 teaspoon white peppercorns, slightly crushed
  1 teaspoon chopped fresh chervil
  8 tablespoons unsalted butter, cut into pieces, room temperature
     Salt and freshly ground white pepper

  2 tablespoons unsalted butter
  2 pounds medium prawns, shelled, deveined
     Fresh chervil sprigs

1. For sauce: Stir together orange juice, wine, shallots, peppercorns and chervil in heavy medium saucepan over high heat. Bring to boil and reduce by half.
2. Strain liquid through fine-mesh sieve into clean saucepan, pressing on solids with back of spoon to extract as much liquid as possible.
3. Whisk in butter, 1 piece at a time, over low heat. Season with salt and white pepper. Set aside and keep warm.
4. Melt butter in heavy large skillet over medium heat.
5. Add prawns and sauté until just pink, 3 to 4 minutes.
6. Stir in sauce and coat prawns well. To serve, divide prawns among warm plates and garnish with fresh chervil sprigs.

Cook's Tip

Try this lovely dish with Gewürztraminer and your choice of complementary herb.

Wine Selection
Alpine Vineyards Dry Riesling

Hot and Spicy Shrimp

Talented in the kitchen as well as the winery, Gail Puryear of **Bonair Winery** crafts delicious Chardonnays, Rieslings and Cabernets from grapes grown in the vicinity of their location in Zillah, Washington. He and his wife Shirley share with us this tasty, simple-to-prepare appetizer, featuring shrimp, one of the Northwest's true delicacies. The best shrimp in our region come from the inland waters of Hood Canal in Washington and from certain coastal areas of Oregon. This preparation demands a rich, full-bodied wine like Bonair Chardonnay to stand up to its hot and spicy character.

4 to 6 servings

1½ pounds medium shrimp
8 tablespoons unsalted butter
1 cup Bonair Chardonnay
¼ teaspoon Tabasco sauce
2 red serrano chilies, stemmed, seeded, deribbed, julienne cut (optional)
4 garlic cloves, minced
  Salt and freshly ground black pepper
  Fresh parsley sprigs

1. Peel and devein shrimp, leaving tails on, if desired. Rinse well under cold, running water. Drain on paper towels and set aside.
2. Melt butter in heavy medium skillet over medium heat.
3. Stir in wine with Tabasco sauce.
4. Increase heat and add shrimp with chilies, if desired. Cook until shrimp are just pink, stirring frequently, 2 to 3 minutes.
5. Stir in garlic last 30 seconds of cooking time and season with salt and pepper. To serve, divide shrimp among warm plates and garnish with fresh parsley sprigs.

Cook's Tip

Fresh cilantro is a nice garnish if you choose to add the chilies.

Wine Selection
Bonair Winery Chardonnay

Barrel Aging – Toast in Your Wine?

Throughout our book we often describe Chardonnay wines as having a toasty/smoky character. These components come from the wine being aged, or fermented and aged, in French oak barrels. Winemakers have found that many consumers prefer a Chardonnay with a smooth palate and the intriguing complexities this treatment affords.

French oak comes from several regions of the country and the barrels are identified by their origin. You will hear of Nevers, Allier, Limousin and other types when you discuss winemaking techniques with the proprietors of Northwest wineries.

Regardless of the region, all French oak barrels are assembled using a technique that adds the toasty complexity to wine. In fact, the "toast" of each barrel is graded as heavy, medium or light depending on the strength of "toast" character that will be imparted.

To assemble a barrel, staves must be warped into a shape that will keep the barrel watertight. Traditionally, the staves are soaked in water then partially assembled into the barrel shape (see illustration). This "half-barrel" is then inverted over a fire heating the wet wood to create steam and thus making the staves pliable. Bending them into the final barrel shape is then accomplished. But what of the smoke from the fire? Indeed, the smoke does penetrate the wood and imparts the "toast" character sought after by winemakers. The inside of the barrel is then scraped to remove as much of the flavor as desired to create a light, medium or heavy toast barrel.

Savory Lamb Pies

Bert Grant, owner of one of the Northwest's pioneer microbreweries, **Grant's Ale Brewery** in Yakima, Washington, has spent a lifetime striving to craft the perfect ale. His Scottish Ale, a rich and aromatic brew styled after the premium ales of Scotland, is testament to his success. This popular local brew is ideal to accompany our Savory Lamb Pies, tailored after the meat pies of Great Britain. In the individual pies, quality Northwest lamb, available year-round, is encased in a flaky pastry with potatoes, fresh herbs and a rich broth reduction. Baked to perfection, these continental snacks are just the ticket for meals-to-go on football Sundays or anytime. This is pub-grub at its finest!

Makes 12

$3/4$	pound lean boneless lamb, finely diced
1	medium potato, finely diced
1	medium onion, finely diced
1	teaspoon minced fresh parsley
1	teaspoon minced fresh thyme
$1^1/_2$	cups Veal Stock, reduced to $^1/_3$ cup (see **Basics**)
	Salt and freshly ground pepper to taste
2	recipes Pâte Brisée, made without sugar (see **Basics**)
2	large egg yolks, lightly beaten with 2 tablespoons water (glaze)

1. Position rack in center of oven and preheat to 350° F. Lightly grease 2 baking sheets and set aside.
2. For filling: Combine all ingredients in medium bowl until well blended and set aside.
3. Roll out dough on lightly floured surface to $^1/_8$-inch thickness. Cut into $6^1/_2$-inch circles.
4. Place 2 tablespoons filling in center of circles. Brush edges with glaze. Fold over to evenly align sides. Press with tines of fork to seal.
5. Place on prepared baking pan and brush with glaze. Bake until light golden brown, about 35 minutes. Serve immediately.

Cook's Tip

The Celts were innovative with the fillings they used in their pies. Feel free to try beef or veal and maybe a few of your favorite root vegetables.

Beer Selection
Grant's Scottish Ale

German Sausages *(Bratwurst)*

Hood River Brewery, the only micro-brewery located along the Columbia Gorge, has become a favorite of the thousands of wind surfers who flock to the area for the thrill of riding the big winds that blow up the Columbia River. HRB's Full Sail Ale is available in both a light version called Golden Ale and a heavier, more flavorful Amber Ale. Additionally, a Brown Ale and a Porter are accompanied by seasonal brews of great character. For the month of October, we suggest taking a lead from the Bavarians with some serious quaffing of these wind-blown brews. To accompany them, celebrate your own Munich Oktoberfest by making authentic, delicate German Sausages. All that's needed for this "oompah-pah madness" is hungry, fun-loving friends.

6 to 8 servings

Filling

  1 cup fresh white bread crumbs
1/2 cup milk
  2 pounds finely ground lean veal
  2 pounds finely ground pork butt
  1 tablespoon plus 1 teaspoon salt
  1 teaspoon freshly ground nutmeg
  1 teaspoon freshly ground white pepper

4 to 5 feet small (1 1/2-inch) hog casing*
  2 tablespoons distilled white vinegar
    Beer
    Butter
    Assorted mustards

1. For filling: Combine bread crumbs with milk in small bowl until well blended. Let stand 10 minutes. Meanwhile, knead veal with pork in large bowl until well blended. Knead in bread crumb mixture with remaining ingredients until well blended. Cover and refrigerate 1 to 2 hours.
2. Rinse casing well under cold, running water to remove salt. Fill medium bowl with cold water and soak casing 30 minutes.
3. Rinse casing well. Fit one end over faucet head and thoroughly flush out any salt with cold, running water. (If you discover any holes, snip them out with scissors.)
4. Place casing in bowl of cold water and stir in vinegar. Set aside until needed. (Rinse well and drain before stuffing.)
5. Fit large pastry bag with wide, 3/4-inch (#9) plain tip. Fill halfway with filling and twist to close.
6. Cut casing into 3 manageable lengths. Working with one wet casing at a time, slip one end onto plain tip of pasty bag and ease on entire length. Tie knot in exposed end.
7. To fill, gently squeeze pastry bag, holding casing in place as it fills. Twist, every 4 inches, in opposite directions. Roll back and forth on work surface to evenly distribute filling. (Do not fill tightly or sausages will burst; filling expands during cooking.) Pierce air bubbles with toothpick. Continue with remaining casings and filling.
8. Place sausages on lightly greased baking sheet and cover. Refrigerate overnight to let flavors blend.
9. To cook, cut sausages into links and pierce all over. Place snugly in heavy large skillet (in batches, if necessary) and pour in 1/2-inch beer. Cover and bring to boil over medium-high heat. Immediately reduce heat and simmer until well cooked, 15 to 20 minutes.
10. Drain beer from skillet and add butter. Increase heat and lightly brown sausages, turning occasionally, about 10 minutes. Drain well on paper towels and serve immediately with assorted mustards. (Makes about 4 pounds.)

* See **Special Ingredients**

Beer Selection

**Hood River Brewery
Full Sail Amber Ale**

Smoked Chicken Salad *with Feta Vinaigrette*

The Greek tradition at **Tagaris Winery** is a family affair. Michael Taggares' grandfather emigrated through Ellis Island at the turn of the century where his name was changed from Tagaris to Taggares. The original Greek spelling was recently revived as the name for their new winery. Our Greek-inspired Smoked Chicken Salad with Feta Vinaigrette is the perfect dish to pair with Tagaris Fumé Blanc. This flavorful luncheon entrée highlights Mediterranean flavors that complement the smoky, flinty character of the wine, while the wine's freshness handles the slight edge of acidity the Feta Vinaigrette lends to the dish. Round out this favorite with hot sourdough bread lavished with your favorite herb butter – yummy!

4 to 6 servings

    1   large head romaine lettuce
    2   large tomatoes, cored, seeded, chopped
    1   medium red onion, peeled, thinly sliced,
            separated into rings
    1   medium cucumber, peeled, halved
            lengthwise, seeded, cubed
    1   pound smoked chicken, cubed
  $^1/_2$ pound Greek-style olives*, rinsed, pitted,
            chopped
        Feta Vinaigrette (recipe follows)
        Salt and freshly ground black pepper
    3   ounces toasted pine nuts

1. Separate lettuce head into leaves and rinse well under cold, running water. Pat dry with paper towels and tear into bite-size pieces. Place in large mixing bowl.
2. Add tomatoes, onion, cucumber, chicken and olives. Toss to mix.
3. Add desired amount of Feta Vinaigrette and toss to mix. Season with salt and pepper. To serve, divide salad among chilled plates and sprinkle with toasted pine nuts.

Feta Vinaigrette

    2   garlic cloves
    4   ounces feta cheese*, crumbled
  $^1/_4$ cup red wine vinegar
    2   teaspoons chopped fresh oregano
  $^1/_8$ teaspoon freshly ground black pepper
    1   cup olive oil
        Salt to taste (optional)

1. Mince garlic in bowl of food processor, fitted with steel knife.
2. Blend in feta cheese, vinegar, oregano and pepper until smooth.
3. With machine running, slowly pour oil through feed tube. Season with salt, if desired. (Makes about $1^3/_4$ cups.)

* See **Special Ingredients**

Cook's Tips

Chill your salad forks for that extra-special touch.

Don't forget to save leftover vinaigrette for a quick salad some other time!

Wine Selection
Tagaris Winery Fumé Blanc

Pork Tenderloin Oriental

Latah Creek Wine Cellars near Spokane, Washington, welcomes visitors year-round to their Spanish mission-styled winery, offering samples of their latest releases. They are one of the few Northwest wineries to produce a Maywine – a blended white wine flavored with strawberry and woodruff herb. Owner/winemaker Mike Conway is highly respected for his varietal wines and his wife Ellena adds to their success by creating wonderful dishes to accompany her husband's efforts. We loved her Pork Tenderloin Oriental with its exotic flavors, paired with Mike's Spokane Blush, made from Merlot. The wine displays fruity overtones of cherries and berries and picks up mutually complementary flavors in the dish – the ideal wine for lazy afternoon sipping, or to accompany Ellena's creative appetizer!

Makes 6 servings

Marinade

- $1/4$ cup soy sauce
- 2 tablespoons Latah Creek Spokane Blush or Merlot
- 1 tablespoon light brown sugar
- 1 tablespoon honey
- $1/2$ teaspoon red food coloring (optional)
- $1/2$ teaspoon cinnamon
- 1 garlic clove, crushed
- 1 green onion, diagonally sliced very thin

- 2 pork tenderloins (about 12 ounces each), trimmed of fat
  Salt and freshly ground black pepper
  Toasted sesame seeds
  Fresh cilantro sprigs
  Chinese mustard (optional)

1. For marinade: Whisk together all ingredients in small bowl until well blended and sugar dissolves. Set aside.
2. Place tenderloins in nonreactive dish, large enough to hold tenderloins with marinade. Pour marinade over, cover and refrigerate at least 1 hour or overnight.
3. Position rack in lowest third of oven and preheat to 350° F.
4. Remove tenderloins from marinade and pat dry with paper towels. Season with salt and pepper. Reserve marinade for basting.
5. Place tenderloins on lightly greased wire rack over baking pan. Bake until thermometer inserted into thickest part registers at least 160° F., about 45 minutes. Turn and baste occasionally with reserved marinade.
6. Transfer tenderloins to carving board and let stand 5 minutes. To serve, slice and place on warm platter. Sprinkle with toasted sesame seeds and garnish with fresh cilantro sprigs. Accompany with Chinese mustard, if desired.

Cook's Tip

Try grilling this tasty appetizer for that next backyard barbecue – it's sure to be a hit!

Wine Selection
Latah Creek Wine Cellars
Spokane Blush

Escargots à la Oregon Blue

Oregon's creamy blue cheese goes haute cuisine and struts its stuff beautifully alongside snails (escargots in France), a member of the mollusk family. Unlike his bivalve brethren who inhabit the waters, the snail carries his house with him on land, feasting on grape leaves and other greens in the vineyards of Southern France. Is this why they marry so beautifully with wine? A wine match from an Italian variety comes to us via **Cavatappi Winery's** Maddelena, made from the Nebbiolo grape. This flavorful, fruity-yet-pungent red wine offers both body and character to stand up to the blue cheese and escargots.

6 servings

  2 cans (7 ounces each) snails
$^3/_4$ cup dry white wine or vermouth

Snail Butter

  4 sprigs fresh Italian flat-leaf parsley
  3 garlic cloves
  1 large shallot
  8 tablespoons unsalted butter, cut into
      pieces, room temperature
  6 ounces Oregon Blue cheese, crumbled,
      room temperature,
      Dash Cognac or other brandy
      Pinch cayenne pepper
      Salt and freshly ground black pepper
        to taste

1. Position rack in center of oven and preheat to 400° F.
2. Rinse snails well under cold, running water to remove briny taste. Pat dry with paper towels and place in bowl, large enough to hold snails with wine. Pour wine over, cover and marinate 15 minutes.
3. Meanwhile prepare snail butter: Finely chop together parsley, garlic and shallot in bowl of food processor, fitted with steel knife. Set aside.
4. Using electric mixer, cream butter with cheese in medium bowl until smooth. Stir in above mixture with remaining ingredients until well blended. Set aside.
5. Drain snails and pat dry with paper towels.
6. Place snails in snail dishes (each dish holds 6 snails) or stuff into individual shells. Top each snail with dollop of snail butter.
7. Place snail dishes or individual shells on baking sheet and bake until bubbly, about 10 minutes. Serve immediately.

Cook's Tip

We use Roland Brand snails. Each can contains about 18 extra-large snails. Shop for them at specialty food markets, like Delaurenti in Seattle.

Wine Selection
Cavatappi Winery Maddelena

Terrine Forestier

The distinctive character of wild mushrooms forms the backbone for our version of the classic preparation, Terrine Forestier. Our selection for a complementary wine comes from **Evesham Wood Vineyard**, operated by Russ and Mary Raney of Salem, Oregon. Together with vineyard owner Tom Robbins, the Raneys produce exciting Pinot Noirs and Chardonnays – Burgundian varietals that offer both fruity and earthy components. To accompany the terrine, their Evesham Wood Chardonnay is our choice. Toasty nuances from barrel-aging and the underlying depth of ripe Chardonnay fruit mingle seductively with the complex flavors of the terrine, while crisp Northwest acidity plays a key role in maintaining a fresh palate with this rich and flavorful first course.

12 servings

    2   tablespoons butter
    1   small onion, chopped
    4   medium garlic cloves, minced
  1/2   pound wild mushrooms*, cleaned, thinly
        sliced
    3   tablespoons Madeira
    1   tablespoon Cognac or other brandy
 1 1/3 pounds unseasoned ground pork
  2/3   pound chicken livers, cleaned
  1/4   pound bacon ends, chopped
  3/4   cup Veal Stock, reduced to 2 tablespoons
        (see **Basics**)
    1   large egg, beaten to blend
    2   tablespoons chopped fresh parsley
 1 1/2 teaspoons chopped fresh thyme
    1   teaspoon salt
    1   teaspoon juniper berries, crushed
  2/3   teaspoon ground allspice
  1/2   teaspoon ground cumin
  1/2   teaspoon freshly ground black pepper
    3   tablespoons chopped walnuts
    2   bay leaves

Wine Selection
Evesham Wood Vineyard
Chardonnay

---

1. Position rack in center of oven and preheat to 350° F. Lightly grease 1 1/2-quart terrine mold and set aside.
2. Melt butter in heavy medium skillet over medium heat. Add onion with garlic. Cook until soft and translucent, stirring occasionally, about 5 minutes.
3. Add mushrooms, cover and cook 3 minutes. Uncover and cook until soft and liquid has evaporated, stirring occasionally, about 5 minutes.
4. Stir in Madeira with Cognac. Bring to boil over high heat and reduce by half. Set aside.
5. Blend pork, chicken livers and bacon ends in bowl of food processor, fitted with steel knife, until smooth, about 1 minute.
6. Blend in above mushroom mixture with next 9 ingredients until smooth, about 45 seconds.
7. Mix in walnuts just to incorporate, using several on/off turns.
8. Spoon mixture into prepared mold, patting firmly to pack tightly. Top with bay leaves and cover tightly with heavy-duty aluminum foil (or terrine top). Poke skewer in center for steam vent.
9. Place terrine in shallow baking pan, just large enough to accommodate it. Pour in boiling water to come halfway up sides of mold.
10. Place in oven and cook until instant-read thermometer, inserted into center, registers 150° F., about 45 minutes.
11. Transfer to wire rack and cool 1 hour. Weight and refrigerate overnight. Unmold and wipe off excess fat. Wrap in plastic wrap and refrigerate several days before serving.

* See **Special Ingredients**

Cook's Tip

We highly recommend an enamel, cast-iron mold for this terrine, such as one by Le Creuset.

Chef Cheri Walker's Cranberry Blueberry Mustard, found on page 58, is a nice accompaniment to this terrine.

Pork Terrine *with Apples and Walnuts*

Master the art of charcuterie by way of the food processor and present our rich, country style terrine at your next dinner party. A lively combination of flavors, textures and tantalizing aromas, this easy-to-prepare appetizer or first course is designed to accompany a slightly chilled glass of **Salishan Vineyard's** Dry Riesling. Winemaker Joan Wolverton of the La Center, Washington, winery specializes in crafting wines to accompany foods. Her Dry Riesling offers fresh aromas of apples and pears with crisp acidity that beautifully cuts the richness of the terrine. Accompany this classic Northwest food and wine pairing with our Fall Fruit Chutney, found on page 68, for yet another flavor dimension.

12 servings

 2 tablespoons unsalted butter
 1 medium onion, finely chopped
 3 garlic cloves, minced
 1 cup Veal Stock (see **Basics**)
 $\frac{1}{2}$ cup Madeira
 2 pounds unseasoned ground pork
 $\frac{1}{2}$ pound chicken livers, cleaned
 1 egg, beaten to blend
 2 teaspoons salt
 $2\frac{1}{2}$ teaspoons chopped fresh thyme
 $2\frac{1}{2}$ teaspoons chopped fresh sage
 1 teaspoon freshly ground black pepper
 $\frac{1}{2}$ teaspoon ground allspice
 $\frac{3}{4}$ cup (3 ounces) walnuts, coarsely chopped
 2 medium green Granny Smith apples, cored, peeled, finely chopped
 2 bay leaves

1. Position rack in center of oven and preheat to 350° F. Lightly grease $1\frac{1}{2}$-quart terrine mold and set aside.
2. Melt butter in heavy medium skillet over medium heat. Add onion with garlic. Cook until soft and translucent, stirring occasionally, about 5 minutes.
3. Purée mixture in bowl of food processor, fitted with steel knife. Set aside.
4. Add stock with Madeira to skillet. Bring to boil over high heat and reduce by half. Add to bowl of processor and pulse to mix, using several on/off turns.
5. Blend in next 8 ingredients until smooth, about 45 seconds.
6. Mix in walnuts with apples just to incorporate, using several on/off turns.
7. Spoon mixture into prepared mold, patting firmly to pack tightly. Top with bay leaves and cover tightly with heavy-duty aluminum foil (or terrine top). Poke skewer in center for steam vent.
8. Place terrine in shallow baking pan, just large enough to accommodate it. Pour in boiling water to come halfway up sides of mold.
9. Place in oven and cook until instant-read thermometer, inserted into center, registers 150° F., about 45 minutes.
10. Transfer to wire rack and cool 1 hour. Weight and refrigerate overnight. Unmold and wipe off excess fat. Wrap in plastic wrap and refrigerate several days before serving.

Cook's Tip

We highly recommend an enamel, cast-iron mold for this terrine, such as one by Le Creuset.

Wine Selection
**Salishan Vineyards
Dry Riesling**

Pad Thai *(Spicy Thai Noodles)*

Bridgeport Brewery has established itself as one of the leaders of the Oregon microbrewery scene and consistently brews top-quality ale to suit the most discriminating palate. Many of their beers have proven to be delightful companions to highly seasoned cuisine, especially that of Thailand. Flamboyant, forthright, and bursting with complex flavors, this current star in the culinary arena calls for a dinner companion with definite character and class. Bridgeport Brewery's fine Blue Heron Best Bitter with its aggressive, hoppy bitterness meets head-on with our rendition of Pad Thai, considered the national dish of Thailand. Have it mild or "spicy" hot – just adjust the Sriracha Sauce (Thai chili sauce) and red peppers to your liking. Try this great party dish for your fire-eating friends!

6 to 8 servings

  1/2   pound rice noodles*
   2   tablespoons vegetable oil (or more)

Sauce

   2   small red serrano chilies, stemmed, seeded, deribbed, finely chopped
   7   tablespoons water
   5   tablespoons ketchup
   5   tablespoons fish sauce*
   3   tablespoons fresh cilantro leaves
2 1/2   tablespoons Sriracha Sauce*
   2   tablespoons shredded pickled radish*
   2   tablespoons tamarind water*
1 1/2   tablespoons sugar
1 1/2   tablespoons fresh lime juice

   2   tablespoons vegetable oil
   1   medium onion, chopped
   4   garlic cloves, minced
  3/4   pound small shrimp, shelled, deveined
   3   large eggs, beaten to blend
  1/2   cup extra-firm tofu*, cubed (optional)
1 1/2   cups bean sprouts, divided
   4   green onions, diagonally sliced very thin, divided
  3/4   cup salted peanuts, chopped, divided
      Lime slices
      Fresh cilantro sprigs
      Green onion brushes*

1. Cover noodles with boiling water in large bowl and let stand until soft, 15 to 20 minutes. Drain well. Toss with oil in large bowl and set aside.
2. For sauce: Stir together all ingredients in 2-cup measure until well blended and set aside.
3. Heat wok over medium-high heat. Add oil and swirl to coat. Add onion with garlic. Stir-fry until soft and translucent, about 5 minutes.
4. Add shrimp and stir-fry until just pink, about 2 minutes.
5. Reduce heat to low and stir in half sauce.
6. Push mixture to sides of wok and add eggs to center. Cover and let set slightly, 2 to 3 minutes. Uncover and toss to mix.
7. Increase heat and stir in reserved noodles with tofu, if desired. Toss to mix.
8. Add remaining sauce with half of each of next 3 ingredients. Toss to mix. Cover about 2 minutes to let flavors blend. To serve, place noodles on warm platter and arrange remaining bean sprouts at one end. Sprinkle with remaining green onions and remaining peanuts. Decoratively garnish with lime slices, fresh cilantro sprigs and green onion brushes.

* See **Special Ingredients**

Cook's Tip

For the serious cook tackling Thai cuisine, we suggest purchasing several Thai cookbooks. The following are our favorites:

Keo's Thai Cuisine by Keo Sananikone
The Taste of Thailand by Vatcharin Bhumichitr
The Original Thai Cookbook by Jennifer Brennan

Beer Selection

**Bridgeport Brewery
Blue Heron Best Bitter**

Nachos Grande

Celebrate Cinco de Mayo with our Nachos Grande – the perfect appetizer when Northwest weather suggests a warm and hearty dish on a spring or summer day! For a crowd, make ahead on your largest ovenproof platter and simply pop into the oven just before serving. The dish features local cheeses from Rogue River Creamery in Central Point, Oregon – use equal amounts of their pepper jack and Rogue Gold Cheddar. A shot of Tequila would be tempting, but we prefer Red Hook Brewery's ESB or Black Hook Porter to quench the fire and enliven the soul. The **Red Hook Brewery** is located in the Fremont District of Seattle and offers tours most days and a chance to relax with a brew in their Trolleyman Pub.

10 to 12 servings

- 2 tablespoons vegetable oil
- 1 large onion, chopped
- 5 garlic cloves, minced
- 3 red serrano chilies, stemmed, seeded, deribbed, finely chopped
- 1½ pounds lean ground beef
- ½ pound bulk pork sausage
- 1½ tablespoons chopped fresh oregano
- 1½ teaspoons ground cumin
  Salt and freshly ground black pepper to taste
- 1 can (31 ounces) refried beans
- 1 jar (8 ounces) salsa, mild or hot
- 3 cups (¾ pound) shredded, sharp Cheddar cheese
- 3 cups (¾ pound) shredded, pepper jack cheese
- 1 package (15 ounces) tortilla chips
- ½ bunch green onions, diagonally sliced very thin
- 1 can (2¼ ounces) sliced olives
  Fresh cilantro sprigs
- 1 container (16 ounces) sour cream
  Guacamole (optional)

1. Position rack in lowest third of oven and preheat to 350° F.
2. Heat oil in heavy large skillet over medium heat. Add onion, garlic and chilies. Cook until onion is soft and translucent, stirring occasionally, about 5 minutes.
3. Add beef with sausage. Fry until meat is well cooked, breaking up large pieces with wooden spoon and stirring occasionally, about 15 minutes. Drain fat and set aside.
4. Combine oregano, cumin, salt and pepper in small bowl. Stir into meat mixture and set aside.
5. To assemble, spread beans over bottom of large ovenproof platter. Top evenly with meat mixture, drizzle generously with salsa and sprinkle with cheeses.
6. Cover loosely with aluminum foil and bake until heated through and cheese starts to bubble, 20 to 25 minutes. To serve, tuck chips around edge of platter and sprinkle with green onions and olives. Garnish decoratively with fresh cilantro sprigs. Accompany with sour cream and guacamole, if desired.

Beer Selection
Red Hook Brewery ESB

Emerald Butterflies

Ranked as one of Washington's finest ethnic restaurants, **The Emerald of Siam** in Richland, Washington, specializes in authentic Thai cuisine. Elegantly presented and prepared daily with the freshest local ingredients, the creative endeavors of chef/owner Ravadi Quinn please locals as well as visitors from afar. One of the most requested appetizers is presented here for your gustatory approval. Freshly cooked crab, cream cheese, green onions and a dash of soy sauce are enclosed in a delicate won ton wrapper and transform into a tantalizing, deep-fried palate teaser. Chef Quinn touts a Northwest wine list, sure to please any wine-conscious gourmand fond of Thai cuisine. She suggests a restaurant favorite, **Barnard Griffin** Johannisberg Riesling to accompany her delightful appetizer. The wine's fresh acidity is an effective contrast to the deep-fried delicacy, while the floral flavors come alive with the addition of your favorite sweet and sour sauce.

Makes 48

Filling

    8 ounces fresh cream cheese, room
          temperature
    1 ounce crabmeat, flaked
    1 green onion, minced
 1¹/₂ teaspoons light soy sauce

    1 package (12 ounces) won ton wrappers*
          (48 wrappers)
       Lukewarm water
       Vegetable oil (for deep-frying)
       Sweet and sour sauce (optional)

1. For filling: Using electric mixer, soften cream cheese in medium bowl 3 minutes. Mix in crabmeat, green onion and soy sauce until well blended. Cover and refrigerate 1 hour.
2. To assemble, place 1 won ton wrapper on work surface with corners at top, bottom, left and right.
3. Place 1 generous teaspoon filling in center of wrapper. Brush edges with warm water and fold top corner down to align with bottom corner. Press to seal.
4. Place on lightly greased baking sheet. Repeat with remaining wrappers and filling. Cover and refrigerate 30 minutes before deep-frying.
5. Heat oil in wok or deep-fryer to 375° F. Deep-fry won tons (in batches; do not crowd) until crisp and lightly browned, about 1¹/₂ minutes. (Flip over once, if necessary.)
6. Using slotted spoon, remove won tons and transfer to paper towels. Drain well and serve immediately with your favorite sweet and sour sauce, if desired.

* See **Special Ingredients**

Cook's Tip

Substitute 1 package (8 ounces) Philadelphia brand cream cheese, if fresh is not available.

Wine Selection
Barnard Griffin
Johannisberg Riesling

Summer Vichyssoise

The following soup is a variation of the classic created by French chef Louis Diat in 1917. With its cornucopia of fresh flavors, highlighting dill and cucumber – a sommelier's nightmare to match with wine, it's a stunning first course for that upcoming backyard barbecue. Susan Martin of Idaho's **Rose Creek Vineyards** feels the dense and crunchy texture of her soup suggests an appropriate wine pairing. Her winemaker/husband Jamie's light and slightly sweet Johannisberg Riesling offers just enough bright young fruit to form a refreshing backdrop to the grassy flavors of the dill, while cleansing the palate before the next bite. Present Susan's Summer Vichyssoise in your finest soup tureen or individual chilled mugs. Accompany with fresh garlic bread toasted on the grill.

6 servings

3 tablespoons unsalted butter
3 garlic cloves, minced
1 bunch green onions, diagonally sliced
    very thin
2 medium cucumbers, peeled, halved
    lengthwise, seeded, diced
1 bunch fresh spinach, well rinsed, dried,
    stemmed, chopped
1 large russet potato, diced
1 turnip, diced
3 cups Chicken Stock, (see **Basics**)
1 tablespoon balsamic vinegar*
1 tablespoon chopped fresh dill
1/4 teaspoon ground cumin
    Dash cayenne pepper
    Salt and freshly ground black pepper
1 cup heavy cream
    Crème Fraîche (see **Basics**) or sour cream
    Fresh dill sprigs

1. Melt butter in medium Dutch oven over medium heat. Add garlic with green onions. Sauté until soft, about 3 minutes.
2. Stir in cucumbers, spinach, potato and turnip. Cover and cook 2 minutes.
3. Add stock, vinegar, dill, cumin and cayenne pepper. Bring to boil over high heat. Immediately reduce heat and simmer until vegetables are soft, about 40 minutes. Season with salt and pepper.
4. Transfer mixture to bowl of food processor, fitted with steel knife (in batches, if necessary). Pulse to almost purée, using several on/off turns. (Do not purée completely, as soup should retain some crunch.)
5. Transfer mixture to plastic storage container and stir in cream. Cover and refrigerate until well chilled. To serve, ladle soup into chilled mugs and top each with dollop of crème fraîche and fresh dill sprig.

* See **Special Ingredients**

Wine Selection

**Rose Creek Vineyards
Johannisberg Riesling**

Phyllo Purses *with Wild Mushrooms,*
Walla Walla Sweets and Roasted Red Pepper Purée

Unbridled creativity is the culinary trademark of Executive Chef Caprial Pence of **Fullers Restaurant** at the Seattle Sheraton. She intuitively creates breathtakingly beautiful and flavorful dishes, making the most of the seasonal bounty of the Pacific Northwest. In the following recipe, chef Pence's inspiration focuses on intense flavors and a picture-perfect presentation – almost too good to eat! Walla Walla sweets, wild mushrooms, goat cheese and roasted red peppers combine beautifully into an unforgettable constellation of shining Northwest stars, warning you that summer is fading quickly and fall is just around the corner. For her earthy first course, chef Pence highly recommends **Rex Hill Vineyards** Pinot Noir as your choice of wine. Rich aromas of fruit and game – a classic sign of good Pinot – mingle with the earthy combination, while the full-bodied palate of the wine contrasts the intense flavors of each ingredient.

6 servings

Roasted Red Bell Pepper Purée

  2   medium red bell peppers
  1   tablespoon olive oil
  3   garlic cloves, roasted

Filling

  1   tablespoon olive oil
  3   shallots, chopped
  2   garlic cloves, chopped
  ½   pound wild mushrooms*, cleaned,
        thinly sliced
  1   small Walla Walla sweet onion, diced
  4   ounces mild soft goat cheese (chèvre),
        such as Montrachet*, room temperature
  1   teaspoon chopped fresh lemon thyme
  ½   teaspoon freshly cracked black pepper
        Salt to taste

  12   phyllo pastry sheets*, thawed if frozen
  4   tablespoons unsalted butter, melted

1. For red pepper purée: Rub peppers with oil and char over gas flame or under broiler on all sides. Let steam in paper bag 10 minutes. Peel, stem, seed and derib. Purée with garlic in blender or food processor, fitted with steel knife. Transfer to serving bowl, cover and set aside until needed. (Purée should be served at room temperature.)

2. For filling: Heat oil in heavy large sauté pan over high heat. Add shallots with garlic. Sauté until you smell aroma of shallots, about 1 minute. Add mushrooms with onion. Sauté until soft, 3 to 4 minutes. Cool mixture slightly, then stir in goat cheese, thyme, pepper and salt. Set aside.

3. Position rack in center of oven and preheat to 350° F.

4. Cut phyllo pastry sheets in half and place atop one another. Cover with waxed paper, then damp cloth.

5. To assemble, place 2 pastry sheets on work surface and brush lightly with butter. Top with 2 more pastry sheets and brush lightly with butter.

6. Place about 3 tablespoons filling in center of pastry sheet. Gather corners and twist. Trim excess. Transfer to lightly greased baking sheet and brush top and sides lightly with butter. Repeat with remaining pastry sheets and filling.

7. Bake until golden brown, about 15 minutes. To serve, place purses on warm plates and accompany with Roasted Red Bell Pepper Purée.

* See **Special Ingredients**

Cook's Tip

Sprigs of fresh lemon thyme make a stunning garnish for chef Pence's show-stopping starter.

Wine Selection
Rex Hill Vineyards Pinot Noir

Tarragon Sour Cream Dip

Dorothy Rogers and Karman McReynolds of Cedarbrook Herb Farm in Sequim, are the authors of *Can't Cook Without Herbs,* a series of popular mini-cookbooks highlighting the use of local herbs. They advise Northwest gardeners (and those elsewhere too) to grow their own herbs during the spring and summer and then pick them at their peak of flavor to dry for winter use. Whether using fresh or dried, cooking with herbs often has the pleasant side result of making any dish more wine-friendly. Some wines have particular affinities for certain herbs as noted in our wine and herb chart below. For example, try Dorothy and Karman's delightfully simple Tarragon Sour Cream Dip with **Neuharth Winery** Chardonnay. The wine offers bright fruity aromas with just a hint of oak, which nicely highlights the tarragon flavors in the dip.

Wine Selection

Neuharth Winery Chardonnay

Makes about 1³/₄ cups

  1 cup sour cream
¹/₂ cup mayonnaise
  2 tablespoons chopped fresh chives
  1 tablespoon chopped fresh tarragon
¹/₂ tablespoon tarragon vinegar *
¹/₂ tablespoon salad burnet vinegar * or white
        wine vinegar

        Crudites

1. Stir together sour cream, mayonnaise, chives, tarragon, tarragon vinegar and salad burnet vinegar in small bowl until well blended.
2. Cover with plastic wrap and refrigerate at least 2 hours or overnight before serving. Accompany with crudites.

* See **Special Ingredients**

Matching Wines with Herbs

Many wines have herbaceous characteristics in their aromas and flavors making them more compatible with dishes in which herbs are part of the seasoning. The chart below lists the most common culinary herbs and the wines that best match them.

Dominant Herb	White Wine Match	Red Wine Match
Basil	Sauvignon Blanc, Semillon	Pinot Noir, Merlot
Coriander	Sauvignon Blanc, Gewürztraminer	Cabernet Sauvignon
Dill	Sauvignon Blanc, Semillon	Cabernet Sauvignon
Mint	Chardonnay, Riesling	Cabernet Sauvignon
Oregano	Sauvignon Blanc, Semillon	Pinot Noir, Merlot
Rosemary	Sauvignon Blanc, Chardonnay	Pinot Noir, Cabernet Sauvignon
Sage	Riesling	Lemberger, Pinot Noir
Tarragon	Chardonnay	Pinot Noir
Thyme	Semillon	Lemberger, Merlot

Walla Walla-Stuffed Mushrooms

For a tempting palate teaser during the month of June, try our Walla Walla-Stuffed Mushrooms, made with Washington State's own famous Walla Walla sweet onions. The season is short, so don't let this regional specialty pass you by! Mushrooms are a natural with Chardonnay and we highly recommend **Waterbrook Winery's** toasty Reserve bottling to sip as you savor these tasty appetizers. Their buttery-earthy character highlights the wine's tropical fruit and toasty butterscotch nuances gained from barrel-fermentaton in French oak. Make ahead and pop in the oven just before your guests arrive!

12 servings

12 large mushrooms (2 inches diameter), cleaned
4 tablespoons unsalted butter
3 garlic cloves, minced
2 medium celery stalks, diced
1 medium Walla Walla sweet onion, finely chopped
$^1/_2$ cup Waterbrook Winery Chardonnay
$1^1/_2$ teaspoons chopped fresh savory
   Dash cayenne pepper
1 cup (4 ounces) shredded Monterey Jack cheese, divided
$^1/_2$ cup fine dry bread crumbs
   Salt and freshly ground black pepper

1. Position rack in center of oven and preheat to 350° F. Lightly grease baking dish, large enough to just accommodate mushrooms.
2. Remove stems from mushrooms and reserve. Hollow out inside of mushrooms and reserve meat. Set mushrooms aside. Finely chop together mushroom stems with mushroom meat. Set aside.
3. Melt butter in heavy medium skillet over medium heat. Add garlic and sauté until tender, about 2 minutes.
4. Stir in mushroom mixture, celery, onion, wine, savory and cayenne pepper. Cook until almost dry, stirring occasionally, about 10 minutes.
5. Stir in $^3/_4$ cup cheese with bread crumbs. Season with salt and pepper. Cool slightly.
6. Stuff mushroom caps, heaping into rounds. Sprinkle with remaining cheese.
7. Place mushrooms in prepared baking dish and bake until almost tender and cheese melts, about 8 minutes. Serve immediately.

Wine Selection
Waterbrook Sauvignon Blanc

Stuffed Grape Leaves

If you're a country music fan, don't miss **Oak Knoll Winery's** "Bacchus Goes Bluegrass" festival held each year on the third weekend in May. It's Oregon's largest winery-sponsored event, attracting over 30,000 music lovers to the Hillsboro winery. Oak Knoll's owners, the Vuylsteke family, offer Stuffed Grape Leaves – a Middle Eastern-inspired creation of Marj Vuylsteke – to the hungry throngs, along with sips of their Vintage Select Pinot Noir. The slight tartness of the grape leaves contrasts the wonderful fruity flavors of the wine and beautifully complements the wine's acidity. Try this tasty combination at home or, better yet, head on down to the festival - we know you'll have a great time!

Makes about 60

Filling

   1 pound lean ground lamb
   1 can (8 ounces) tomato sauce
   1 small onion, finely chopped
  $^1/_2$ cup uncooked rice, rinsed until clear
  $^1/_2$ teaspoon garlic powder
     Salt and freshly ground black pepper
       to taste

 65 fresh grape leaves (about) or 1 jar
       (7 ounces)*
$1^1/_2$ cups water
  2 tablespoons fresh lemon juice
  2 beef bouillon cubes
     Lemon wedges
     Fresh Italian flat-leaf parsley sprigs

1. For filling: Knead together all ingredients in large bowl until well blended. Cover and refrigerate about 1 hour.
2. Cut tough stems from grape leaves and discard. Place leaves in large bowl, cover with boiling water and let stand several minutes to become pliable. Drain well, pat dry with paper towels and set aside.
3. Position rack in lowest third of oven and preheat to 350° F.
4. Line bottom of $3^1/_2$-quart Dutch oven or ovenproof casserole (with tight fitting lid) with several leaves. Set aside.
5. To roll, place 1 grape leaf, vein side up, on work surface with stem end facing you. Place 1 tablespoon filling in center, $^1/_2$-inch from stem end. Fold stem end over filling. Fold right side in to enclose filling, then fold left side in to enclose filling. Roll up and place snugly, seam side down, in Dutch oven. (Do not roll too tightly or grape leaf will burst; filling expands during cooking.) Repeat with remaining grape leaves and filling.
6. Stir together water, lemon juice and bouillon cubes in 2-cup measure. Pour over grape leaves.
7. Place inverted heatproof dish (one that just fits inside Dutch oven) atop grape leaves to prevent them from unrolling during cooking. Cover tightly with lid or heavy-duty aluminum foil.
8. Place in oven and cook until grape leaves are tender, about 45 minutes. Transfer to wire rack and cool slightly. To serve, drain liquid and invert casserole onto serving dish. Garnish with lemon wedges and fresh parsley sprigs.

* See **Special Ingredients**

Cook's Tip

Make these tasty appetizers ahead through step #5 and freeze. To complete the preparation, simply thaw and proceed with step #6.

Hummus *(Garbanzo Bean Dip)*

Garbanzo (or chick-pea), a warm-weather bush bean native to the subtropics, has recently proven quite successful in dry areas of the Pacific Northwest. In 1987, Eastern Washington was the leading garbanzo-producing region in the U.S. Hummus, a Middle Eastern-inspired bread dip made with garbanzo beans, was made popular in our region by the many Lebanese families living in the area. This tasty mezza (appetizer in Lebanese) is a snap to prepare and freezes beautifully – ideal for those last minute gatherings. Our version draws inspiration from many Lebanese cooks, all of whom claim their version to be the best! The somewhat mouth-coating texture calls for a dry, crisp white wine with lots of character. **Cascade Estates Winery** Chardonnay offers a kiss of oak from barrel-aging to provide a delicious flavor interest, while the wine's acidity complements the tang from the freshly squeezed lemon juice. Pass the pita bread – a must for scooping!

Makes 2 cups

       3 garlic cloves
    1¹/₂ cups dried garbanzo beans, cooked and
             drained or 2 cans (15¹/₂ ounces each)
             garbanzo beans, drained, well rinsed
     ¹/₂ cup tahini (sesame seed paste)
       7 tablespoons fresh lemon juice
          Salt and freshly ground black pepper
          Olive oil
          Paprika
          Fresh cilantro sprigs
          Pita bread

1. Mince garlic in bowl of food processor, fitted with steel knife.
2. Blend in garbanzo beans (set several aside for garnish), tahini and lemon juice until smooth. Season with salt and pepper. To serve, pour mixture into shallow serving dish and drizzle with oil. Sprinkle with paprika and garnish with reserved garbanzo beans and fresh cilantro sprigs. Accompany with pita bread.

Cook's Tip

To savor the full flavors of this tasty dip, serve at room temperature.

Wine Selection

**Cascade Estates Winery
Chardonnay**

Marinated Chèvre

Chèvre, a name increasingly heard in our region, is the French word for goat cheese and, by extension, cheese made from goat's milk. Locally, several producers are enjoying success at crafting this delightfully versatile cheese which adapts beautifully to a number of fine Northwest wines. **Stimson Lane Wines & Spirits** in Woodinville, Washington, offers a line of méthode champenoise sparkling wines under the brand **Domaine Ste. Michelle**. Talented winemaker Allan Pangborn crafts their Blanc de Noir to yield toasty, yeasty aromas and lovely austere fruit, making it the perfect foil for our Marinated Chèvre. The soft, tangy character of the cheese, punctuated with the intensity of oven-dried tomatoes and the pungency of fresh oregano, challenges the earthy qualities of the wine, while the crisp acid backbone wins out to cleanse the palate.

Wine Selection

**Domaine Ste. Michelle
Blanc de Noir Brut**

Serves 25 to 30

Marinade

- ³/₄ cup extra-virgin olive oil
- ¹/₄ cup pure olive oil
- 10 black Greek-style olives, rinsed
- 3 garlic cloves, halved
- 3 Oven-Dried Tomatoes, chopped (see **Basics**)
- 1 tablespoon Oven-Dried Tomato Oil (see **Basics**)
- 1 tablespoon chopped fresh oregano

- 8 ounces mild soft goat cheese (chèvre), such as Montrachet*
- 1 loaf French bread, diagonally sliced ³/₄-inch-thick (25 to 30 slices)

1. For marinade: Combine all ingredients in small bowl until well blended and set aside.
2. Place goat cheese in serving bowl, large enough to accommodate it with marinade.
3. Pour marinade over, cover and refrigerate at least 3 hours to let flavors blend. To serve, soften cheese slightly at room temperature. Accompany with French bread slices.

* See **Special Ingredients**

Méthode Champenoise
The Making of Sparkling Wine

The best sparkling wines are made by a process called méthode champenoise, perfected during the 300 years since Dom Perignon first exclaimed "I'm drinking stars!" at the Abbaye d' Hautvilliers.

Champagne and other sparkling wines begin as still wine (wine without bubbles) fermented as is any other wine. These various lots of still wine are blended into a cuvée (blend) to which a mixture of wine, sugar and yeast is added to start the secondary fermentation. After this "liqueur de tiriage" is added, the wine is bottled into champagne bottles and capped with a crown cap (beer cap).

After several months the bottles are placed into riddling racks or onto gyropallets to undergo a process by which the yeast sediment is gently shaken down into the neck of the bottle.

To remove this collected sediment, the bottles are placed, neck down, into a freezing brine solution. This freezes a plug of wine and sediment in the neck which is "disgorged" by removing the crown cap. The built-up pressure in the bottle forces the plug out leaving clean, sediment-free sparkling wine behind.

Before the final corking, a "dosage" of brandy, sugar and wine is added to create a slight, offsetting sweetness in the finished wine. In Brut wines this sugar amount is very small.

After several months of rest in the bottle, the finished sparkling wine is on its way to your celebration!

Garlic Pesto Bruschetta

With local basil season in the Northwest at its peak in August, and last minute entertaining upon us, pesto-making is a must! In our Garlic Pesto Bruschetta, fresh basil and other wonderful ingredients team up with the fragrance of a whole head of garlic and freshly grated Parmesan cheese to make an appetizer sure to please any garlic-loving dinner guest. An excellent accompanying wine is **Staton Hills Winery** Sauvignon Blanc. Their crisp and herbaceous version has the necessary acidity to cut through the richness of the dish, while hints of oak and herbs complement the flavors of the garlic and basil. Make this tasty appetizer ahead and pop it in the oven when your guests arrive.

About 25 servings

1 loaf French bread, diagonally sliced
  $3/4$-inch-thick (about 25 slices)
1 cup extra-virgin olive oil
1 head fresh garlic (12 to 15 cloves),
  minced
1 cup Garlic Pesto or more (recipe follows)
$1^1/2$ cups heavy cream
2 ounces freshly grated Parmesan cheese
  Chopped fresh Italian flat-leaf parsley

1. Position rack in center of oven and preheat to 350° F.
2. Loosely wrap bread in aluminum foil, leaving top open. Set aside.
3. Whisk together oil with garlic in small bowl until well blended.
4. Generously brush mixture between bread slices, then brush Garlic Pesto between bread slices. Set aside.
5. Bring cream to boil in heavy medium saucepan over medium-high heat. Reduce by half. Stir in cheese until well blended.
6. Drizzle mixture between and atop bread slices.
7. Close foil and bake 15 minutes. Remove bread from oven and open foil to expose top of loaf.
8. Return to oven and bake until top is lightly browned, 8 to 10 minutes. Leave bread in foil and sprinkle generously with chopped parsley. Serve immediately with tongs.

Garlic Pesto

2 cups loose-packed fresh basil leaves (no thick stems)
$1/2$ cup extra-virgin olive oil
$1/2$ cup (4 ounces) freshly grated Parmesan cheese
6 garlic cloves, minced
2 tablespoons freshly grated Romano cheese
2 tablespoons toasted pine nuts
2 sprigs fresh Italian flat-leaf parsley
  Salt and freshly ground black pepper to taste

Blend above ingredients in bowl of food processor, fitted with steel knife, until smooth. (Makes about $1^1/2$ cups.)

Cook's Tip

For a stunning presentation, nestle this tasty bread in a pretty napkin atop a silver tray and garnish lavishly with fresh basil sprigs.

Wine Selection

**Staton Hills Winery
Sauvignon Blanc**

Gewürztraminer Garlic Toast

Amity Vineyards is one of Oregon's pioneer wineries in the production of award-winning Pinot Noir, but owner Myron Redford continues to have a fondness in his heart for other varietals, especially locally-grown Gewürztraminer. Myron's significant other, Vikki Wetle, shares with us her wonderful cold weather appetizer, Gewürztraminer Garlic Toast, to accompany Myron's delightful wine. She adapted the recipe from a dish they enjoyed on one of their trips to the Burgundy region of France. The potency of garlic is well-known, but Vikki "tames the tiger" by gently sautéing the garlic, then lightly poaching it in Amity Vineyards' distinctive Gewürztraminer. You may choose to pour Myron's Gewürztraminer with the dish or opt instead for a glass of his magnificent Pinot Noir. Both wines marry beautifully with this garlic-lovers' delight.

12 servings

- 6 tablespoons unsalted butter
- 6 tablespoons olive oil
- 50 medium garlic cloves (3 to 4 medium heads)
- 1½ cups Amity Vineyards Gewürztraminer
  Freshly ground black pepper to taste
- 12 slices toasted French bread
- 12 tablespoons minced fresh basil or parsley
- 12 tablespoons minced fresh chives

1. Melt butter with oil in heavy medium skillet over medium heat.
2. Add garlic and sauté until slightly softened, about 5 minutes.
3. Reduce heat and stir in wine with pepper. Simmer about 10 minutes.
4. With slotted spoon, transfer garlic to bowl of food processor, fitted with steel knife, and purée.
5. Spread purée on toasted French bread slices and place on serving plate. Set aside.
6. Quickly reduce skillet liquid by half and drizzle over toasted French bread slices. Generously sprinkle with minced fresh basil and minced fresh chives. Serve immediately.

Wine Selection
Amity Vineyards Gewürztraminer

Pesto Chèvre Bread

Mary Benoit of **Chateau Benoit** in Carlton, Oregon, shares her idea for the perfect summer appetizer – a thinly sliced baguette of French bread lavished with tangy goat cheese (chèvre in France), freshly made pesto and homemade, oven-dried tomatoes. Top with a drizzle of fruity olive oil and you've got a simple, yet delicious, starter for that next special evening. To accompany, pour Chateau Benoit's award-winning Sauvignon Blanc and savor the flavors of this sensational, seasonal match. The herbaceous flavors of the wine are delicious with the fresh, earthy flavors of the bread's toppings – a classic wine country combination!

About 25 servings

  2 ounces mild soft goat cheese (chèvre),
      such as Montrachet*, room temperature
  2 tablespoons heavy cream
1¹/₂ cups Pesto (see **Basics**)
  1 loaf French bread, diagonally sliced
      ³/₄-inch-thick (about 25 slices)
     Oven-Dried Tomatoes, slivered
      (see **Basics**)
     Olive oil
     Fresh Basil sprigs

1. Combine goat cheese with cream in small bowl until well blended. Set aside.
2. Generously spread pesto on bread slices.
3. Generously spread goat cheese mixture on bread slices.
4. Top bread slices with oven-dried tomato slivers, then drizzle with olive oil. To serve, arrange bread slices on large serving tray and decoratively surround with fresh basil sprigs.

* See **Special Ingredients**

Cook's Tip

For this lovely appetizer, we like to use a fruity olive oil, such as Antinori or Badia a Coltibuno from Italy.

Wine Selection
Chateau Benoit Sauvignon Blanc

Northwest Cheeses with Northwest Wines

The term "Northwest cheese" invokes images of fresh homestead cheeses and caring producers of bulk cheese taking advantage of the freshest local milk. Both styles have large and devoted followings around the country.

Northwest cheeses are usually differentiated by state; styles between Washington and Oregon are quite different, while Idaho tends to complement Washington's style of small, local producers with little or no mass marketing of their product. It is for this reason that many cheeses are only occasionally available on your local cheesemongers' shelves. Savvy customers become well schooled in asking what is currently fresh rather than demanding the same cheese week after week.

Washington cheese pioneers in promoting this philosophy are Sally Jackson of Oroville,

The Quillasascut Cheese Co. of Rice, and Glencorra Cheeses of Lopez Island. Their products are hand delivered to the Seattle market on an "as ready" basis. In Oregon, the Rogue Valley Creamery near Grants Pass and the Tillamook Cheese Co. follow a decades old tradition of milk co-ops to find the highest quality milk for their cheddars and blues.

Most gourmands acknowledge that fine cheese and fine wines are the perfect match. Very few combinations fail to please the palate. Try the local chèvres and sheep's milk cheeses with your favorite Northwest Sauvignon Blanc, Riesling, Chardonnay or Pinot Noir for an enjoyable beginning to an elegant evening.

*Special thanks to our good friend Kathleen McInnis, proprietor of **Brie and Bordeaux** in Seattle, who shared this knowledge of the Northwest cheese industry.*

Swiss Rye Bread

Philippe Girardet, owner and winemaker of **Girardet Vineyards**, fondly remembers growing up in the Alps of Switzerland and the foods and wines his family served. Hearty loaves of country rye bread, lavished with soft, voluptuous cheeses such as Vacherin and Reblochon, were his inspiration for the crafting of his country style wines, Oregon Vin Blanc and Oregon Vin Rouge. These wines, blended from selected varietals grown at Girardet Vineyards, offer earthy complexity reminiscent of many European bottlings. Try our Swiss Rye Bread with the cheeses of Girardet's homeland, accompanied by a glass of his exquisitely crafted Vin Blanc or Vin Rouge.

Makes two 1¹/₂ pound loaves

  1 tablespoon honey, divided
  2 cups water, divided (¹/₄ cup warm –
        105° F. to 115° F., 1³/₄ cups cool)
1¹/₂ tablespoons active dry yeast
3³/₄ cups bread flour*
  2 cups medium rye flour
2¹/₂ teaspoons salt
  4 tablespoons butter, cut into pieces, room
        temperature
  2 tablespoons dark molasses
  3 tablespoons caraway seeds, divided
      Cornmeal
  1 large egg, lightly beaten with ¹/₂ teaspoon
        salt (glaze)

1. Stir together 1 teaspoon honey with warm water in small bowl until well blended. Sprinkle over yeast and stir to dissolve. Let stand until foamy, about 10 minutes.
2. Mix both flours with salt in bowl of food processor, fitted with steel knife, using several on/off turns.
3. With machine running, add butter through feed tube, 1 piece at a time, until thoroughly incorporated.
4. Mix in yeast mixture, remaining honey, molasses and 1 tablespoon caraway seeds until just incorporated, using several on/off turns.
5. With machine running, slowly pour cool water through feed tube until dough cleans sides of bowl and forms ball atop blade. Process 45 seconds longer to thoroughly knead.
6. Transfer dough to lightly greased bowl and rotate to coat surface with oil. Cover with towel and let rise in warm, draft-free area until doubled, about 1 hour.
7. Meanwhile, position rack in center of oven and preheat to 375° F.
8. Punch down dough and turn out onto lightly floured surface. Divide in half and shape into round loaves.
9. Transfer loaves to lightly greased baking sheet (or sheets) sprinkled with cornmeal. Cover with towel and let rise in warm, draft-free area until doubled, about 45 minutes.
10. Slash tops of loaves crosswise, several times, with sharp knife and brush with glaze. Sprinkle with remaining caraway seeds.
11. Bake until loaves sound hollow when tapped on bottom, 35 to 40 minutes. Transfer loaves to wire rack and cool. Thinly slice and serve.

* See **Special Ingredients**

Wine Selection

**Girardet Vineyards
Oregon Vin Blanc**

Gourmet Harvest Pizza

When it comes to pizza, the possibilities for crusts and toppings are almost endless. In our Gourmet Harvest Pizza, we celebrate the end of summer with some of the finest bounty the Northwest has to offer – juicy vine-ripe tomatoes, freshly made pesto, bright red bell peppers and earthy chanterelle mushrooms. Top a pizza with all of this, along with other traditional favorites, and you've got a pizza with pizazz! Enjoy our favorite wine for this pizza-lovers' delight, a glass of **Barnard Griffin's** richly flavored Fumé Blanc. The wine's richness and complexity is the perfect foil for the herbaceous and earthy flavors of the pizza. Like many Northwest white wines, this Fumé Blanc offers crisp acidity to refresh and cleanse the palate, while also providing a complement to the tomato sauce.

6 to 8 servings

Pizza Dough

    1   tablespoon active dry yeast
    1   cup water, divided (¹/₄ cup warm –
          105° F. to 115° F., ³/₄ cup cool)
    2   tablespoons olive oil
    1   tablespoon honey
    3   garlic cloves
    3   cups bread flour*
    1   teaspoon salt
        Olive oil

Topping

    2   tablespoons olive oil
    2   garlic cloves, minced
¹/₄   pound chanterelles*, cleaned, thinly
          sliced
    2   cups Spicy Tomato Sauce (see **Basics**)
³/₄   cup Pesto (see **Basics**)
    1   small red bell pepper, stemmed, seeded,
          deribbed, cut julienne
    4   Oven-Dried Tomatoes,
          minced (see **Basics**)
1¹/₂ cups (about 6 ounces) shredded Fontina
          cheese
1¹/₂ cups (about 6 ounces) shredded
          Mozzarella cheese
³/₄   cup (about 3 ounces) freshly grated
          Parmesan cheese
        Oven-Dried Tomato Oil (see **Basics**)

        Fresh basil sprigs (optional)
        Freshly grated Parmesan cheese
          (optional)

1. For pizza dough: Sprinkle yeast over warm water in small bowl and stir to dissolve. Let stand until foamy, about 10 minutes. Whisk together cool water, oil and honey in measuring cup. Set aside.

2. Mince garlic in bowl of food processor, fitted with steel knife. Mix in flour with salt, using several on/off turns. With machine running, slowly pour yeast mixture, then cool water mixture, through feed tube until dough cleans sides of bowl and forms ball atop blade. Process 45 seconds longer to thoroughly knead.

3. Transfer dough to lightly greased bowl and rotate to coat surface with oil. Cover with plastic wrap and let rise in warm, draft-free area until doubled, about 1 hour.

4. Position rack in center of oven and preheat to 400° F. Lightly grease 16-inch-diameter pizza pan.

5. Punch down dough and roll out on lightly floured surface into 16-inch round. Transfer to prepared pan and brush with olive oil.

6. Bake until starting to brown, 5 to 7 minutes. Set aside and proceed with topping.

7. For topping: Heat oil in heavy medium skillet over medium-low heat. Add garlic with chanterelles. Sauté until soft, about 4 minutes. Set aside.

8. Spread tomato sauce over crust, leaving 1-inch border. Drizzle with pesto and top with chanterelles, red bell peppers and oven-dried tomatoes. Sprinkle with Fontina, Mozzarella and Parmesan. Brush edges with oven-dried tomato oil.

9. Bake until cheese melts and crust is golden brown, 12 to 15 minutes. Cut into wedges and serve immediately. Garnish with fresh basil sprigs and offer additional freshly grated Parmesan cheese, if desired.

* See **Special Ingredients**

Wine Selection

Barnard Griffin Fumé Blanc

Walnut Brie in Brioche

Foris Vineyards owner and winemaker Ted Gerber produces fine quality Muscat from his vineyard near Cave Junction in Southern Oregon. An intriguing varietal, this off-dry version, with a pungent aroma and crisp acidity, is the perfect complement to our Walnut Brie in Brioche. The firm acid backbone cuts through the butterfat of the cheese, while the delicious toasty dimension of the wine is highlighted by the addition of walnuts – a sublime match! Fresh apple slices make a nice accompaniment to this before-or-after-dinner treat!

4 to 6 servings

Brioche Dough

1 teaspoon Quick-Rise active dry yeast
2 tablespoons warm water (105° F. to 115° F.)
2 tablespoons sugar, divided
1 cup bread flour*, divided
2 large eggs, room temperature
7 tablespoons butter, cut into pieces, room temperature
Bread flour

$^1/_2$ cup (2 ounces) chopped walnuts
1 wheel Brie cheese (8 ounces), room temperature
1 large egg, slightly beaten with 1 teaspoon warm water (glaze)
Cornmeal

1. For brioche dough: Combine yeast, water and 1 tablespoon sugar in tilted bowl of food processor. Let stand until foamy, about 10 minutes.
2. Engage processor bowl and mix in $^1/_4$ cup flour with 1 egg, using several on/off turns. Sprinkle in remaining flour, cover and let stand 1 hour at room temperature.
3. Blend in remaining sugar with remaining egg, processing about 20 seconds.
4. With machine running, add butter through feed tube, 1 piece at a time, until thoroughly incorporated.
5. Scrape mixture into lightly greased bowl and sprinkle lightly with flour. Cover with towel and let rise $2^1/_2$ to 3 hours in warm, draft-free area.
6. With handle of plastic spatula, deflate dough. Cover with towel and refrigerate 20 minutes.
7. Turn out dough onto lightly floured surface and knead gently 2 minutes. Dust lightly with flour, wrap in plastic wrap and let rest at least 8 hours or overnight before using. (Makes about $^3/_4$ pound.)
8. To assemble, roll out dough on lightly floured surface into 12-inch round. Sprinkle center with walnuts and place cheese atop walnuts. Bring sides up and over to enclose cheese. Seal with glaze and pinch to secure. Reserve glaze.
9. Invert brioche onto lightly greased baking sheet sprinkled with cornmeal. Cover with plastic wrap and let rise 1 hour in warm, draft-free area.
10. Meanwhile, position rack in center of oven and preheat to 425° F.
11. Brush brioche with remaining glaze and bake 10 minutes. Immediately reduce heat to 350° F. and bake until lightly browned, about 10 minutes longer. Transfer baking sheet to wire rack and let brioche rest 5 minutes. To serve, transfer brioche to bread board and cut into wedges.

* See **Special Ingredients**

Wine Selection
Foris Vineyards Early Muscat

Entrées

Northwest Dungeness Crab Feed ~ 54

Fisherman's Soup ~ 55

Chargrilled Halibut ~ 56

Grilled Halibut Kebabs ~ 57

Grilled Pacific Salmon ~ 58

Salmon and Oysters ~ 59

Grapewood-Grilled Salmon ~ 60

Mussels Marinara ~ 61

White Clam Linguine ~ 62

Pacific Snapper Creole ~ 63

Paella Northwest Style ~ 64

Chicken Tarragon ~ 66

Stuffed Chicken Breasts ~ 67

Roast Breast of Turkey ~ 68

Almond Chicken Curry ~ 69

Szechwan Pork with Broccoli ~ 70

Grilled Pork Chops ~ 71

Baby Back Ribs
   with Spicy Peanut Sauce ~ 72

Veal Marengo ~ 73

Grilled Veal Loin Chops ~ 74

Flank Steak Salsa ~ 75

Grilled New York Steaks ~ 76

Beef Tournedos
   with Oregon Blue Cheese ~ 77

Pan-Fried Filet Mignons ~ 78

Wheeler's Supreme Chili ~ 79

Corned Beef and Cabbage ~ 80

Garlic Beef Stew ~ 81

Canard Beaujolais ~ 82

Breast of Pheasant
   with Fresh Mint and Kirsch ~ 83

Rosemary-Stuffed Quail ~ 84

Rabbit Merlot ~ 85

Venison Medallions
   with Garlic Cream ~ 86

Grilled Lamb Chops Polaise ~ 88

Rack of Lamb
   with Cabernet Mint Sauce ~ 89

Spit-Roasted Leg of Lamb ~ 90

Butterflied Leg of Lamb
   in Limberger ~ 91

Middle Eastern Lamb Brochettes ~ 92

Garlic Spinach Cannelloni ~ 93

Pesto Hazelnut Lasagna ~ 94

Asparagus Morel Risotto ~ 95

Northwest Dungeness Crab Feed

On Seattle's waterfront **Elliott's Oyster House** has long provided the freshest shellfish to locals and visitors alike. Fresh Dungeness crab is the centerpiece for their Northwest crab feed, a marvel in culinary simplicity taking advantage of the finest in fresh crustaceans accompanied only by a simple salad and fresh bread. Of course, no Northwest seafood feast would be complete without an appropriate wine. A recent tasting confirmed that **Paul Thomas Winery** Johannisberg Riesling is the perfect foil to the slightly sweet crab, providing a cleansing acidity to refresh the palate. Often overlooked for this elegant entrée, Northwest Riesling is just the ticket! Special thanks to chef Tony Casad and consultant Jon Rowley for revealing the secrets to a perfect crab cracking as presented below.

Fresh cooked Dungeness crab, 1 per person
Simple salad of fresh greens
Fresh French bread or sourdough

1. Crack crabs as described below. Present legs, claws and body pieces in serving bowls, along with salad and bread.
2. Table setting should include bibs for each person, finger bowls with warm lemon water or weak tea, and plenty of paper napkins. "Litter Patrol" should be handy in removing bowls of empty shells and used napkins.
3. The sharp pointed "toe" off a crab leg makes an excellent "crab pick" for removing bits of meat from legs and claws.

Cleaning the Crabs

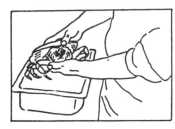

1. With cooked crab facing away from you, pry top shell off and discard. Just inside are small pockets of cream-colored "crab butter," considered a delicacy by crab fanciers. Scoop out with a piece of French bread.

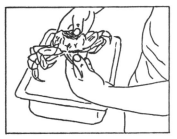

2. Reach under the crab and, using your thumb, pry off v-shaped plate and bottom shell.

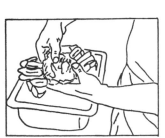

3. Run thumb along sides of body cavity to scrape away gills and liver. Rinse away remaining liver under running water.

Cracking the Crabs

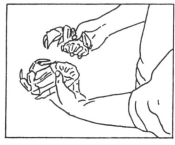

1. Break crab body into two halves as shown.

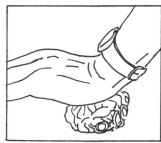

2. Remove legs and claws from body sections, then crack body sections by pressing down with palm of hand as shown. Cut each body section into two pieces with chefs knife.

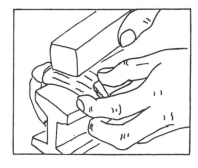

3. Using an aluminum crab cracker or oak dowel, crack each claw section by gently rapping. Don't hit so hard that you crush the crabmeat. Using the same technique, crack each leg section. Be sure to strike on the edge, not the flat side. Guests should only have to twist sections to remove whole pieces of meat.

Fisherman's Soup

Romeo Conca of **Lost Mountain Winery** in Sequim, Washington, shares his wonderful recipe for Fisherman's Soup – a hearty soup developed over the years for family and friends, using fresh, local ingredients. To accompany this one-dish meal, Romeo suggests a tossed green salad, lots of good Italian bread (to soak up the yummy broth) and a glass of his delightful Washington Merlot. Punctuated with the licorice-anise flavors of fennel and the citrusy nuances of fresh orange peel, this tomato-based soup is a prime candidate for his red wine. The rich and spicy character of Lost Mountain Merlot plays off the Mediterranean flavors with just the right degree of contrast.

6 to 8 servings

- 1 firm-fleshed fish (2¹⁄₂ to 3 pounds), such as true cod, ling cod, Pacific snapper or sea bass
- 32 medium prawns (about ³⁄₄ pound)
- 2 quarts cold water (or to cover)
- ¹⁄₂ cup dry white wine
  Juice of 1 small lemon
- 2 cardamom pods, crushed
- 1 large leek, cleaned, sliced, divided
- 1 bay leaf
- ¹⁄₄ cup olive oil
- 4 garlic cloves, minced
- 1¹⁄₂ pounds very ripe plum tomatoes, cored, seeded, coarsely chopped
- 2 generous pinches saffron
- 2 equatorial strips (¹⁄₂-inch-wide each) orange zest
- 1 teaspoon fennel seeds
- 4 tablespoons chopped fresh Italian flat-leaf parsley
  Salt and freshly ground black pepper
- 32 small clams (about 1 pound), scrubbed, degorged of sand (see **Cook's Tip**)
- 32 mussels (about ³⁄₄ pound), scrubbed, degorged of sand (see **Cook's Tip**)
- 32 small bay scallops (about ³⁄₄ pound), well rinsed, patted dry
- 4 squid, cleaned, cut into ¹⁄₂-inch-thick ringlets

1. Fillet fish (or have your fishmonger do it). Cut fillets into 1¹⁄₂-inch pieces and refrigerate until needed. Reserve trimmings to prepare broth.
2. Peel and devein prawns. Refrigerate until needed and reserve shells to prepare broth.
3. Prepare broth: Combine fish trimmings with prawn shells in large pot. Cover with water, wine and lemon juice. Bring to boil over high heat and skim foam from surface. Add cardamom pods, green part of leek and bay leaf. Immediately reduce heat and simmer about 30 minutes. Strain through fine-mesh sieve into clean pot and set aside.
4. Heat oil in large Dutch oven over medium heat. Add garlic with remaining leek. Sauté until garlic is lightly golden brown and leek is soft and translucent, about 3 minutes.
5. Reduce heat and stir in reserved broth, tomatoes, saffron, orange zest and fennel seeds. Simmer about 30 minutes.
6. Stir in chopped parsley and season with salt and pepper.
7. Add clams with mussels. Cover and simmer about 3 minutes.
8. Add reserved fish pieces, reserved prawns, scallops and squid. Cover and simmer until shells open and other seafood is slightly firm, 3 to 5 minutes longer. Discard any unopened shells, orange peels and bay leaf. Ladle soup into warm bowls and serve immediately.

Cook's Tips

Substitute 1 can (16 ounces) whole peeled tomatoes, cored, seeded, coarsely chopped with juices, if very ripe plum tomatoes are not available.

Clams and mussels tend to be sandy. To degorge them of their sand, simply soak them in a solution of 1 part coarse sea salt dissolved in 8 parts water (to cover) at least 1 hour. Rinse well before using.

Wine Selection
Lost Mountain Winery Merlot

Chargrilled Halibut *with Lemon Oregano Butter*

True halibut lovers living in the Puget Sound region have reason to rejoice when the long-awaited halibut season opens each April. No one does this seasonal specialty better than Executive Chef Sally McArthur at **Anthony's HomePort** waterfront restaurants. We love her Chargrilled Halibut with Lemon Oregano Butter – the perfect choice for that next gathering of special friends. The nature of the fish, its preparation, and herbaceous accompaniment make it a prime candidate for **Paul Thomas Winery's** highly touted Sauvignon Blanc. Hints of citrus and herbs in the wine's aroma complement the oregano flavors in the dish, while the refreshing acidity is a fine match for the citrus tastes.

4 servings

Marinade

- 1 cup extra-virgin olive oil
- 2 tablespoons unsalted butter, melted
- 1$^{1}/_{2}$ teaspoons dried whole oregano, crumbled
- 1 teaspoon anchovy paste*
- 1 teaspoon grated lemon zest
- $^{3}/_{4}$ teaspoon minced garlic
- $^{3}/_{4}$ teaspoon kosher salt*

- 4 fresh halibut fillets (about 8 ounces each), preferably Alaskan
- 4 pinches kosher salt
  Lemon Oregano Butter (recipe follows)

1. For marinade: Whisk together all ingredients in small bowl until well blended and set aside.
2. Rinse fillets well and pat dry with paper towels. Place in nonreactive dish, large enough to hold fillets with marinade. Pour marinade over, cover and refrigerate 30 minutes. Turn once.
3. Preheat grill with medium-hot coals. Adjust rack 3 to 4 inches from heat and lightly oil.

4. Remove fillets from marinade and drain well. Reserve marinade for basting.
5. Place fillets on grill and cook 60% done, basting occasionally with reserved marinade. Turn and complete cooking, about 12 minutes total. As fillets complete cooking, sprinkle with kosher salt. To serve, place fillets on warm plates and top each with 2 slices Lemon Oregano Butter. (Butter should just melt and glaze fillet.)

Lemon Oregano Butter

- 8 tablespoons unsalted butter, softened
- 1 tablespoon fresh lemon juice
- 2 teaspoons grated lemon zest
- $^{1}/_{2}$ teaspoon minced garlic
- $^{1}/_{4}$ teaspoon sugar
- 1 teaspoon chopped fresh oregano
- $^{1}/_{4}$ teaspoon dried whole oregano, crumbled

1. Combine butter, lemon juice, lemon zest, garlic and sugar in small bowl until well blended.
2. Rub oreganos together and stir into above mixture.
3. Spread mixture on plastic wrap and form into 1$^{1}/_{2}$-inch-diameter cylinder.
4. Wrap in aluminum foil and refrigerate until firm, about 2 hours.
5. Cut into $^{1}/_{2}$-ounce slices, as needed. (Any leftover butter may be frozen for later use.)

* See **Special Ingredients**

Cook's Tip

We like to garnish chef McArthur's wonderful dish with sprigs of fresh oregano.

Wine Selection
**Paul Thomas Winery
Sauvignon Blanc**

Grilled Halibut Kebabs

Pacific waters teem with halibut, the most highly prized whitefish among Northwest aficionados. Naturally lean and distinguished by firm, snow-white flesh, this exquisitely mild flavored fish adapts well to a number of cooking methods. Marilyn Webb of **Bethel Heights Vineyard** favors grilling and shares with us her delightful Grilled Halibut Kebabs – just one example of the many outstanding ways this premium quality seafood can be savored. Their crisp and medium-bodied Chardonnay offers the complex flavors of aging in French oak while preserving a fruity aroma and balanced palate. The wine is structured perfectly to accompany the grilled flavors of this Northwest specialty.

6 servings

Marinade

$^1/_2$	cup Bethel Heights Vineyard Chardonnay
$^1/_4$	cup olive oil
2	tablespoons fresh lime juice
2	tablespoons finely chopped red onion
2	garlic cloves, chopped
1	tablespoon unsalted butter, melted
1	tablespoon chopped fresh oregano

$1^1/_2$	pounds fresh Pacific halibut, cut into $1^1/_2$-inch cubes
12	small cherry tomatoes
12	large mushrooms, cleaned
1	large green bell pepper, stemmed, seeded, deribbed, cut into $1^1/_2$-inch cubes
1	red onion, cut into large chunks
	Salt and freshly ground black pepper
	Fresh oregano sprigs

1. For marinade: Combine all ingredients until well blended in nonreactive bowl, large enough to hold halibut with marinade.
2. Add halibut to marinade and toss to coat. Cover and refrigerate about 2 hours, adding tomatoes, mushrooms, green bell pepper and onion last 30 minutes of marinating time.
3. Prepare grill with medium-hot coals. Adjust rack 3 to 4 inches from heat and lightly oil.
4. With slotted spoon, remove halibut with vegetables from marinade. Drain well. Reserve marinade for basting.
5. Thread halibut alternately with vegetables onto 6 long metal skewers. Season with salt and pepper.
6. Place skewers on grill and cook to desired doneness or 8 to 10 minutes total, turning and basting occasionally with reserved marinade. Serve immediately and garnish with fresh oregano sprigs.

Cook's Tip

The halibut tends to cook a little faster than the vegetables, resulting in 'al dente' vegetables – if you prefer more well-done vegetables, skewer them separately and adjust your cooking time.

Wine Selection

Bethel Heights Vineyard Chardonnay

Grilled Pacific Salmon
with Cranberry Blueberry Mustard Sauce

The Shoalwater Restaurant, located in the historic Shelburne Inn in Seaview, Washington, specializes in Northwest regional cuisine. Owners Tony and Ann Kischner keep an extensive Northwest wine cellar to accompany the creative efforts of chef Cheri Walker. For your culinary enjoyment they share the following entrée, Grilled Pacific Salmon with Cranberry Blueberry Mustard Sauce. This masterpiece of simplicity and intriguing flavors focuses on several of the finest ingredients from the Northwest – Pacific salmon, cranberries and blueberries. **Veritas Vineyards Winery's** rich and complex Chardonnay, with its superb fruit/acid balance is just the wine to show off this outstanding creation. Chardonnay forms a wonderfully delicate background for the flavors of grilled salmon and the fruity, mustard-based sauce.

4 servings

4 fresh Pacific salmon fillets (6 to 8 ounces each)
Salt and freshly ground black pepper

Cranberry Blueberry Mustard Sauce

$^1/_4$ cup Veritas Vineyard Chardonnay
$^1/_4$ cup dry vermouth
$^1/_4$ cup Cranberry Blueberry Mustard (recipe follows)
4 tablespoons butter, cut into small pieces

1. Prepare grill with medium-hot coals. Adjust rack 3 to 4 inches from heat and lightly oil.
2. Rinse fillets well and pat dry with paper towels. Season with salt and pepper.
3. Place fillets on grill and cook 4 to 5 minutes per side. (Proceed with sauce as fillets cook.)
4. For sauce: Combine wine with vermouth in heavy small saucepan over high heat. Bring to boil and reduce by half.

5. Whisk in mustard and bring to boil.
6. Remove pan from heat and whisk in butter, 1 piece at a time, until sauce thickens and turns glossy. (Do not reheat or let cool.) To serve, arrange fillets on warm plates and accompany with Cranberry Blueberry Mustard Sauce.

Cranberry Blueberry Mustard

$^3/_4$ cup fresh cranberries, well rinsed, drained, picked over
$^1/_2$ cup fresh blueberries, well rinsed, drained, picked over
$^1/_3$ cup raspberry vinegar*
$^1/_3$ cup sugar
2 tablespoons port
$^2/_3$ cup water
$^1/_3$ cup dry mustard
3 large egg yolks, room temperature

1. Combine berries, vinegar, sugar and port in heavy medium saucepan over high heat. Bring to boil and cook, stirring occasionally, until berries pop, about 5 minutes.
2. Purée mixture in blender or bowl of food processor, fitted with steel knife.
3. Strain mixture through fine-mesh sieve into medium bowl and set aside.
4. Combine water with mustard in top of double boiler over gently simmering water, stirring until smooth.
5. Whisk in egg yolks, 1 at a time, until well blended and mixture begins to thicken.
6. Whisk in reserved purée until smooth. Transfer to glass jar, cover and refrigerate.

* See **Special Ingredients**

Cook's Tip

Chef Walker recommends serving their delicious Cranberry Blueberry Mustard with pâtés, grilled meats and on sandwiches. We love it with our Terrine Forestier, found on page 35.

Wine Selection
Veritas Vineyards
Chardonnay

Salmon and Oysters
with Chardonnnay Sabayon Cream Sauce

Hyatt Vineyards, nestled up against the Rattlesnake Hills north of Zillah, Washington, produces a delicious version of Chardonnay that marries especially well with food. This award-winning wine inspired us to create Salmon and Oysters with Chardonnay Sabayon Cream Sauce – a lovely dish highlighting two of the Northwest's finest, local ingredients. The rich tastes and textures of the dish call for a fresh, fruity wine with a firm acid backbone and just a kiss of oak. Hyatt Vineyards distinctive Chardonnay fills the bill nicely for this all-Northwest preparation!

2 servings

- 2 tablespoons unsalted butter
- 2 shallots, chopped
- 2 Pacific salmon fillets (6 to 8 ounces each)
- 1 tablespoon Dijon mustard, divided
  Salt and freshly ground black pepper
- 10 Olympia oysters, shucked, juices reserved
- 3/4 cup Hyatt Vineyards Chardonnay, divided
- 1 teaspoon fresh lemon juice
- 1/2 cup Shellfish Stock (see **Basics**)
- 1/2 cup warm water (or more)
- 1 cup heavy cream
  Dash cayenne pepper
- 2 large egg yolks, room temperature
  Chopped fresh chervil

1. Position rack in center of oven and preheat to 425°F.
2. Melt butter in 11-inch, cast-iron, oval au gratin dish over medium heat. Add shallots and cover with parchment paper, cut to fit dish. Sweat until soft, shaking dish to evenly distribute shallots, about 2 minutes. Set aside.
3. Rinse fillets well and pat dry with paper towels. Arrange atop shallots and brush each fillet with 1 teaspoon mustard. Season with salt and pepper. Set aside.
4. Stir together reserved oyster juices, 1/2 cup wine, lemon juice, stock and water in heavy small saucepan over medium-high heat. Bring almost to boil and pour over fillets, adding more warm water just to cover, if necessary. Top with buttered parchment paper.
5. Place dish in oven and poach fish until just opaque and almost flaky, adding oysters last half of cooking time. (We use the Canadian Cooking Method of 10 minutes per inch. In this case, poach a little less, due to the additional cooking procedures.)
6. With slotted spatula, transfer fillets with oysters to warm plate and tent with foil.
7. Transfer dish with poaching liquid to stovetop and bring to boil over high heat. Reduce by half. Add cream and reduce by half. Stir in remaining mustard with cayenne pepper. Set aside and keep warm.
8. Make sabayon by whisking together egg yolks with remaining wine in top of double boiler over simmering water until frothy, about 3 minutes. Slowly stir into cream mixture, adjusting seasonings, as necessary. Set aside and keep warm.
9. Briefly reheat fillets with oysters (in microwave). To serve, arrange fillets in center of warm plates and top each with 5 oysters, letting them fall naturally. Strain sauce through fine-mesh sieve over each serving. Place under broiler and brown tops lightly. Sprinkle with chopped fresh chervil.

Cook's Tips

The au gratin dish we use is by Le Creuset and goes from stovetop to oven, making this preparation a one-dish meal (in more ways than one). Shop for it at any fine kitchen shop.

It is important to use small (even tiny) oysters for this preparation. Olympias are available in the Northwest, but Kumamotos or Blue Points also work well.

Wine Selection
Hyatt Vineyards Chardonnay

Grapewood-Grilled Salmon *with Lettuce Sauce*

Winemaker Rick Small, at **Woodward Canyon Winery**, in Lowden, Washington, obviously believes that good things come in small packages. He concentrates on a few varietals, producing only top-quality wines in limited volume. Much success has come to Rick for his conservative philosophy, and recently his efforts with the Semillon grape have been outstanding. Lean and fruity with toasty oak overtones, this Bordeaux varietal makes an exquisite dinner partner for his wife Darcey's Grapewood-Grilled Salmon with Lettuce Sauce. Rich and herbaceous, it's irresistible alongside Rick's white Charbonneau (a blend of 80% Semillon with 20% Sauvignon Blanc). The scarce availability of this bottling is testament to its fine structure, intense varietal character and affinity for fine cuisine.

6 servings

Lettuce Sauce

  1 head romaine lettuce or 2 heads butter lettuce
  2 tablespoons unsalted butter
  1 cup heavy cream
  ¹/₄ cup Woodward Canyon Charbonneau
  Salt and freshly ground white pepper

  5 pieces (6 to 8 inches long each) dried grape vine cuttings *, soaked 1 hour in water (longer for thicker stems and trunks)
  6 Pacific salmon fillets (6 to 8 ounces each), preferably King
  4 tablespoons unsalted butter, melted
  Juice of 1 lemon
  Salt and freshly ground black pepper to taste
  Lemon wedges
  Fresh Italian flat-leaf parsley sprigs

Wine Selection

Woodward Canyon Winery
White Charbonneau

---

1. For sauce: Separate lettuce head into leaves and rinse well under cold, running water. Pat dry with paper towels and cut into large julienne. Set aside.
2. Melt butter in heavy large skillet over medium heat. Add lettuce and cover. Cook until wilted and moisture has almost evaporated, shaking pan and stirring occasionally, about 5 minutes.
3. Purée mixture in bowl of food processor, fitted with steel knife. Set aside.
4. Combine cream with wine in heavy medium saucepan over high heat. Bring to boil and reduce by about half. Stir in lettuce purée and season with salt and white pepper. Set aside and keep warm.
5. Prepare grill with medium-hot coals. Remove grill rack and place grape vine cuttings atop coals. Smolder briefly. Replace grill rack 4 to 5 inches from heat and lightly oil.
6. Rinse fillets well and pat dry with paper towels. Remove any visible bones and set aside.
7. Whisk together melted butter, lemon juice, salt and pepper in small bowl until well blended.
8. Generously brush fillets with mixture and place on grill. Cook about 4 minutes per side, basting frequently with remaining mixture. (Fish is cooked when it flakes easily and is just opaque.) To serve, arrange fillets on warm plates and garnish with lemon wedges and fresh parsley sprigs. Accompany with Lettuce Sauce.

* See **Special Ingredients**

Cook's Tip

Get a bird's-eye-view of this beautiful dish on our front cover. Congratulations to Woodward Canyon for a stunning presentation!

Mussels Marinara

The northern Puget Sound of Washington State is home to the most famous mussel farming area in the world, Whidbey Island's Penn Cove. Grown on ropes suspended in the cold, pristine waters of Puget Sound, they are the sweetest, most tender mussels you'll ever eat. Susan Killermann, Marketing Director for **Stewart Vineyards**, provided the creative inspiration for Mussels Marinara and highly recommends the accompaniment of Stewart Vineyards Cabernet Sauvignon. Red wine with mussels? We tried it and loved it! The addition of Cabernet to the sauce provides a direct link from wine to food, while adding an intriguing complexity to the dish. Herbaceous nuances in the sauce are reflected beautifully in the wine and put this match in total harmony.

4 to 6 servings

Sauce

¼ cup olive oil
4 large garlic cloves, chopped
1 large red onion, finely chopped
1 green bell pepper, stemmed, seeded, deribbed, finely chopped
2 pounds very ripe Italian plum tomatoes, cored, seeded, finely chopped
1 can (15 ounces) tomato sauce
¾ cup water
¼ cup Stewart Vineyards Cabernet Sauvignon
2 teaspoons chopped fresh basil
2 teaspoons chopped fresh oregano
1 teaspoon chopped fresh rosemary
1 bay leaf
Pinch of sugar
Salt and freshly ground black pepper to taste

1½ cups dry white wine (or more)
4 dozen small mussels, scrubbed, debearded, degorged of sand (see **Cook's Tip**)
1½ pound fresh linguine
Fresh Italian flat-leaf parsley sprigs

1. For sauce: Heat oil in medium Dutch oven over medium heat. Add garlic and sauté until soft, about 2 minutes. Do not burn.
2. Add onion with green bell pepper. Cook until tender, stirring occasionally, about 5 minutes.
3. Reduce heat and stir in remaining ingredients. Simmer until thick, stirring occasionally, about 1 hour. Remove bay leaf, set aside and keep warm.
4. Bring wine to boil in heavy large pot over high heat.
5. Add mussels, cover and steam until shells open, shaking pan occasionally, about 4 minutes.
6. Remove mussels from pan and strain liquid through double thickness of cheesecloth. (Liquid may be used to thin sauce, if necessary.) Discard unopened shells.
7. Remove mussels from shells (leave several in shells per person for garnish) and stir into sauce.
8. Cook linguine in large pot of boiling, salted water until just tender, but still firm to bite, stirring occasionally. Drain well. To serve, divide pasta among warm (shallow) bowls and top with sauce. Garnish with reserved mussels and fresh parsley sprigs.

Cook's Tips

To degorge mussels of sand, soak them in a solution of 1 part coarse sea salt dissolved in 8 parts water (to cover) at least 1 hour. Rinse well before using.

If fresh Italian plum tomatoes are not available, substitute 1 can (28 ounces) whole peeled tomatoes, cored, seeded, crushed with juices.

Wine Selection
Stewart Vineyards
Cabernet Sauvignon

White Clam Linguine

Ponzi Vineyards, located in Oregon's northern Willamette Valley, has been one of the pioneers in the production of Pinot Gris. This varietal is not highly regarded in its native France, but the version produced by Dick Ponzi offers both ageability and an excellent affinity for Northwest seafood. Crisp and refreshing, Ponzi Pinot Gris is the perfect partner for our White Clam Linguine. The wine's excellent acidity cuts the heaviness of the oil in the dish, while its enigmatic round-ness of palate is accentuated by the contrast of the bouquet of fresh herbs. Italian focaccia bread and a crisp green salad are all that is needed to accompany this tantalizing pasta favorite.

6 servings

Sauce

- 10 tablespoons olive oil
- 8 medium garlic cloves, minced
- 5 cans (6^1/$_2$ ounces each) chopped clams, drained, 2 cups juice reserved
- ^{1}/$_4$ cup Ponzi Vineyards Pinot Gris
- 6 tablespoons minced fresh Italian flat-leaf parsley
- 2 tablespoons minced fresh basil
- 2 tablespoons minced fresh oregano
- 1 bay leaf
- ^{1}/$_2$ teaspoon salt
- ^{1}/$_2$ teaspoon red pepper flakes
- ^{1}/$_4$ teaspoon freshly ground black pepper

- 1^1/$_2$ pounds fresh linguine
  Freshly grated Parmesan cheese (optional)
  Chopped fresh Italian flat-leaf parsley
  Steamed clams

1. For sauce: Heat oil in medium Dutch oven over medium heat.
2. Add garlic and cook until slightly golden, about 1 minute. Do not burn.
3. Add reserved clam juice (set drained clams aside) with remaining ingredients. Increase heat and boil 2 minutes.
4. Immediately reduce heat and remove bay leaf. Stir in clams and simmer 2 minutes. Set aside and keep warm.
5. Cook linguine in large pot of boiling, salted water until just tender, but still firm to bite, stirring occasionally. Drain well. To serve, toss pasta with sauce and divide among warm (shallow) bowls. Top with freshly grated Parmesan cheese, if desired, and garnish with fresh parsley and steamed clams.

Cook's Tips

Fresh clams are especially tasty during the winter months in the Northwest. To use fresh clams in our recipe, simply steam 5 to 6 pounds of them in 2 cups water, ^{1}/$_2$ cup dry white wine, several sprigs fresh parsley and a bay leaf until they open. Remove them from their shells and coarsely chop. Strain liquid through a fine-mesh sieve and reserve 2 cups. Continue with recipe as directed.

If you prefer a creamy sauce, reduce 1^1/$_2$ cups of heavy cream to ^{1}/$_2$ cup and stir into sauce, prior to tossing with pasta.

Wine Selection

Ponzi Vineyards
Pinot Gris

Pacific Snapper Creole

You don't have to go to the bayous to enjoy a great Creole dish in the Northwest. Pacific snapper, a member of the rockfish family, is available year-round and just waiting to celebrate the spicy cuisine of Louisiana. In our Pacific Snapper Creole, luscious, vine-ripe tomatoes, fragrant fresh herbs and other wonderful ingredients combine with this versatile fish to make a traditional Southern specialty. The peppery, aggressive flavors of the dish overwhelm even the most assertive white wines, while the Oregon Pinot Noir made by **Yamhill Valley Vineyards** has the gutsy character necessary to stand up to the Creole flavors. The herbal-spicy qualities of the wine are a wonderful complement to the tomato-based sauce, while the fruity nuances add additional complexity. Northwest red wine with Northwest fish – we love it!

6 servings

Sauce

3 tablespoons vegetable oil
1 medium onion, finely chopped
3 garlic cloves, finely minced
2 celery stalks, finely chopped
$1/2$ green bell pepper, stemmed, seeded, deribbed, finely chopped
2 pounds very ripe tomatoes (about 6 medium), cored, seeded, coarsely chopped
2 tablespoons chopped fresh parsley
1 tablespoon chopped fresh basil
1 tablespoon chopped fresh thyme
2 teaspoons tomato paste
$1/4$ teaspoon cayenne pepper (or more)
1 bay leaf
Dash sugar
Salt and freshly ground black pepper to taste

Melted butter
6 snapper fillets (6 to 8 ounces each)
Fresh parsley sprigs

1. For sauce: Heat oil in medium Dutch oven over medium heat. Add onion with garlic. Cook until starting to brown and almost caramelized, stirring occasionally, about 20 minutes.
2. Stir in remaining ingredients and bring to boil over medium-high heat. Immediately reduce heat and simmer 45 minutes. Remove bay leaf and set aside.
3. Position rack in lowest third of oven and preheat to 400° F. Generously butter two 9- by 13-inch baking dishes and set aside.
4. Rinse fillets well and pat dry with paper towels. Arrange in prepared baking dishes and top with sauce.
5. Bake until fillets flake easily and are just opaque, about 25 minutes. To serve, place fillets on warm plates and top with remaining sauce. Garnish with fresh parsley sprigs.

Cook's Tip

If very ripe tomatoes are not available, substitute 1 can (28 ounces) whole peeled tomatoes, cored, seeded, chopped with juices.

Wine Selection
**Yamhill Valley Vineyards
Pinot Noir**

Paella Northwest Style

For your next ethnic evening of entertainment, hire a flamenco dancer, invite a few good friends over and try our Paella Northwest Style. The name Paella originates from the utensil in which it is cooked, the paellera – the Catalan word for skillet. Much like a wok with a flat bottom, the paellera is a large, round iron skillet with two handles that comes in many sizes. The multiflavored character of this dish makes for exciting choices of wine, so treat yourself and your guests to **Zillah Oakes** Grenache – even the Spanish prefer a red wine with this favorite. The bright fruit flavors and aromas of this light red wine play off the myriad of ingredients in the dish to provide a delightful complexity. Winemaker David Crippen's medal-winning version of this Rhone varietal is in short supply, but is well worth seeking out.

4 to 6 servings

- 1/4 cup Spanish olive oil
- 1/2 pound Spanish chorizo*, cut into 1/4-inch-thick slices
- 4 garlic cloves, minced
- 1 large onion, coarsely chopped
- 1 small red bell pepper, stemmed, seeded, deribbed, diced
- 1 large tomato, cored, seeded, coarsely chopped
- 2 bay leaves
- 1 1/2 teaspoons chopped fresh thyme
- 1 teaspoon chopped fresh rosemary
- 1/2 teaspoon saffron threads*, crushed
- 1/4 teaspoon paprika
- 2 cups arborio rice* (or other short grain rice)

- 4 cups Shellfish Stock (see **Basics**)
- 2 tablespoons dry white wine
- 1 tablespoon fresh lemon juice
  Salt and freshly ground black pepper
- 1/2 pound medium shrimp, shelled, deveined, tails intact
- 1/2 pound small sea scallops
- 1/2 pound squid, cleaned, cut into 1/4-inch-thick ringlets
- 1 jar (6 ounces) marinated artichoke hearts, drained, quartered
- 1/2 cup frozen peas
- 1/2 cup (2 ounces) diced smoked ham
- 1/2 jar (2 ounces) pimentos, drained
- 10 littleneck clams, scrubbed, degorged of sand (see **Cook's Tip**)
- 10 Penn Cove mussels, scrubbed, debearded, degorged of sand (see **Cook's Tip**)
- 1 cup dry white wine (or more)
- 10 pimiento-stuffed Spanish olives
  Fresh Italian flat-leaf parsley sprigs
- 1 lemon, quartered

1. Position rack in lowest third of oven and preheat to 350° F.
2. Heat oil in at least 11-inch paella pan over medium-high heat.
3. Add Chorizo and brown well. Transfer to warm plate and tent with foil.
4. Reduce heat to medium and add garlic. Sauté 30 seconds. Add onion with red bell pepper. Sauté until soft and translucent, about 5 minutes.
5. Stir in tomato, bay leaves, thyme, rosemary, saffron threads and paprika. Cook about 3 minutes.

6. Stir in rice and coat grains well with mixture. Cook until opaque, stirring frequently, about 4 minutes.
7. Stir in stock, wine and lemon juice. Season with salt and pepper. Bring to boil over high heat. Immediately reduce heat and simmer 15 minutes.
8. Tuck Chorizo, shrimp, scallops, squid and artichokes into rice. Scatter peas, ham and pimientos over.
9. Cover loosely with aluminum foil and bake until liquid is absorbed, 20 to 25 minutes.
10. Meanwhile, steam clams with mussels in wine in large pot over medium-high heat until shells open, about 3 minutes. Discard unopened shells with liquid. To serve, decoratively top paella with clams, mussels, olives, and fresh parsley sprigs. Tuck in lemon quarters.

* See **Special Ingredients**

Cook's Tips

If you do not have a paella pan, a heavy, ovenproof skillet (11 inches or larger) will do. Also, the lovely terra cotta paella dishes make for a beautiful presentation – just do all of your stove-top preparation in a heavy skillet.

Clams and mussels tend to be sandy. To degorge them of their sand, simply soak them in a solution of 1 part coarse sea salt dissolved in 8 parts water (to cover) at least 1 hour. Rinse well before using.

Wine Selection
**Zillah Oakes Winery
Grenache**

Wine Serving Temperatures

With the advent of modern refrigeration, most white wines are now served about 15 degrees colder than the ideal. While the refrigerator is designed to keep milk from spoiling at a temperature of about 40° F., the best serving temperature for wines, red or white, is considerably higher. The following discussion of wine types and temperatures should provide some guidelines.

White Wines

Still white wines (not sparkling) are best served at "cellar temperature" or about 55° F. This temperature allows the aromatic components of the wine to be released and thus be appreciated by the taster. A wine serving temperature of 40° F. keeps these enticing aromas locked in the wine. If your white wine has been refrigerated, allow one to two hours at room temperature for it to warm up.

Red Wines

Light red wines, older red wines and young, hearty red wines all are subject to slightly different considerations in serving temperature. Light and fruity reds may be served at cellar temperature (55° F.) to preserve their fruity aromas and flavors, and to provide a refreshing coolness on the palate. Young, hearty reds like Cabernet and Merlot may be served at a slightly higher 65° to 75° F. which accelerates their breathing time and allows more aromatic components to be released. Older red wines if served too warm will rapidly release the beautiful bouquet for which the wine was aged in the first place. This ten minute rush of ecstacy is too short to enjoy a snack, much less a meal. Serve the wine at 55° F. and allow it to warm up to room temperature gradually, appreciating the nuances that evolve with the warming.

Sparkling Wine

Chill it down and keep it in the ice bucket. A serving temperature of 40° F. is just right for sparklers, keeping the bubbles flowing in a fine bead for several hours.

Chicken Tarragon

Saddle Mountain Winery, 13 miles east of Mattawa, Washington, crafts wines to please the consumer. Their Fumé Blanc stands out as one of our favorites. Winery representative Julie Rose shared her recipe for Chicken Tarragon to accompany this popular Northwest varietal. Anise-like tarragon, one of the best savory herbs for cooking, punctuates the dish, bringing out the lovely herbaceous nuances of the wine, while a touch of wine to the sauce provides the unifying element. Julie's preferred cooking method is baking, but we fired up the grill on a "hot August night" and chicken never tasted so good! A slightly chilled glass of Saddle Mountain's delightful Fumé Blanc was heavenly relief to the evening's heat and the perfect partner to this delicious entrée!

4 servings

1/4 cup Saddle Mountain Winery Fumé Blanc
3 tablespoons Dijon mustard
2 tablespoons olive oil
2 tablespoons unsalted butter, melted
2 tablespoons chopped fresh tarragon
1 broiler-fryer chicken (3 to 4 pounds), quartered
Salt and freshly ground black pepper
Fresh tarragon sprigs

1. Position rack in lowest third of oven and preheat to 375°F.
2. Whisk together wine, mustard, oil, butter and tarragon in small bowl until well blended. Set aside.
3. Rinse chicken well and pat dry with paper towels. Arrange, skin side up, in baking dish, large enough to accommodate it. Pour sauce over.
4. Bake until chicken is cooked through and juices run clear, when pierced with skewer, 45 minutes to 1 hour. To serve, arrange chicken on warm serving platter and pour pan juices over. Garnish with fresh tarragon sprigs.

Wine Selection

**Saddle Mountain Winery
Fumé Blanc**

Stuffed Chicken Breasts
with Chardonnay Cream Sauce

Award-winning wines in many styles are crafted at **Covey Run Winery** in Zillah, Washington, under the direction of U.C. Davis-trained winemaker David Crippen. Their lovely Chardonnay sets a dramatic backdrop for this wonderful recipe the winery shared with us, Stuffed Chicken Breasts with Chardonnay Cream Sauce. Boned breasts of chicken become tasty envelopes for a medley of prosciutto, fontina and sage; and a delicious sauce, incorporating the wine, adds the finishing touch. As with all Covey Run wines, their Chardonnay offers intense varietal character and balanced acidity to accompany this rich dish. For a stunning presentation, fan-slice the breasts and drizzle with sauce.

4 servings

    2   tablespoons olive oil
    2   garlic cloves, minced
    $^1/_2$ cup (2 ounces) chopped prosciutto*
    $^1/_4$ teaspoon minced fresh sage
    $^1/_4$ cup (1 ounce) grated Fontina or Swiss cheese
    4   boneless chicken breast halves, (about 6 ounces each), skinned
    2   tablespoons unsalted butter
        All-purpose flour
    1   cup Covey Run Chardonnay
    1   cup heavy cream
    1   teaspoon Dijon mustard
        Salt and freshly ground black pepper
        Fresh sage sprigs

1. Heat oil in heavy medium skillet over medium heat. Add garlic, prosciutto and sage. Sauté 3 minutes. Remove from heat and cool slightly. Combine with cheese in small bowl and set aside.

2. Rinse breasts well and pat dry with paper towels. With sharp knife, cut 3-inch-long by 2-inch-deep pocket in breasts, moving knife in arc to create pocket.

3. Stuff each pocket with about 2 tablespoons filling and secure with toothpicks. Set aside.

4. Heat butter in heavy medium skillet over medium heat.

5. Dredge breasts in flour and shake off excess. Add to skillet and brown lightly.

6. Reduce heat and pour in wine. Partially cover and simmer until breasts are almost cooked through, 5 to 7 minutes. Transfer to warm plate, remove skewers and tent with foil.

7. Bring skillet liquid to boil over high heat and reduce to $^1/_4$ cup. Stir in cream with mustard. Bring to boil and reduce until sauce coats back of spoon, 3 to 5 minutes. Season with salt and pepper.

8. Return breasts to pan and coat well with sauce. Reheat briefly. To serve, arrange breasts on warm plates and top with sauce. Garnish with fresh sage sprigs.

* See **Special Ingredients**

Cook's Tip

For easier cutting, place breasts in freezer about 30 minutes prior to cutting pocket.

Wine Selection
Covey Run Winery Chardonnay

Roast Breast of Turkey *with Fall Fruit Chutney*

Celebrate the bounty of the Northwest at Thanksgiving with our easy-to-prepare Roast Breast of Turkey with Fall Fruit Chutney. Accented with the lemony perfume of fresh sage and roasted to a succulent golden brown, our rendition of everybody's favorite bird is sure to please the most discriminating turkey lover. **Tualatin Vineyards** medium-dry White Riesling offers hints of apples and herbs that beautifully complement the succulent turkey and accompanying chutney in this Thanksgiving mini-feast. Your traditional favorites and side dishes are welcome – Happy Thanksgiving Northwest style!

3 to 4 servings

Basting Mixture

- 1 cup Tualatin Vineyards White Riesling
- 4 tablespoons butter, melted
- 2 tablespoons olive oil
- 1 tablespoon chopped fresh sage
- $^1/_4$ teaspoon cinnamon
- $^1/_8$ teaspoon ground cloves
- $^1/_8$ teaspoon ground nutmeg

- 1 boneless turkey breast half ($2^1/_2$ to 3 pounds)
  Salt and freshly ground black pepper
  Fresh sage sprigs
  Fall Fruit Chutney (recipe follows)

1. Position rack in lowest third of oven and preheat to 325°F.
2. For basting mixture: Whisk together all ingredients in medium bowl until well blended and set aside.
3. Rinse turkey breast well and pat dry with paper towels. Season with salt and pepper.
4. Place breast on lightly greased rack in shallow roasting pan and generously brush with basting mixture.
5. Roast until thermometer inserted into thickest part of breast registers 165° F. to 170° F., basting occasionally with remaining basting mixture, about 1 hour 10 minutes.
6. Transfer to carving board and let stand about 15 minutes. Carve and serve immediately. Garnish with fresh sage sprigs and accompany with Fall Fruit Chutney.

Fall Fruit Chutney

- $^3/_4$ cup sugar
- $^3/_4$ cup cider vinegar
- $^1/_2$ cup raisins
- 1 small onion, finely chopped
- $^1/_2$ lime, thinly sliced, halved, seeded
- 1 tablespoon Tualatin Vineyards White Riesling
- $^3/_4$ teaspoon cinnamon
- $^1/_2$ teaspoon chopped fresh sage
- $^1/_4$ teaspoon ground allspice
- $^1/_4$ teaspoon ground cloves
- $^1/_4$ teaspoon salt
- 1 pound Golden Delicious apples, cored, peeled, seeded, coarsely chopped
- 1 pound Bartlett pears, cored, peeled, seeded, coarsely chopped

1. Bring to boil all ingredients, except apples and pears, in medium Dutch oven over medium-high heat, stirring until sugar dissolves.
2. Immediately reduce heat and stir in apples with pears. Simmer until soft, stirring occasionally, about 50 minutes. (If necessary, increase heat and further reduce liquid.)
3. Partially mash mixture with back of slotted spoon. Transfer to serving bowl, cover and refrigerate until serving time. (Makes about $3^1/_2$ cups.)

Cook's Tip

If you have leftover chutney, try it with our delicious Pork Terrine with Apples and Walnuts, found on page 36.

Wine Selection
**Tualatin Vineyards
White Riesling**

Almond Chicken Curry

A touch of mystique and intrigue surrounds the exotic dishes of Southeast Asia called curries. Curry, actually, is not a dish, but a process by which piquant mixtures of ground herbs and spices blend with other ingredients into delightfully aromatic combinations. Our spicy, yet mild, Almond Chicken Curry takes on characteristics of all Southeast Asian curries. To accompany this exotic dish, we suggest the flavorful Gewürztraminer produced by **Hoodsport Winery**, located along Washington's scenic Hood Canal. This deliciously spicy wine echoes hints of the dish's complex flavors and tantalizes the palate with each sip. The slightly bitter finish of Gewürztraminer balances the intensity of the rich and spicy curry.

6 to 8 servings

    2 broiler-fryer chickens (3 to 4 pounds
          each)
    6 tablespoons vegetable oil (or more)
    2 large onions, finely chopped
    6 garlic cloves, minced
    1 tablespoon finely grated fresh ginger
    3 red serrano chilies, stemmed, seeded,
          deribbed, finely chopped
    1 tablespoon ground coriander
    1 tablespoon ground cumin
    1 teaspoon ground turmeric
  1/2 teaspoon ground black pepper
  1/2 teaspoon ground fennel
  1/4 teaspoon cardamom
  1/4 teaspoon cinnamon
  1/4 teaspoon ground cloves
  1/4 teaspoon cayenne pepper
  1/8 teaspoon freshly grated nutmeg
    1 pound very ripe tomatoes (about 3
          medium), cored, seeded, chopped
  1/2 cup loose-packed cilantro leaves
  1/2 cup (2 ounces) sliced almonds, divided (1
          ounce toasted, ground, 1 ounce
          toasted only)
1 1/2 cups coconut cream*, stirred until smooth
1 1/2 cups coconut milk*, stirred until smooth
  1/4 cup fish sauce*
  1/4 cup loose-packed Thai basil*, shredded
          Steamed jasmine rice*
          Fresh Thai basil sprigs

1. Cut chicken into bite-size pieces. Rinse well and pat dry with paper towels. Set aside.
2. Heat oil in large Dutch oven over medium-high heat.
3. Add chicken pieces and brown (in batches; do no crowd) on all sides. Drain well on paper towels. Transfer to warm platter and tent with foil.
4. Reduce heat to medium and add onions, garlic and ginger. Cook until starting to brown and almost caramelized, stirring occasionally, and adding more oil, if necessary, about 25 minutes.
5. Add next 11 ingredients and cook, stirring occasionally, about 5 minutes.
6. Add tomatoes, cilantro leaves and ground almonds. Cook until tomatoes are pulpy, stirring occasionally, about 10 minutes.
7. Stir in coconut cream, coconut milk and fish sauce. Cook 5 minutes.
8. Return chicken to Dutch oven and coat well with mixture.
9. Partially cover and cook on low heat until tender, 45 minutes to 1 hour. Just before serving, stir in shredded basil. Serve immediately over steamed jasmine rice and garnish with toasted almonds and fresh Thai basil sprigs.

* See **Special Ingredients**

Wine Selection
**Hoodsport Winery
Gewürztraminer**

Szechwan Pork *with Broccoli*

Szechwan dishes present a special challenge in matching food with wine. No one does it better in the Northwest than creative winemaker Jeffrey Lamy of **Montinore Vineyards**. After 13 years of preparing this firey cuisine, Jeff concludes that Germanic style white wines of pronounced citrus-varietal character with residual sugars of 2-3% and acidity levels of 0.75 - 0.9% are the perfect accompaniments. His Szechwan Pork with Broccoli, a tantalizing orchestration of many flavors, is beautifully matched with a chilled glass of Montinore Vineyard's off-dry Oregon White Riesling. The slight sweetness of the wine is a foil for the salty-spicy flavors of Szechwan cuisine, while the aromas of fresh fruit are a welcome resting point between bites. The wine becomes a sensuous background, like a subtle tapestry, to the dominant flavors of this inspiring dish.

4 to 6 servings

- 2 pounds boneless pork loin, trimmed of fat
- $3/4$ pound fresh broccoli
- 12 dried Szechwan red peppers*, seeded, chopped, divided
- 3 tablespoons minced fresh ginger, divided
- 2 tablespoons light soy sauce
- 2 tablespoons light brown sugar
- 1 tablespoon Black Bean Sauce with Garlic*
- 1 tablespoon Hoisin Sauce*
- 1 tablespoon Montinore Vineyards Dry Riesling
- 8 garlic cloves, minced
- $3/4$ cup water
- 2 tablespoons cornstarch
   Peanut or vegetable oil
- 1 can (8 ounces) sliced water chestnuts, drained
- 1 carrot, peeled, diagonally sliced thin, parboiled 2 minutes
- 8 dried Chinese black mushrooms*, rehydrated, stems removed, cut into $1/4$-inch-wide strips
- 1 can (15 ounces) straw mushrooms*, drained, rinsed
- 2 teaspoons Oriental sesame oil*
   Steamed white rice
- 3 green onions, diagonally sliced very thin

1. Cut pork loin into $1/2$-inch-thick slices. Cut slices into $1/4$-inch-wide shreds. Cut shreds into $1^1/2$-inch-long lengths. Set aside.
2. Cut broccoli into bite-size florets. Peel stalks and thinly slice. Set aside.
3. To make sauce, stir together half red peppers, half ginger, soy sauce, brown sugar, Black Bean Sauce, Hoisin Sauce, wine and garlic in small bowl until well blended. Set aside.
4. Combine water with cornstarch in small bowl until well blended. Stir together with above sauce until well blended and set aside.
5. Heat wok over high heat until hot enough to evaporate bead of water on contact. Add oil to coat and swirl.
6. Immediately reduce heat to medium-high and add pork (in batches; do not crowd). Stir-fry until no longer pink, $1^1/2$ to 2 minutes. With slotted spoon, transfer to warm plate and tent with foil.
7. Add remaining peppers with remaining ginger. Stir-fry until fragrant, adding more oil, if necessary, about 30 seconds.
8. Reduce heat and add broccoli with water chestnuts. Stir-fry 2 to 3 minutes.
9. Add carrots with mushrooms. Stir-fry 1 minute.
10. Push mixture to sides of wok and add sauce to center. Cook until thick and bubbly, 2 to 3 minutes. (Cover, if desired.)
11. Drain pork well and return to wok. Toss well to coat with mixture and cook 2 to 3 minutes. Remove wok from heat and drizzle with sesame oil. Toss to mix well. Serve immediately over steamed white rice. Garnish with sliced green onions.

* See **Special Ingredients**

Wine Selection

**Montinore Vineyards
White Riesling**

Grilled Pork Chops *with Cranberry Mint Relish*

Bill and Susan Blosser, owners of one of Oregon's largest wineries, **Sokol Blosser**, work miracles with the Pinot Noir grape. The grapes of three separate vineyards are blended to produce wines of great complexity and character. Their "Redland Reserve" label is the most complex of the releases, with berry-like qualities that team up beautifully with our tasty Grilled Pork Chops with Cranberry Mint Relish. The wine's medium-bodied structure of tannin and acidity complements the texture of the meat, while the berry nuances in the accompanying relish echo the wine's flavors. Fire up the grill for this great summertime marriage of food and wine!

6 servings

Marinade

  1 cup olive oil
$^1/_2$ cup Sokol Blosser Winery Pinot Noir
$1^1/_2$ tablespoons chopped fresh mint
  3 garlic cloves, chopped

  6 rib pork chops (6 to 8 ounces each), trimmed of fat
    Salt and freshly ground black pepper
    Fresh mint sprigs
    Cranberry Mint Relish (recipe follows)

1. For marinade: Whisk together all ingredients in small bowl until well blended and set aside.
2. Place pork chops in nonreactive dish, large enough to hold chops with marinade. Pour marinade over, cover and refrigerate several hours. Turn once.
3. Prepare grill with medium-hot coals. Adjust rack 3 to 4 inches from heat and lightly oil.
4. Remove chops from marinade and pat dry with paper towels. Season with salt and pepper. Reserve marinade for basting.
5. Place chops on grill and cook until thermometer inserted into center registers at least 160° F., basting occasionally with reserved marinade. Serve immediately and garnish with fresh mint sprigs. Accompany with Cranberry Mint Relish.

Cranberry Mint Relish

12 ounces fresh whole cranberries, washed, drained, picked over
$^1/_2$ cup sugar
$^1/_2$ cup water
$^1/_4$ cup honey
$^1/_4$ cup Sokol Blosser Winery Pinot Noir
$^1/_2$ cup (2 ounces) chopped walnuts
  1 tablespoon chopped fresh mint
    Zest of $^1/_2$ orange, finely minced

1. Combine cranberries, sugar, water, honey and wine in heavy medium saucepan over high heat. Bring to boil and cook, stirring occasionally, until berries pop, about 5 minutes.
2. Reduce heat and cook until thick consistency, about 30 minutes.
3. Partially mash berries with back of slotted spoon. Stir in walnuts, mint and orange zest. Transfer to serving bowl, cover and refrigerate until serving time. (Makes about 2 cups.)

Cook's Tip

If you have leftover Cranberry Mint Relish, try it with our Terrine Forestier, found on page 35.

Wine Selection

**Sokol Blosser
Redland Reserve Pinot Noir**

Baby Back Ribs *with Spicy Peanut Sauce*

Northwest summers and backyard barbecues go well together and no summer should pass without savoring our delicious Baby Back Ribs! We love them grilled Asian style, combining the tantalizing tastes and textures from two of our favorite cuisines, Thai and Chinese. Dip them in our "famous" Spicy Peanut Sauce to give an added dimension to lip-smackin' summer barbecue. Red wine lovers might prefer a hearty Cabernet or Merlot, but for a wine encounter of the lighter style, try **Pintler Cellars** Idaho Chenin Blanc. The spicy fruitiness of the wine, with flavors of pears and apricots, complements the complex flavors from the marinade and cools the heat of the peanut sauce – oh, so nicely!

6 servings

Asian Marinade

- 2 cups water
- 2 cups light brown sugar
- 1 cup soy sauce
- $1/2$ cup honey
- 1 stalk fresh lemon grass, very thinly sliced
- $1/2$ small onion, minced
- 2 tablespoons Oriental sesame oil *
- 1 tablespoon chopped fresh cilantro
- 1 tablespoon minced ginger
- 1 tablespoon rice vinegar*
- 2 teaspoons toasted sesame seeds
- $1^1/2$ teaspoons dried red pepper flakes

   6 pounds baby back pork ribs
   Fresh cilantro sprigs
   Spicy Peanut Sauce (recipe follows)

1. For marinade: Stir together all ingredients in medium bowl until well blended and set aside. (Makes about 1 quart.)
2. Cut ribs into 6 serving portions and place in nonreactive dishes, large enough to hold them. Pour marinade over, cover and refrigerate 2 to 3 hours. Turn once.
3. Prepare grill with medium-hot coals. Adjust rack 3 to 4 inches from heat and lightly oil.
4. Remove ribs from marinade and pat dry with paper towels. Reserve marinade for basting.

5. Place ribs on grill and cook until desired doneness, turning and basting occasionally with reserved marinade. To serve, place ribs on large platter and garnish generously with fresh cilantro sprigs. Accompany with Spicy Peanut Sauce.

Spicy Peanut Sauce

- $1^1/2$ tablespoons garlic oil (see **Cook's Tip**)
- 2 tablespoons Muslim Curry Paste*
- 2 cans (14 ounces each) coconut milk*, stirred until smooth, divided
- $1/2$ cup loose-packed cilantro leaves
- $1/4$ cup chopped salted peanuts
- 6 tablespoons unsalted crunchy peanut butter, preferably Adams Old-Fashioned
- 3 tablespoons dark brown sugar
- 2 tablespoons fish sauce*
- $3/4$ teaspoon tamarind concentrate*
- $1/4$ teaspoon cinnamon

1. Heat oil in heavy large saucepan over high heat 1 to 2 minutes.
2. Add curry paste and fry several minutes to release flavors.
3. Stir in 1/2 cup coconut milk to make thick paste
4. Reduce heat to low and stir in remaining coconut milk. Cook 2 minutes.
5. Stir in remaining ingredients and cook until thick and uniform consistency, about 10 minutes. (Makes about 4 cups.)

* See **Special Ingredients**

Cook's Tip

To make garlic oil, we add several cloves of crushed garlic to a container of vegetable oil and let it steep several days. It's great to have on hand for all of your Asian cuisines!

Wine Selection
Pintler Cellars
Chenin Blanc

Veal Marengo

A la Marengo, a style usually applied to chicken, takes on a new twist in Diane Howieson's snappy version of the French classic. In the following recipe, tender chunks of milk-fed veal are lightly browned, then slowly braised in a savory blend of wine, tomatoes and fresh herbs. As the stew cooks, these delicious, herbaceous flavors intensify and call for a complementary wine to match. Diane suggests **Veritas Vineyards** delightful Pinot Noir, and we agree. The wine contrasts the dish with fruity aromas of cherries and spice as well as complementing the flavors of earth and herbs. Serve this regal dish as the French do with a garnish of heart-shaped croutons lightly sautéed in butter.

6 to 8 servings

¼ cup olive oil (or more)
3 pounds boneless lean veal, cut into 1-inch cubes
   Salt and freshly ground black pepper
1 large onion, chopped
2 garlic cloves, finely chopped
1 tablespoon chopped fresh basil
1 tablespoon chopped fresh thyme
   Pinch cayenne pepper
1½ cups Veal Stock (see **Basics**)
½ cup Veritas Vineyards Pinot Noir
1 large tomato, cored, seeded, coarsely chopped
2 strips (2 inches long each) lemon peel
12 pearl onions, peeled, left whole
1½ cups button mushrooms, cleaned, thinly sliced
1 can (2¼ ounces) sliced black olives
   Hot cooked rice
2 tablespoons chopped fresh parsley

1. Heat oil in medium Dutch oven over medium-high heat.
2. Season veal with salt and pepper. Add to Dutch oven and brown (in batches; do not crowd) on all sides. With slotted spoon, transfer to warm plate and tent with foil.
3. Reduce heat to medium and add onion, garlic, basil, thyme and cayenne pepper. Cook until onion is soft and translucent, stirring occasionally, and adding more oil, if necessary, about 5 minutes.
4. Stir in stock, wine, tomato and lemon peel. Simmer 10 minutes.
5. Drain veal well and return to Dutch oven. Stir well to coat with sauce. Partially cover and cook on low until almost tender, 45 minutes to 1 hour.
6. Stir in pearl onions, mushrooms and olives. Partially cover and cook 15 minutes longer. Season with salt and pepper. (If sauce is too thin, remove veal with slotted spoon and reduce sauce to desired consistency; return veal to Dutch oven.) Serve immediately over hot cooked rice and garnish with chopped fresh parsley.

Wine Selection

**Veritas Vineyards
Pinot Noir**

Grilled Veal Loin Chops
with Walla Walla Sweet Onion Confit

Dick Erath, owner/winemaker of one of Oregon's largest wineries, **Knudsen Erath**, produces some of the state's finest Pinot Noirs. He takes his success one step further with his "Vintage Select" designation – reserve style wines of greater depth and complexity meant for long-time cellaring. These wines display the power and finesse of Pinot Noir, offering rich, ripe fruit and generous flavor and body. Such characteristics in Pinot are delightful dinner companions to grilled meats, especially our Grilled Veal Loin Chops with Walla Walla Sweet Onion Confit. The berry-peppery nuances in the wine highlight the grilled flavors of the meat, while the slightly sweet onion confit accentuates the wine's fruity palate. Show off that special Oregon Pinot with this elegant grilled dish!

6 servings

Marinade

    1 cup olive oil
  $^1/_2$ cup Knudsen Erath Pinot Noir
    2 teaspoons chopped fresh rosemary
    3 garlic cloves, chopped

    6 veal loin chops (about 8 ounces each), trimmed of fat
       Salt and freshly ground black pepper
       Fresh rosemary sprigs
       Walla Walla Sweet Onion Confit (recipe follows)

1. For marinade: Whisk together all ingredients in small bowl until well blended and set aside.
2. Place veal loin chops in nonreactive dish, large enough to hold chops with marinade. Pour marinade over, cover and refrigerate several hours. Turn once.
3. Prepare grill with medium-hot coals. Adjust rack 3 to 4 inches from heat and lightly oil.

4. Remove chops from marinade and pat dry with paper towels. Season with salt and pepper. Reserve marinade for basting.
5. Place chops on grill and cook to desired doneness or 5 to 7 minutes per side for medium meat, basting occasionally with reserved marinade. Serve immediately and garnish with fresh rosemary sprigs. Accompany with Walla Walla Sweet Onion Confit.

Walla Walla Sweet Onion Confit

    2 tablespoons unsalted butter
    2 tablespoons vegetable oil
    1 large Walla Walla sweet onion, thinly sliced
  $1^1/_2$ cups Veal Stock (see **Basics**)
    3 tablespoons red wine vinegar
    3 tablespoons golden raisins
    2 tablespoons dark brown sugar
  $1^1/_2$ tablespoons tomato paste
  $^1/_2$ teaspoon chopped fresh rosemary
    3 garlic cloves, chopped
       Salt and freshly ground black pepper to taste

1. Melt butter with oil in medium Dutch oven over medium heat.
2. Add onion and cook until golden brown, stirring occasionally, about 20 minutes.
3. Reduce heat and stir in remaining ingredients. Partially cover and simmer about 45 minutes.
4. Uncover, increase heat and cook until thick glaze forms and liquid is reduced, stirring occasionally, 15 to 20 minutes. Transfer to serving bowl, cover and refrigerate until serving time. (May be warmed prior to serving time or served at room temperature. Makes about $1^1/_2$ cups.)

Wine Selection
Knudsen Erath
Vintage Select Pinot Noir

Flank Steak Salsa

Dedicated winemaker John Paul of **Cameron Winery** gained international wine-making experience studying in the Burgundy region of France as well as New Zealand and Australia. He now puts his well-traveled knowledge to work and crafts lovely Burgundian style wines, with great success. His Pinot Noirs are fine examples of Oregon's potential with this sometimes troublesome varietal. His wife, Teri Wadsworth, shares with us her wonderful Mexican-inspired Flank Steak Salsa, designed to accompany John's Pinot Noir. As far as the wine matchup, John says, "The dish requires the intensity of young fruit and some youthful structure from our Abby Ridge Vineyard. The tart and spicy character is great with the grilled flavors." We fired up our grill more than once for this one, and loved it!

4 to 6 servings

Salsa

2 ripe large tomatoes, cored, seeded, finely chopped
3 garlic cloves, minced
1 green bell pepper, stemmed, seeded, deribbed, finely chopped
2 jalapeño chilies, stemmed, seeded, deribbed, chopped
$^1/_2$ small onion, finely chopped
$^1/_2$ cup tomato sauce
2 tablespoons chopped fresh cilantro
1 tablespoon red wine vinegar
1 teaspoon olive oil
Salt and freshly ground black pepper to taste

1 flank steak ($1^1/_2$ to 2 pounds), surface fat trimmed
Fresh cilantro sprigs

1. For salsa: Combine all ingredients in medium bowl until well blended and set aside.
2. Pound steak to tenderize and place in nonreactive dish, large enough to hold steak with salsa. Pour salsa over, cover and refrigerate at least 6 hours or overnight. Turn occasionally.
3. Prepare grill with medium-hot coals. Adjust rack 3 to 4 inches from grill and lightly oil.
4. Remove steak from salsa and pat dry with paper towels. Season with salt and pepper. Transfer salsa to serving bowl, cover and set aside until serving time.
5. Place steak on grill and cook to desired doneness or about 8 minutes per side for medium-rare meat.
6. Transfer steak to carving board and let stand about 5 minutes. To serve, slice meat, across grain, into thin, diagonal slices. Arrange on warm plates and garnish with fresh cilantro sprigs. Accompany with reserved salsa.

Cook's Tips

For an impressive appetizer, cut meat into strips and thread onto bamboo skewers for grilling. Be sure to soak skewers about 30 minutes in water.

For another delicious alternative, wrap strips of meat in warm tortillas with other Mexican favorites, such as guacamole, sour cream, chopped tomatoes, shredded lettuce and fresh cilantro sprigs, and top with salsa.

Wine Selection
Cameron Winery
Pinot Noir

Grilled New York Steaks *with Parsley Beurre Blanc*

Fire up the grill and enjoy these delectable New Yorks for an exciting taste sensation. Enhanced by a velvety textured, herbaceous butter sauce, this grilled favorite is a winner every time. Our inspiration for this hearty entrée came from Alex Golitzin, owner and winemaker of **Quilceda Creek Vintners**. His rich and flavorful Cabernet Sauvignons burst with fruit and complexity and offer the required tannin backbone to stand up to the richness of the steak and accompanying sauce. The power and longevity of these wines are well-documented, with Alex crediting some of his success to early encouragement and advice from his uncle, Andre Tchellistcheff, one of the modern day fathers of California winemaking.

4 servings

Marinade

 1 cup Quilceda Creek Vintners Cabernet Sauvignon
 1/2 cup olive oil
 1/2 small onion, chopped
 2 tablespoons chopped fresh Italian flat-leaf parsley

 4 New York steaks (about 8 ounces each), trimmed of fat
   Salt and freshly ground black pepper
   Fresh Italian flat-leaf parsley sprigs
   Parsley Beurre Blanc (recipe follows)

1. For marinade: Combine all ingredients in small bowl until well blended and set aside.
2. Place steaks in nonreactive dish, large enough to hold steaks with marinade. Pour marinade over, cover and refrigerate 1 to 2 hours. Turn once.
3. Prepare grill with medium-hot coals. Adjust rack 3 to 4 inches from heat and lightly oil.

4. Remove steaks from marinade and pat dry with paper towels. Reserve marinade for basting. Season steaks with salt and pepper.
5. Place steaks on grill and cook to desired doneness or 4 to 5 minutes per side for medium-rare meat, basting occasionally with reserved marinade. Serve immediately and garnish with fresh parsley sprigs. Accompany with Parsley Beurre Blanc.

Parsley Beurre Blanc

 3 shallots, finely chopped
 3/4 cup dry white wine
 1/4 cup heavy cream
 12 tablespoons unsalted butter, cut into pieces, chilled
 1 tablespoon chopped fresh Italian flat-leaf parsley
   Salt and freshly ground white pepper

1. Combine shallots with wine in heavy small saucepan over high heat. Bring to boil and reduce to 1 tablespoon. (If smooth sauce is desired, strain liquid through fine-mesh sieve into clean saucepan, pressing on shallots with back of spoon to extract as much liquid as possible.)
2. Stir in cream and warm briefly.
3. Whisk in butter, 1 piece at a time.
4. Stir in parsley and season with salt and white pepper. Serve immediately or store in well insulated thermos up to 2 hours. (Makes about 3/4 cup.)

Cook's Tip

Try Top Sirloins for a tasty, economical alternative to New Yorks. We like to buy them on sale and stock the freezer, especially during the summer!

Wine Selection

**Quilceda Creek Vintners
Cabernet Sauvignon**

Beef Tournedos
with Oregon Blue Cheese and Cabernet Sauce

Brother and sister John and Kristi Jorgensen own and run **Pacifica**, a lovely wine country restaurant nestled in the picturesque town of Woodinville, Washington. John presides over the kitchen, stressing his preference for fresh, regional products, while Kristi is in charge of the extensive wine cellar, favoring Northwest wines to accompany her brother's delightful culinary inspirations. Together they create dynamic duos of food and wine, and one of their favorites is Beef Tournedos with Oregon Blue Cheese and Cabernet Sauce. Teamed up with **Columbia Winery's** rich and flavorful Cabernet Sauvignon, it's wine country cooking at its best! The wine's youthful tannins and intense fruit stand up beautifully to the rich flavors of the meat and blue cheese, while a touch of wine to the sauce provides the necessary unifying element to round out the elegant dish.

2 servings

2 beef tournedos (5 to 6 ounces each)
2 tablespoons (1 ounce) Oregon Blue cheese, softened, divided
1¹/₂ tablespoons unsalted butter
2 tablespoons gin
1 small shallot, finely chopped
¹/₃ cup Columbia Winery Cabernet Sauvignon
¹/₃ cup heavy cream
Salt and freshly ground black pepper
Fresh herb sprigs

1. With sharp paring or boning knife, cut pocket in tournedos (on side), making incision no more than ¹/₂-inch-long on outer surface, yet increasing interior cut.
2. Stuff each tournedo with 2¹/₂ teaspoons cheese, reserving 1 teaspoon for sauce. Take two toothpicks (per tournedo) and make an x-cross over opening to prevent cheese from leaking out during cooking. Set aside.
3. Melt butter to point before browning in heavy medium sauté pan over medium-high heat.
4. Add tournedos and sear on both sides. Immediately reduce heat and cook to almost preferred doneness, turning occasionally.
5. With tournedos in pan, increase heat to high. Deglaze with gin and ignite; avoid flame. Immediately transfer tournedos to warm plate and tent with foil.
6. Add shallots and sauté quickly. Stir in wine and bring to boil. Reduce by about half. Add cream and boil until sauce coats back of spoon. Whisk in remaining blue cheese and season with salt and pepper. To serve, arrange tournedos on warm plates and top with sauce. Garnish with fresh herb sprigs.

Cook's Tip

Be sure to cook your tournedos to almost preferred doneness – they will continue to cook as you make the sauce.

Wine Selection
**Columbia Winery
Cabernet Sauvignon**

Pan-Fried Filet Mignons
with Crème de Cerise Mushroom Sauce

Columbia Crest Winery, part of the Stimson Lane Wine & Spirits group that includes Chateau Ste. Michelle, is one winery not to miss if you're touring the beautiful Eastern Washington wine country. Located just above the Columbia River in Paterson, this impressive facility has everything to offer wine buffs – picnic areas, guided tours, tasting room and an interesting gift shop. More impressive than the ambiance of the expansive facility are the delightful wines crafted to accompany food, by talented winemaker Doug Gore. We love his rich and flavorful Merlot, loaded with cherry and mint nuances – it's just right with our Pan-Fried Filet Mignons with Crème de Cerise Mushroom Sauce. Fruity nuances in the sauce are complemented by the wine's aromas of cherries and spice, while the full-bodied palate stands up to the richness of this hearty meat preparation.

4 servings

5 tablespoons unsalted butter, divided
1 tablespoon vegetable oil
4 beef filet mignon steaks (6 to 8 ounces each), trimmed of fat
    Salt and freshly ground black pepper
1 shallot, finely chopped
1 garlic clove, minced
1 pound small button mushrooms, cleaned, thinly sliced
2 tablespoons crème de cerise liqueur (sweet cherry)
$^1/_2$ cup Columbia Crest Merlot
1 cup Veal Stock (see **Basics**)
$1^1/_2$ teaspoons chopped fresh mint
    Fresh mint sprigs

1. Melt 1 tablespoon butter with vegetable oil in heavy medium skillet over medium-high heat.
2. Season steaks with salt and pepper. Add to skillet and sear on both sides. Immediately reduce heat to medium and cook to almost preferred doneness. Transfer to warm plate and tent with foil.
3. Degrease skillet and add 2 more tablespoons butter. Add shallot with garlic. Cook until soft and translucent, stirring occasionally, about 2 minutes.
4. Add mushrooms and cook until soft and almost dry, stirring occasionally, 8 to 10 minutes.
5. Stir in liqueur and cook 2 minutes. With slotted spoon, transfer mushrooms to warm plate and tent with foil.
6. Add wine with stock to skillet. Bring to boil over high heat and reduce by half.
7. Reduce heat and stir in remaining butter, chopped fresh mint and reserved mushrooms. Season with salt and pepper.
8. Return steaks to skillet and coat well with sauce. Reheat briefly. To serve, arrange steaks on warm plates and top with sauce. Garnish with fresh mint sprigs.

Cook's Tip

The steaks will continue to cook as you make the sauce, so be sure to cook to almost preferred doneness. Also, they are briefly reheated prior to serving, cooking a little further — so, do plan your timing for a perfect end result!

Wine Selection
Columbia Crest Winery Merlot

Wheeler's Supreme Chili

Chili lovers gather 'round for "Jazz at the Winery" most Sundays, during the summer, at **Ste. Chapelle Vineyards** winery in Caldwell, Idaho. Enjoy the music of famous jazz artists and even the Boise Philharmonic Orchestra while you sip the internationally acclaimed wines of the Northwest's second largest winery. Bring a picnic lunch or purchase freshly baked breads, a variety of cheeses or other tempting snacks. If Wheeler's Supreme Chili happens to be bubbling on the stove, go for it – the best darn chili in the Northwest! Winery friends and family unanimously confirm Ste. Chapelle Vineyard's Cabernet Sauvignon the appropriate wine to sip with this hearty dish and we agree. The contrasting fruit flavors in the wine team up beautifully with the spicy, full flavors in the chili. Now, who can second guess a "chili-bean-wine-lover" from Idaho? Not us!

8 to 10 servings

- ¼ cup vegetable oil
- 2 medium onions, chopped
- 3 garlic cloves, minced
- 2 pounds lean ground beef
- 4 tablespoons chili powder, (mild or hot)
- 1 fresh jalapeño chili, stemmed, seeded, deribbed, chopped
- ¾ teaspoon ground cumin
- 2 pounds very ripe tomatoes, cored, seeded, finely chopped
- 1 can (15 ounces) tomato sauce
- ¼ cup Ste. Chapelle Vineyards Cabernet Sauvignon
  Salt and freshly ground black pepper to taste
- 1 can (27 ounces) kidney beans, drained, rinsed

1. Heat oil in large Dutch oven over medium-high heat. Add onions with garlic. Cook until onions are soft and translucent, stirring occasionally, about 5 minutes.
2. Add beef and fry until well cooked, breaking up meat with wooden spoon and stirring occasionally, about 15 minutes. Drain fat.
3. Stir in remaining ingredients, except beans. Reduce heat and simmer about 1 hour 30 minutes, adding beans last 30 minutes of cooking time. Serve immediately.

Cook's Tip

If ripe, juicy tomatoes are not available, do not hesitate to substitute 1 can (28 ounces) whole peeled tomatoes, cored, seeded and finely chopped with juices.

Wine Selection
**Ste. Chapelle Vineyards
Cabernet Sauvignon**

Corned Beef and Cabbage

The popular holiday of Ireland comes once a year and Northwesterners celebrate from dawn till dusk, carousing with friends at local pubs and consuming copious quantities of green beer. As the day winds down, round out the evening's celebration with Ireland's most famous dish, Corned Beef and Cabbage. Our rendition of the Emerald Isle favorite takes on a slightly new twist, as we embellish it with "stick-to-your-ribs" potatoes to create a hearty supper for slightly tired celebrators! Gulps of Irish whiskey would be in order, but we suggest Mike Hale's Special Bitter from **Hale's Ales Brewery**. This well-hopped bitter ale offers rich clean flavors and a malty finish, perfect for the pungency of corned beef.

Serves 4 to 6

1 fresh corned beef brisket (about 3 pounds)
   Water to cover
4 large russet potatoes, cut into 1¹/₂-inch chunks
4 large carrots, peeled, diagonally sliced into ¹/₂-inch pieces
1 head white cabbage, wilted outer leaves removed, cored, cut into chunks
   Butter
   Salt and freshly ground black pepper

1. Place brisket, fat side up, in Dutch oven (with tight-fitting lid), large enough to accommodate it with vegetables.
2. Cover with water and bring to boil over high heat. Immediately reduce heat and skim foam from surface. Gently simmer 2 hours 30 minutes.
3. Add potatoes with carrots. Simmer until vegetables are almost tender, about 20 minutes.
4. Add cabbage and simmer until tender, about 10 minutes.
5. Drain meat with vegetables. Transfer meat to carving board and let stand 5 minutes.
6. Transfer vegetables to serving bowl and dot with butter. Season with salt and pepper. To serve, slice corned beef, across grain, and accompany with vegetables.

Cook's Tip

A good rule of thumb for cooking a corned beef brisket is about 1 hour per pound.

Beer Selection

Hale's Ales Special Bitter

Garlic Beef Stew

As snow frequently blankets the Northwest during the winter months, cozy, satisfying meals come to mind – hearty stews, like Mom used to make. Our Garlic Beef Stew is just the "comfort food" to soothe that yearning. A whole head of garlic, Pike Place XXXXX Stout and Whidbey's Port complement the lean stewing beef, while fresh vegetables and herbs join in to create a delicious one-dish meal fit for a king. A hearty brew like **Pike Place Brewery's** XXXXX Stout is a wonderful companion to the flavors and richness of this delightful stew. A small brewery, even by microbrew standards, Pike Place Stout is only available in the Seattle area.

4 to 6 servings

3   tablespoons all-purpose flour
2   tablespoons cornstarch
    Salt and freshly ground black pepper to taste
6   tablespoons vegetable oil (or more), divided
2   large onions, chopped
1   large head garlic, separated into cloves, (6 minced, remaining peeled, left whole)
2½ pounds stewing beef, trimmed of fat, cut into large pieces
3   large Russet potatoes, cut in 1-inch chunks
3   carrots, peeled, diagonally cut into 1-inch pieces
1   small red bell pepper, stemmed, seeded, deribbed, diced
1   pound very ripe tomatoes (about 3 medium), cored, seeded, chopped
1   cup Veal Stock (see **Basics**)
½   cup Pike Place Brewery XXXXX Stout
½   cup Whidbey's Port
3   tablespoons chopped fresh Italian flat-leaf parsley
1½ tablespoons chopped fresh thyme
1   tablespoon honey
½   teaspoon ground cumin
2   bay leaves
    Fresh Italian flat-leaf parsley sprigs

1. Position rack in lowest third of oven and preheat to 325° F.
2. Combine flour, cornstarch, salt and pepper in medium, shallow bowl until well blended. Set aside.
3. Heat 4 tablespoons oil in heavy large skillet over medium heat. Add onions with minced garlic. Cook until starting to brown and almost caramelized, stirring occasionally, about 25 minutes.
4. With slotted spoon, transfer mixture to medium Dutch oven (with tight-fitting lid) and set aside.
5. Increase heat and add remaining oil to skillet.
6. Dredge beef in seasoned flour and shake off excess. Brown in fat (in batches; do not crowd), adding more oil, if necessary. With slotted spoon, transfer beef to Dutch oven and place atop onions.
7. Arrange potatoes, carrots, red bell pepper and remaining garlic cloves atop beef. Set aside.
8. Add remaining seasoned flour (if any) to skillet and stir to brown.
9. Stir in remaining ingredients, except parsley sprigs and bring to boil over high heat. Immediately stir mixture into Dutch oven mixture and season with salt and pepper.
10. Cover Dutch oven, place in oven and cook until meat is almost tender, about 1 hour 30 minutes. Turn off heat and let stand in oven 30 minutes longer. Remove bay leaves and serve immediately. Garnish with fresh parsley sprigs.

Cook's Tips

Substitute 1 can (14½ ounces) whole peeled tomatoes, cored, seeded, chopped with juices, if very ripe tomatoes are not available.

This wonderful stew is even better the next day. Reheat in the oven about 50 minutes at 350° F.

Beer Selection
Pike Place Brewery
XXXXX Stout

Canard Beaujolais

Duck hunting season in the Pacific Northwest opens around mid-October and fanciers of this seasonal waterfowl take to the lakes, ponds and rivers in hopes of bringing the true pleasures of the great outdoors to the table. Elizabeth Tross-Deamer, marketing representative for **Mont Elise Vineyards** of Bingen, Washington, shares her delightful recipe for this Northwest specialty, Canard Beaujolais. To accompany her elegant dish, she highly recommends Mont Elise Vineyard's lovely Beaujolais, the only one of its kind in the Northwest. The wine's brilliant young fruit is a fine match for the gamy flavors of the duck, while nuances of wood and earth accentuate the fine marriage of food and wine.

2 servings

Stuffing

- $1/2$ cup pitted cherries, preferably Bings
- 2 tablespoons toasted pine nuts
- 3 garlic cloves, minced
- 3 sprigs fresh mint
- 1 small onion, quartered
- 1 celery stalk, coarsely chopped

- 1 fresh wild duck ($3^1/2$ to 4 pounds) or 2 small wild ducks (about $1^1/2$ pounds each), ready to cook
  Fatback strips
  Melted unsalted butter (optional)

Sauce

- 2 tablespoons unsalted butter
- 1 shallot, minced
- 2 sprigs fresh mint
- $1/4$ cup Mont Elise Vineyards Gamay Beaujolais
- $1/2$ cup Dark Poultry or Game Stock (see **Basics**)
- $1/2$ cup pitted cherries, preferably Bings
- 1 tablespoon toasted pine nuts
- 2 tablespoons unsalted butter or Crème Fraîche (see **Basics**)
  Salt and freshly ground black pepper

  Fresh mint sprigs

1. Position rack in lowest third of oven and preheat to 425° F.
2. For stuffing: Toss together all ingredients in medium bowl until well blended.
3. Spoon into cavity of duck and close with skewers.
4. Drape strips of fatback over breasts and secure with twine. Pierce duck all over, especially under thighs and around legs. Truss.
5. Place duck, breast side up, on lightly greased rack in shallow roasting pan.
6. Reduce heat to 350° F. and roast duck until juices run clear, when thigh is pierced with skewer and skin is well browned, 18 to 20 minutes per pound. Baste occasionally with pan juices or melted butter.
7. Transfer to carving board and proceed with sauce.
8. For sauce: Melt butter in heavy medium skillet over medium heat. Add shallot with mint. Sauté briefly. Stir in wine with stock. Bring to boil over high heat and reduce by half.
9. Strain sauce through fine-mesh sieve into clean saucepan, pressing on solids with back of spoon to extract as much liquid as possible.
10. Stir in cherries with pine nuts. Swirl in butter and season with salt and pepper. To serve, discard stuffing and carve duck, as desired. Place on warm plates and garnish with fresh mint sprigs. Accompany with sauce.

Cook's Tip

Wild ducks are not as fatty as the domestic Long Island-style variety called the White Pekin, so caution must be taken in cooking. Internal breast temperature should not exceed 140° F. – the meat toughens when cooked longer. A good rule of thumb is 18 to 20 minutes per pound.

Wine Selection
Mont Elise Vineyards
Gamay Beaujolais

Breast of Pheasant *with Fresh Mint and Kirsch*

Taming the tempermental Pinot Noir varietal in Oregon's Willamette Valley is a yearly challenge for both grape grower and winemaker. **Rex Hill Vineyards** has chosen to confront this difficulty by vinting several Pinot Noirs from each vintage. Products of individual vineyard sites, each wine offers unique aromas and flavors. A quality shared by these delightful wines is their affinity for feathered game, particularly pheasant, the most sought-after gamebird in the Pacific Northwest. Delightful combinations such as these send hunters to the field, gastronomes to the kitchen, and enophiles to the wine cellar. Our Breast of Pheasant with Fresh Mint and Kirsch lets Rex Hill's lovely wine take center stage. Punctuated with fresh mint and kirsch, both components that echo the wine's flavor and bond the food and wine more closely together, this dish will please connoisseurs of all three disciplines.

4 servings

   2 fresh hen pheasants (about $2^1/_2$ pounds each), ready to cook

Stock

   1 small onion, coarsely chopped with skin
   1 small carrot, peeled, coarsely chopped
   1 celery stalk, coarsely chopped
$^1/_2$ cup Rex Hill Vineyards Pinot Noir
   6 cups water (or to cover)
   5 sprigs fresh mint (or more)
   2 sprigs fresh parsley
   1 sprig fresh thyme
   5 black peppercorns
   4 juniper berries, crushed
   2 coriander seeds
   1 bay leaf

   3 tablespoons unsalted butter, divided
   1 tablespoon vegetable oil
$1^1/_2$ tablespoons kirsch (clear cherry brandy)
$^1/_4$ cup Rex Hill Vineyards Pinot Noir
   2 teaspoons chopped fresh mint (or more)
     Salt and freshly ground black pepper
     Fresh mint sprigs

1. Position rack in lowest third of oven and preheat to 375° F.
2. Lift breasts from pheasants with sharp knife and wrap in plastic wrap. Refrigerate until needed. Reserve carcasses to prepare stock.
3. For stock: Chop carcasses and arrange in lightly greased, shallow roasting pan. Roast about 30 minutes. Top with onion, carrot and celery. Roast 30 minutes longer or until vegetables start to brown.
4. Transfer bones with vegetables to stockpot, draining fat, as necessary.
5. Degrease roasting pan and set over high heat atop stove. Deglaze with wine, scraping up all browned bits. Add mixture to stockpot with water. Bring to boil over high heat and skim foam from surface.
6. Immediately reduce heat and add remaining ingredients. Simmer, uncovered, 2 hours, skimming foam and fat occasionally. (Do not stir or stock will become cloudy.)
7. Strain stock through fine-mesh sieve into clean pot and reduce to $1^1/_2$ cups. Set aside.
8. Heat 1 tablespoon butter with oil in heavy large skillet over medium heat.
9. Add breasts and cook until lightly browned on both sides and internal temperature registers no more than 140° F. (Gamebirds cooked longer become tough.) Transfer to warm plate and tent with foil.
10. Deglaze pan with kirsch and wine over high heat, scraping up any browned bits. Stir in mint and reduce liquid by half. Add reserved stock and reduce by half.
11. Strain stock through fine-mesh sieve into clean saucepan. Whisk in remaining butter and season with salt and pepper. To serve, briefly reheat breasts and fan-slice. Arrange on warm plates and drizzle with sauce. Garnish with fresh mint sprigs.

Cook's Tip

Chicken is a lovely, economical alternative to this seasonal dish, for about $^1/_4$ the cost!

Wine Selection
Rex Hill Vineyards
Pinot Noir

Rosemary-Stuffed Quail *with Balsamic Vinegar Sauce*

Oregon Pinot Noirs are among the most sought-after in the world, consistently challenging the reputation of the highly touted wines of Burgundy. Among those who have consistently shown an intuitive hand with this temperamental varietal are Pat and Joe Campbell of **Elk Cove Vineyards**. Their estate-bottled Pinot Noir offers elegance and exquisite balance, displaying herbal and spicy notes with a rich, full palate. This lovely wine is a classic match for our Rosemary-Stuffed Quail with Balsamic Vinegar Sauce. The backbone of acidity found in this Oregon Pinot is a fine complement to the slight balsamic bite in the sauce, while gamy/earthy notes in both put the dish in total harmony.

6 servings

Balsamic Vinegar Sauce

- 1/4 cup Cognac or other brandy
- 1/2 cup Elk Cove Vineyards Pinot Noir
- 1 shallot, minced
- 1 sprig fresh rosemary
- 2 1/2 teaspoons balsamic vinegar*
- 1/2 teaspoon black peppercorns, cracked
- 3 cups Dark Poultry or Game Stock (see **Basics**)
- 4 tablespoons unsalted butter, room temperature
  Salt and freshly ground black pepper

- 6 fresh bobwhite quails (6 to 8 ounces each), ready to cook
  Salt and freshly ground black pepper
  Fresh rosemary sprigs
- 8 tablespoons unsalted butter, divided

1. For sauce: Combine cognac, wine, shallot, rosemary, vinegar and black peppercorns in heavy medium saucepan over high heat. Bring to boil and reduce to 1/4 cup. Add stock and reduce to about 3/4 cup.

2. Strain liquid through fine-mesh sieve into clean saucepan, pressing on solids with back of spoon to extract as much liquid as possible.

3. Whisk in butter, 1 tablespoon at a time, and season with salt and pepper. Set aside and keep warm.

4. Position rack in lower third of oven and preheat to 350° F.

5. Rub birds inside and out with salt and pepper. Stuff each cavity with 1 fresh rosemary sprig and 1 teaspoon butter. Truss (as best you can).

6. Place birds on lightly greased rack in shallow roasting pan and set aside.

7. Melt remaining butter in heavy small saucepan over low heat. Mix in several fresh rosemary sprigs and let stand 5 minutes. Generously brush birds with mixture, using sprigs as brush.

8. Roast birds until thermometer inserted into thickest part of breast registers 140° F., basting once with remaining rosemary butter, 20 to 25 minutes. If tops are not lightly browned, briefly place under broiler to do so. To serve, arrange birds on warm plates and top with Balsamic Vinegar Sauce. Garnish with fresh rosemary sprigs.

* See **Special Ingredients**

Cook's Tips

Try the smaller sparrow quails for a real tasty treat. Count on 2 per person, as they weigh only about 4 ounces each.

For those of you who do not hunt, shop University Seafood and Poultry in the University District in Seattle for their supply of fresh and frozen quails.

Wine Selection
Elk Cove Vineyards
Estate Bottled Pinot Noir

Rabbit Merlot

Lou Facelli, talented owner/ winemaker of **Facelli Winery**, and his wife Sandy find much enjoyment creating recipes to accompany their fine wines. Wearing his familiar beret as his chef's toque, he shares a family favorite, Rabbit Merlot, that fits like a glove with its delightfully rich namesake. Slightly gamy and a delicious cross between chicken and veal, fresh rabbit is carefully coaxed, along with an enticing tomato and fresh herb sauce, into an intriguingly delightful symphony of flavors with the Facelli touch! The addition of Lou's fruity and full-bodied Merlot to the dish lends a delicious complexity that ties food and wine more closely together. Try this flavorful Italian-inspired marriage of food and wine – as Lou and Sandy say, "Salute!"

8 servings

2 fresh rabbits (3 to 3^1/$_2$ pounds each), cut into serving pieces
1 cup all-purpose flour (or more)
   Salt and freshly ground black pepper to taste
^{1}/$_4$ cup vegetable oil (or more)
2 medium onions, chopped
10 garlic cloves, chopped
^{1}/$_2$ pound button mushrooms, cleaned, thinly sliced
2 pounds very ripe tomatoes (about 6 medium), cored, seeded, chopped
1 can (8 ounces) tomato sauce
1 cup Facelli Winery Merlot
2 tablespoons chopped fresh Italian flat-leaf parsley
1 tablespoon chopped fresh basil
1 tablespoon chopped fresh oregano
1 teaspoon balsamic vinegar* (optional)
   Salt and fresh ground black pepper to taste

1. Rinse rabbit pieces well and pat dry with paper towels. Set aside.
2. Combine flour with salt and pepper in medium, shallow bowl until well blended. Set aside.
3. Heat oil in medium Dutch oven over medium-high heat.
4. Dredge rabbit pieces in seasoned flour and shake off excess. Add to Dutch oven and brown (in batches; do not crowd) on all sides. Drain on paper towels. Transfer to warm platter and tent with foil.
5. Reduce heat to medium and add onions with garlic. Cook until soft and translucent, stirring occasionally, and adding more oil, if necessary, about 5 minutes.
6. Stir in mushrooms, cover and cook until tender, about 5 minutes. Uncover and cook until almost dry, stirring occasionally, about 5 minutes.
7. Sir in remaining ingredients and bring to boil over high heat. Immediately reduce heat and simmer about 30 minutes.
8. Return rabbit to Dutch oven and coat well with sauce. Partially cover and cook on low until tender, 45 minutes to 1 hour. Serve immediately.

* See **Special Ingredients**

Cook's Tips

Lou and Sandy suggest serving this tasty dish with polenta – now that's Italian!

If very ripe tomatoes are not available, substitute 1 can (28 ounces) whole peeled tomatoes, cored, seeded, chopped with juices.

Wine Selection
**Facelli Winery
Merlot**

Venison Medallions *with Garlic Cream*

Multitalented Executive Chef Barbara Figueroa strives for top-quality Northwest cuisine at her current venue, **The Hunt Club** restaurant in Seattle's lovely Sorrento Hotel. With a strong French background in the fundamentals of cooking, chef Figueroa's style is light and contemporary. Fond of pairing Asian ingredients with the finest from the Northwest, she skillfully blends East with Northwest and French in her Venison Medallions with Garlic Cream – a culinary masterpiece! Her talents also extend to the wine cellar and she highly recommends **Waterbrook Winery's** Merlot to accompany her exotic entrée. This rich and mouth-filling wine offers aromas of cherries and spice with firm structure on the palate – a perfect partner for this game lover's delight.

6 servings

Whidbey's Port Demi-Glace

1	quart Veal or Venison Stock (see **Basics**)
$1^{1}/_{2}$	cups ruby port
2	medium onions, chopped
1	small carrot, peeled, chopped
1	medium celery stalk, chopped
$1^{1}/_{2}$	teaspoons chopped fresh thyme
1	teaspoon chopped fresh rosemary
1	teaspoon chopped fresh sage
2	juniper berries, crushed
1	garlic clove, crushed
6	tablespoons unsalted butter, cut into pieces, room temperature
2	tablespoons Whidbey's Port
$^{1}/_{2}$	teaspoon red wine vinegar
	Salt and freshly ground black pepper to taste

	Peanut oil or vegetable oil
$2^{1}/_{4}$	pounds boneless loin of venison, cut into 12 medallions
	Salt and freshly ground black pepper
6	shiitake mushroom caps* (about 2 inches diameter), cleaned
$^{1}/_{4}$	cup olive oil
	Garlic Cream (recipe follows)
	Fresh herb sprigs

1. For demi-glace: Combine first 10 ingredients in heavy large saucepan over medium-high heat. Bring to boil and reduce by $^{3}/_{4}$ or until sauce coats back of spoon. Strain through fine-mesh sieve into clean saucepan and whisk in remaining ingredients. Set aside and keep warm.

2. In heavy large skillet, cover bottom with oil and heat to almost smoking.

3. Season venison medallions with salt and pepper. Add to skillet and cook (in batches; do not crowd), turning once, until well seared outside and rare inside.

4. Meanwhile, coat mushroom caps with oil and season with salt and pepper. Grill or sauté over moderately-low heat until lightly cooked through. To serve, ladle demi-glace onto warm plates. Arrange 2 venison medallions with 1 piece of garlic cream on each plate. Garnish with grilled shiitake mushroom caps and fresh herb sprigs.

Garlic Cream

$^{1}/_{3}$	cup whole garlic cloves (about 1 medium head), peeled
	Water to cover
$^{2}/_{3}$	cup half-and-half
1	tablespoon highly concentrated Venison or Veal Stock (see **Basics**)
6	large eggs, room temperature, divided
	Salt and freshly ground black pepper
	Vegetable oil (for deep-frying)
$^{1}/_{2}$	cup all-purpose flour
$^{1}/_{2}$	cup fine dry bread crumbs

1. Position rack in center of oven and preheat to 350° F. Lightly grease 5- by 9-inch loaf pan and set aside.

2. Bring to boil garlic cloves with water in heavy small saucepan over medium-high heat. Drain. Repeat procedure twice more or until garlic is slightly softened.

Continued next page

3. Blend garlic, half-and-half, stock, and 4 eggs in blender until smooth. Season with salt and pepper.

4. Pour mixture into prepared pan, cover loosely with aluminum foil and bake until toothpick or skewer inserted near center comes out clean. Cover and refrigerate until thoroughly chilled, at least 4 hours or overnight.

5. Heat oil in deep-fryer to 375° F.

6. Beat remaining 2 eggs in small, shallow bowl and season with salt and pepper. Set aside.

7. Cut garlic cream into 6 rectangular pieces of equal size. Dip in flour, egg and bread crumbs (in that order). Fry until golden brown. Drain well on paper towels and keep warm until serving time.

* See **Special Ingredients**

Cook's Tip

We make chef Figueroa's garlic cream through step #4 the day ahead. The following evening, just before sautéing the venison medallions, the rest is a snap to put together.

Wine Selection
Waterbrook Winery
Merlot

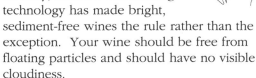

How to Taste Wine

Take a Look

Appearance and color are very important to your enjoyment of wine. Fortunately, modern winemaking technology has made bright, sediment-free wines the rule rather than the exception. Your wine should be free from floating particles and should have no visible cloudiness.

White wines often range in color from almost water-clear to golden yellow. Most Northwest whites are somewhere in-between and are described as "pale straw" in color.

Red wines can be anywhere from dark ruby to pale garnet in hue. Lighter colored wines often have lighter flavor and less tannin.

Take a Sniff

Swirl the wine in your glass and take a deep sniff. Aroma and bouquet are the terms used to describe the smell of the grape (aroma) and the smell of treatment (oak aging, etc.) of the wine (bouquet). Together the two sensations can tell you much about the quality of the wine and its origin. Professional wine tasters often make most of their judgements based on a wine's smell rather than on the taste of the wine.

Take a Sip

Take a small amount of wine in your mouth and swirl it around your tongue. You will notice different impressions in different parts of your mouth. Acidity is detected on the sides of your tongue, sweetness on the tip and bitterness or astringency (tannin) on the back of your tongue and palate.

The flavor of a good quality wine will often echo the aroma and bouquet. Additional factors, as described above, relate to the balance of the wine on your palate. The balance between acidity and sweetness is important to Northwest wines because they often feature higher than average acidity. A little residual sugar is often left in many wines to balance the acidity and thus provide a refreshing feeling on the palate.

Grilled Lamb Chops Polaise

Polaise Sauce, a classic Bearnaise-type sauce enlivened with fresh mint, is the ideal accompaniment to our grilled lamb chops. Big on flavor and richness, this stunning entrée calls for the finest drinking partner you can afford, or a slight twisting of the arm to bring up your most treasured bottle from the cellar. We highly recommend **Leonetti Cellar's** Cabernet Sauvignon, crafted by talented winemaker Gary Figgins. Characterized by intense, ripe varietal character, Figgins' Cabernets are exquisitely structured and balanced. The slightly gamy-smoky notes of the rosy grilled chops, along with the minty flavors in the sauce, connect beautifully to similar qualities in the wine. Irresistible now, and a wine-worthy companion for our chops, Leonetti Cabernets are also excellent candidates for aging.

4 servings

Marinade

1   cup olive oil
1/2   cup Leonetti Cellar Cabernet Sauvignon
1   tablespoon chopped fresh mint
3   garlic cloves, chopped

8   lamb loin chops (about 4 ounces each), trimmed of fat
    Salt and freshly ground black pepper
    Fresh mint sprigs
    Polaise Sauce (recipe follows)

1. For marinade: Whisk together all ingredients in small bowl until well blended and set aside.
2. Place lamb loin chops in nonreactive dish, large enough to hold chops with marinade. Pour marinade over, cover and refrigerate several hours. Turn occasionally.
3. Prepare grill with medium-hot coals. Adjust rack 3 to 4 inches from heat and lightly oil.
4. Remove chops from marinade and pat dry with paper towels. Season with salt and pepper. Reserve marinade for basting.
5. Place chops on grill and cook to desired doneness or 3 to 4 minutes per side for medium-rare meat, basting occasionally with reserved marinade. Serve immediately and garnish with fresh mint sprigs. Accompany with Polaise Sauce.

Polaise Sauce

2   tablespoons white wine vinegar
2   tablespoons vermouth
1   tablespoon chopped fresh mint, divided
1   large shallot, finely chopped
5   white peppercorns, slightly crushed
    Pinch fresh tarragon
2   large egg yolks, room temperature
8   tablespoons unsalted butter, clarified
1/2   teaspoon fresh lemon juice
    Dash cayenne pepper
    Salt and freshly ground white pepper

1. Combine vinegar, vermouth, 1 1/2 teaspoons mint, shallot, peppercorns and tarragon in heavy small saucepan over high heat. Bring to boil and reduce to 1 1/2 tablespoons. Cool completely.
2. Strain liquid through fine-mesh sieve into top of double boiler over gently simmering water, pressing on solids with back of spoon to extract as much liquid as possible. Discard solids.
3. Using whisk or hand-held electric mixer (with whisk attachment), whisk in egg yolks until thick and creamy, about 4 minutes.
4. Drizzle in butter, whisking continuously, until well blended.
5. Stir in remaining mint, lemon juice and cayenne pepper. Season with salt and white pepper. Serve immediately or store in well-insulated thermos up to 2 hours. (Makes about 3/4 cup.)

Cook's Tip

Try lamb sirloin steaks for a tasty, economical alternative to chops.

Wine Selection
**Leonetti Cellar
Cabernet Sauvignon**

Rack of Lamb *with Cabernet Mint Sauce*

Celebrate your next occasion with someone special, our mouth-watering Rack of Lamb with Cabernet Mint Sauce and a bottle of **Chateau Ste. Michelle's** Cold Creek Vineyard Cabernet Sauvignon. This remarkable complex wine is crafted from the best grapes from one of the Northwest's finest Cabernet vineyards. The rich nuances of classic Cabernet aroma are reflected throughout the dish, accentuating the lovely flavors of the fresh mint. The meaty texture and fat of the lamb tame any excess tannins in the wine, while a long and delicious finish allows this distinctive Cabernet a final word.

2 servings

Cabernet Mint Sauce

 1 cup Veal Stock (see **Basics**)
 $1/4$ cup Chateau Ste. Michelle Cabernet
      Sauvignon
 2 sprigs fresh mint
 1 small shallot, chopped
 1 tablespoon unsalted butter
   Salt and freshly ground black pepper

 1 rack of lamb ($1^1/2$ to 2 pounds), trimmed
      of fat, frenched, chine bones cracked
 1 tablespoon olive oil
   Salt and freshly ground black pepper
 $3/4$ cup fine dry bread crumbs
 1 tablespoon finely chopped fresh mint
 2 garlic cloves, minced
 $1/4$ teaspoon freshly ground black pepper
 2 tablespoons Dijon mustard (or more)
 1 tablespoon unsalted butter, melted
   Fresh mint sprigs

1. For sauce: Combine stock, wine, mint and shallot in heavy small saucepan over high heat. Bring to boil and reduce by half.

2. Strain through fine-mesh sieve into clean saucepan, pressing on solids with back of spoon to extract as much liquid as possible. Stir in butter and season with salt and pepper. Set aside and keep warm.

3. Position rack in center of oven and preheat to 350° F.

4. Wipe lamb dry with damp cloth and wrap exposed bones with aluminum foil. Brush with oil and season with salt and pepper.

5. Place lamb, meat side up, on lightly greased rack in shallow roasting pan. Roast 15 minutes per pound. Remove and cool.

6. Meanwhile, combine bread crumbs, mint, garlic and pepper in small bowl until well blended. Set aside.

7. Brush lamb with mustard and pat bread crumb mixture onto mustard, pressing firmly. Drizzle with butter.

8. Return rack to oven and roast until desired doneness or about 140° F. for rare meat.

9. Transfer to carving board and let stand about 5 minutes. To serve, carve chops and arrange on warm plates. Garnish with fresh mint sprigs and accompany with Cabernet Mint Sauce.

Cook's Tip

We use an instant-read thermometer by Cuisinart to quickly test our lamb in this recipe. Purchase it at any fine kitchen shop.

Wine Selection

**Chateau Ste. Michelle
Cold Creek Cabernet Sauvignon**

Spit-Roasted Leg of Lamb

Experience the taste of **The Hogue Cellars** wines at one of their special annual events – the Spring Barrel Tasting in April, the Anniversary Celebration in June or the Harvest Party in October. All are great fun! If you're lucky, you might even get to taste Shyla Hogue's delicious Spit-Roasted Leg of Lamb, marinated in the winery's award-winning Merlot. Crafted by renowned winemaker Rob Griffin, the rich and spicy varietal accompanys this tantalizing family favorite like no other wine. Delightful aromas of cherries and herbs lead to rich, complex flavors from barrel-aging – delicious with the grilled flavors of the lamb. So, crank up the spit and join the Hogue family for some fine dining, Prosser style!

6 to 8 servings

Marinade

   1 cup Hogue Cellars Merlot
   1 cup water
 ¹/₂ cup olive oil
 ¹/₂ cup finely chopped fresh parsley
   2 medium tomatoes, cored, seeded, diced
   1 medium green bell pepper, stemmed, seeded, deribbed, diced
   1 medium onion, sliced
   3 garlic cloves, minced
   1 teaspoon chopped fresh marjoram
 ¹/₄ teaspoon dry mustard
 ¹/₄ teaspoon Tabasco sauce

   1 leg of lamb (6 to 7 pounds), boned, butterflied, surface fat trimmed
      Salt and freshly ground black pepper
      Fresh parsley or marjoram sprigs

1. For marinade: Combine all ingredients in medium bowl until well blended and set aside.
2. Place lamb in nonreactive dish, large enough to hold lamb with marinade. Pour marinade over, cover and refrigerate 1 day. Turn occasionally.
3. Prepare bed of medium-hot coals at rear of grill (firebox).
4. Remove lamb from marinade and pat dry with paper towels. Season with salt and pepper. Roll, tie and set aside.
5. Strain vegetables from marinade and place in serving bowl. Cover and refrigerate until serving time. Reserve liquid for basting.
6. Arrange lamb on spit rod and secure. Test for balance and attach spit. Start motor and place drip pan under lamb to prevent fat from dripping onto fire. Grill until thermometer, inserted into center of meat, registers 175° F. to 180° F., 3 to 4 hours. (A good rule of thumb is 25 to 30 minutes per pound.) Baste occasionally with reserved marinade liquid.
7. Transfer lamb to carving board and let stand about 15 minutes. Carve and serve with chilled, marinated vegetables. Garnish with fresh parsley sprigs.

Cook's Tip

For those of you who do not have a spit, grill this summertime favorite butterflied. Use a covered grill and cook over indirect heat. Turn once and reduce cooking time to about 25 minutes per side.

Wine Selection

The Hogue Cellars
Merlot

Butterflied Leg of Lamb in Limberger

Mercer Ranch Vineyards near Prosser, Washington, began their Lamberger-Limberger Festival to celebrate the annual release of their Limberger wine, a red varietal grown almost exclusively in the Northwest. Grilled while you watch, lamburgers are served with the traditional accompaniments, along with ranch favorites like pickled garlic, jalapeno mint jelly (a specialty at the ranch), marinated onions and Yakima Valley cheeses. Linda Mercer, co-owner of the winery with husband/winemaker Don, prepares other wonderful lamb dishes too, and usually pairs them with Don's medium-bodied Limberger. Its distinctive berry-cherry overtones and depth of flavor make it the classic dinner companion to Linda's wonderful lamb creations, especially her Butterflied Leg of Lamb in Limberger. With this preparation, the intense grilled and gamy flavors of the lamb highlight the wine's wonderful fruit flavors – oh, so nicely – the only way to spend a lazy Northwest summer evening.

6 to 8 servings

Marinade

  1 cup Mercer Ranch Vineyards Limberger
$^1/_2$ cup olive oil
  6 garlic cloves, minced

  1 leg of lamb (6 to 7 pounds), boned, butterflied, surface fat trimmed
  1 large onion, sliced $^1/_4$-inch-thick, halved
     Salt and freshly ground black pepper
     Fresh rosemary or oregano sprigs

1. For marinade: Whisk together all ingredients in small bowl until well blended and set aside.
2. Place lamb in nonreactive dish, large enough to hold lamb with marinade. Pour marinade over and rub in well. Cover and refrigerate at least 2 hours or overnight. Turn occasionally.
3. Prepare grill with medium-hot coals. Place drip pan (a bit larger than butterflied lamb) in center and arrange coals around. Adjust rack 5 to 6 inches from heat and lightly oil.
4. Remove lamb from marinade and pat dry with paper towels. Reserve marinade for basting.
5. Place lamb on work surface, skin side down. Cut slits, $^2/_3$ way through, at 2-inch intervals. Place onion halves, round side up, into meat slits.
6. Thread long metal skewer through longest side of meat, 2 inches in from edge and parallel to opposite side, securing onions. Repeat with another skewer through opposite side; skewers should cross at tips. Season with salt and pepper.
7. Place lamb, onion side up, on grill and cook until thermometer inserted into thickest part registers 140° F., basting occasionally with reserved marinade, about 1 hour 15 minutes. (Due to uneven thickness of meat, you will have both rare and well-done meat. If necessary, close cover at any time to better regulate heat.)
8. Several minutes before lamb is done, tuck rosemary sprigs into slits with onion. Transfer lamb to carving board and let stand about 10 minutes. Remove skewers, carve and serve immediately. Garnish with fresh rosemary sprigs.

Wine Selection

Mercer Ranch Vineyards
Limberger

Middle Eastern Lamb Brochettes

Fresh lamb is always available in the Northwest and takes on a Middle Eastern aura, playing a starring role, in the following tantalizing and exotic recipe. Enhanced with the season's freshest produce and the intense flavors from grilling, this specialty is sure to become a favorite of any backyard barbecue chef! To accompany this hearty entrée, pour **Seven Hills Cellars** rich and highly touted Merlot. The fruity aromas and flavors of cherries and plums contrast the smoky character of the grilled meat, while a touch of wine to the marinade provides the unifying element to round out the dish. Sit back, enjoy and let your grill do the work!

6 servings

Marinade

   1/2 cup olive oil
   1/4 cup Seven Hills Cellars Merlot
   1/2 bunch chopped fresh mint
    3   garlic cloves, chopped

    2   pounds boneless lamb (preferably from
        the leg), trimmed of fat, cut into
        1 1/2-inch cubes
    2   medium tomatoes, cored, cut into large
        cubes
    1   large green bell pepper, stemmed,
        seeded, deribbed, cut into large cubes
    1   large red onion, cut in large cubes
        Salt and freshly ground black pepper

        Fresh mint sprigs
        Cucumber Sauce (recipe follows)

1. For marinade: Whisk together all ingredients until well blended in nonreactive bowl, large enough to hold lamb and vegetables with marinade.
2. Add lamb to marinade and toss to coat. Cover and refrigerate about 2 hours, adding tomatoes, green bell pepper and red onion last 30 minutes of marinating time.
3. Prepare grill with medium-hot coals. Adjust rack 3 to 4 inches from heat and lightly oil.
4. With slotted spoon, remove lamb with vegetables from marinade. Drain well. Reserve marinade for basting.
5. Thread lamb alternately with vegetables onto 6 long, metal skewers. Season with salt and pepper.
6. Place skewers on grill and cook to desired doneness or about 12 minutes for medium-rare meat, turning and basting occasionally with reserved marinade. Serve immediately and garnish with fresh mint sprigs. Accompany with Cucumber Sauce.

Cucumber Sauce

    1   cup plain yogurt
    1   tablespoon olive oil
    1   teaspoon white wine vinegar
    1   medium cucumber, peeled, halved
        lengthwise, seeded, finely diced
    2   garlic cloves, minced
        Salt and freshly ground black pepper to
        taste

Stir together all ingredients in medium bowl until well blended. Cover and refrigerate. (Makes about 2 cups.)

Cook's Tip

Be sure to cut all vegetables about the same size as the lamb cubes. The vegetables will cook a little faster than the lamb – if you prefer 'al dente' vegetables, skewer them separately and adjust your cooking time.

Wine Selection
**Seven Hills Cellars
Merlot**

Garlic Spinach Cannelloni

Garlic lovers, this one's for you! Celebrate your own garlic festival with our Garlic Spinach Cannelloni, an Italian-inspired dish from the Piedmont region of Italy. The cheesy and herbaceous filling, combined with the rich toppings of Béchamel and tomato sauce, might inspire a wine match of Cabernet or Merlot. Our choice, however, is **Panther Creek Cellars** Pinot Noir, a wine with intense flavors and a well-structured backbone of tannin and acidity. Winemaker Ken Wright crafts this hearty wine by utilizing extended skin contact and barrel-aging. His rich and spicy Pinots have found quite a following by those who disdain the "soda pop" style of Pinot Noir.

8 servings

Melted unsalted butter

Filling

    1   pound fresh ricotta cheese, well drained
          or 1 container (15 ounces)
 $^1/_2$ cup (2 ounces) freshly grated Parmesan
          cheese
    1   bunch fresh spinach, well rinsed, dried,
          stemmed, chopped
    1   head garlic (12 to 15 cloves), minced
    1   large egg, beaten to blend, room
          temperature
        Dash nutmeg
        Salt and freshly ground black pepper to
          taste

    1   pound fresh egg pasta sheets, cut into 5-
          to 6-inch-long rectangles (about 16)
    4   cups Béchamel Sauce (see **Basics**)
    3   cups Spicy Tomato Sauce (see **Basics**)
    2   cups (8 ounces) freshly grated Parmesan
          cheese
        Melted unsalted butter
        Fresh basil sprigs

1. Position rack in lowest third of oven and preheat to 350° F. Lightly butter two 9- by 13-inch glass baking dishes and set aside.
2. For filling: Blend together all ingredients in bowl of food processor, fitted with steel knife, until smooth. Set aside.
3. Cook pasta rectangles in large pot of boiling, salted water until just tender, but still firm to bite, stirring occasionally. Drain well and transfer to large bowl of ice water. Set aside.
4. To assemble cannelloni: With slotted spoon, transfer 1 pasta rectangle to work surface and pat dry with paper towels. Spread about 2 tablespoons filling over surface, leaving $^1/_8$-inch border. Roll up, jelly roll style, to form cannelloni and place, seam side down, in prepared baking dish. Continue with remaining pasta rectangles and filling. (Makes about 16 cannelloni.)
5. Spread 2 cups béchamel sauce, followed by $1^1/_2$ cups tomato sauce atop each baking dish. Sprinkle each with 1 cup freshly grated Parmesan cheese and drizzle each with melted butter.
6. Bake until tops are lightly browned and bubbly, about 35 minutes. Transfer dishes to wire rack and let stand 10 minutes. To serve, cut into squares, place on warm plates and garnish with fresh basil sprigs.

Cook's Tip

Make cannelloni ahead through step #4 and freeze. To complete preparation, simply thaw and proceed with step #5.

Wine Selection
**Panther Creek Cellars
Pinot Noir**

Pesto Hazelnut Lasagna

Tucked away in a small McMinnville storefront, **Nick's Italian Cafe** has become a legend, not only for fabulous Italian cuisine, but as the meeting place for the Pinot Noir movers and shakers of Yamhill County. Chef/owner Nick Peirano, is praised for his innovative ways with fresh, seasonal ingredients from local sources. In his Pesto Hazelnut Lasagna, he skillfully blends freshly made pesto, oyster mushrooms, Oregon hazelnuts, and other traditional ingredients into an enticingly delicious pasta entrée. A crisp green salad, lots of good Italian bread and a bottle of **Adelsheim Vineyard's** lovely Elizabeth's Reserve Pinot Noir are all that is needed to make this meal a memorable one! Nuances of berries and spice, along with a background of the elusive Pinot "barnyard" character, play off the myriad of flavors in the lasagna. With such subtlety afoot, the wine becomes more than an accompanying beverage – it is like an elegant, understated sauce.

6 to 8 servings

Melted unsalted butter

Filling

1 pound fresh ricotta cheese, well drained or 1 container (15 ounces)
1 cup Pesto (see **Basics**)
¹/₂ cup Béchamel Sauce (see **Basics**)
1 egg, beaten to blend
    Salt and freshly ground black pepper to taste

³/₄ pound fresh egg pasta sheets, cut into lasagna noodles or 12 ounces dried lasagna noodles
8 ounces oyster mushrooms, cleaned
3 cups Béchamel Sauce (see **Basics**)
¹/₂ cup (2 ounces) freshly grated Parmesan cheese
¹/₂ cup (2 ounces) freshly grated Romano cheese
³/₄ cup (3³/₄ ounces) hazelnuts, roasted, husked, coarsely chopped
1¹/₄ pound grilled chicken breasts, cut into bite-size pieces (optional)
    Fresh basil sprigs

1. Position rack in lowest third of oven and preheat to 350° F. Lightly butter 9- by 13-inch baking dish and set aside.
2. For filling: Blend together all ingredients in medium bowl to make spreadable paste and set aside.
3. Cook lasagna noodles in large pot of boiling, salted water until just tender, but still firm to bite, stirring occasionally. Drain well and transfer to large bowl of ice water.
4. To assemble: With slotted spoon, remove enough noodles from ice water to slightly overlap and cover bottom of baking dish. Pat dry with paper towels and cut to fit dish, if necessary. Arrange in dish. Continue layering with 1³/₄ cups filling, noodles (patting dry and cutting to fit, if necessary), oyster mushrooms, 1¹/₂ cups béchamel sauce, remaining 1³/₄ cups filling, remaining noodles (patting dry and cutting to fit, if necessary) and remaining 1¹/₂ cups béchamel sauce (in that order).
5. Combine cheeses and sprinkle over lasagna. Top with hazelnuts.
6. Bake until top is golden brown and bubbly, about 50 minutes. Transfer dish to wire rack and let stand 15 minutes. To serve, cut into squares, place on warm plates and garnish with fresh basil sprigs.

Cook's Tip

Nick suggests layering grilled chicken breasts throughout the dish for a different taste sensation. We tried it and loved it – the grilled flavors married beautifully with the Pinot.

Wine Selection

**Adelsheim Vineyard
Elizabeth's Reserve Pinot Noir**

Asparagus Morel Risotto

Springtime in the Northwest brings a bounty of fresh asparagus and earthy morels – ideal ingredients for risotto, an old Italian favorite. Dating back to the Renaissance, and a descendant of the Spanish Paella, this tasty dish is one of the most versatile in Italian cuisine. Its preparation with arborio rice by the Lombard technique – simmering broth is added in stages and more is added only when the other is absorbed – requires constant attention, but the creamy, delicious results are well worth the effort. Try your hand at our Asparagus Morel Risotto and partner it with **Quarry Lake's** delightful Sauvignon Blanc. The wine's subtle aroma of herbs and earth beautifully highlight the asparagus and morels, while a firm back-bone of acidity is the perfect foil for the creamy texture of the dish.

4 to 6 servings

$^1/_2$ pound fresh asparagus
$^1/_2$ pound fresh morels* or 2 ounces dried
$^1/_2$ cup Quarry Lake Sauvignon Blanc
$^1/_2$ teaspoon saffron threads*, crushed
 7 tablespoons unsalted butter, divided
 5 tablespoons olive oil, divided
 1 medium onion, chopped
 1 shallot, minced
 2 garlic cloves, minced
 2 cups arborio rice*, rinsed until water runs clear
$5^1/_2$ cups (about) simmering Shellfish Broth, divided (see **Basics**)
$^3/_4$ cup (3 ounces) freshly grated Parmesan cheese
  Salt and freshly ground black pepper
  Freshly grated Parmesan cheese

1. Trim ends of asparagus and peel stalks, if necessary. Cut diagonally into $^3/_4$-inch lengths. Blanch in heavy medium saucepan of boiling, salted water about 2 minutes. Refresh under cold, running water and drain well. Set aside.
2. Halve morels and rinse well inside and out. Pat dry with paper towels and set aside.
3. Combine wine with saffron in small bowl. Let stand until needed.
4. Melt 1 tablespoon butter with 1 tablespoon oil in heavy medium skillet over medium heat. Add asparagus with morels. Sauté until asparagus are crisp-tender, about 3 minutes. Transfer mixture to warm plate and tent with foil.
5. Melt 4 tablespoons butter with remaining oil in heavy large saucepan or medium Dutch oven over medium heat. Add onion, shallot and garlic. Sauté until soft and translucent, stirring occasionally, about 5 minutes.
6. Stir in rice and coat grains well with mixture. Cook until opaque, stirring frequently, about 4 minutes.
7. Add wine with saffron. Cook until liquid is absorbed, stirring constantly, 3 to 4 minutes.
8. Reduce heat and stir in $^1/_2$ cup broth. Cook until liquid is absorbed, stirring constantly. Repeat with remaining broth ($^1/_2$ cup at a time) until rice is tender, but still firm to bite. (This procedure takes about 25 minutes and requires your undivided attention and patience.)
9. Gently stir in remaining butter, Parmesan cheese, asparagus and morels. Season with salt and pepper. Cover and let stand 1 minute. To serve, divide among warm (shallow) bowls and pass freshly grated Parmesan cheese.

* See **Special Ingredients**

Wine Selection
Quarry Lake Vintners
Sauvignon Blanc

Cooking with Wine

A sip for the cook, a splash for the pan . . . and so it goes. Cooking with wine can be an easy and exciting way to add a creative flair to your meals AND to lend greater harmony to the marriage of food and wine. Add a new dimension of flavor and aroma to your favorite recipes or try your hand at experimenting with totally new creations. Remember when cooking with wine that bad wine for drinking is also bad wine for cooking. Use fresh, good quality wines only for your creative endeavors.

Grilled Specialties
Call for Great Marinades

Link those special summertime entrées and appetizers to your favorite wines by marinating them in a little of the wine, some olive oil and fresh herbs. A quick one hour marinade is plenty for fish and shellfish, a little longer for poultry. Meats may be marinated up to three hours since the tenderizing action of the wine's acids helps the toughest of cuts to become fork-tender. Try a butterflied leg of lamb marinated in Cabernet Sauvignon, a touch of olive oil and your favorite summer herb. Fresh oregano, parsley and basil form a wonderful herb base for fish and shellfish when added to your favorite Sauvignon Blanc or Semillon.

Pan Sauces Made Easy

Try deglazing your next sauté with about 2 tablespoons of wine (per serving) and make a tasty pan sauce. For example, after sautéing 4 filet mignons, transfer them to a warm plate and tent with foil. Add 1/2 cup wine (2 tablespoons x four servings) and reduce by half. Next add about 3 tablespoons of stock per serving and reduce by half. For a creamy sauce, add an equal amount of cream, along with the stock, and reduce. Remove the pan from the heat and whisk in 1 to 2 tablespoons butter or crème fraîche per serving – depending on how thick you want your sauce. Fresh herbs are always welcome at this stage also. This method of sauce-making directly links the wine to the dish.

Wine in Your Salad Dressing

Wine has an acid base just like vinegar and performs as a wonderful flavor enhancer in salad dressings. Simply substitute half the amount of vinegar called for in your recipe with a wine you think may complement your salad. Salads of character, especially those with meats and cheeses are especially good paired with a wine-based salad dressing.

Baste with Butter and Wine

That next holiday bird will be a real crowd pleaser if you baste during cooking with equal portions of butter and off-dry Northwest Riesling. Add a few fresh herbs to give even more character to this fruity alternative. Fruit-based stuffings can also serve as an additional bridge from wine to food.

Braising in Wine-Based Liquids

Another wonderful way to include wine in your cooking is to enhance a stew with the addition of your favorite Northwest wine. Whether a ragout of beef or lamb, or a fresh seafood or poultry stew, just select an appropriate wine (often the one you plan to serve with the meal) to add extra complexity and zest to the dish.

Dessert Time Toppers

Late harvest Rieslings and Gewürztraminers are excellent when drizzled over fresh fruit or frozen desserts. These unctuous and richly flavored wines are just the right topping for many simple dessert preparations.

Food and wine pairing is made delightfully simple with the suggestions listed above. Find your best combinations by experimenting with the wonderful fresh foods and delectable wines of the Northwest.

Desserts

Apricot Raspberry Tart

The month of July brings delicate apricots from the Yakima and Columbia valleys of Washington State – great for eating out of hand and especially tasty made into tarts. Our Apricot Raspberry Tart, created to complement **Kiona Vineyards'** luscious Late Harvest Riesling, makes a beautiful summertime dessert. The flavors of apricots and raspberries go well together and make a dramatic backdrop for this lovely wine. The reduced poaching liquid adds the finishing touch and serves as a bridge between tart and wine. We believe fruit-based desserts, a Northwest specialty, are the best match for late harvest Riesling wines – try this flavorful combination and we think you'll agree!

8 to 10 servings

Poaching Liquid

- 2 cups Kiona Vineyards Late Harvest Riesling
- $1/2$ cup sugar
- 1 clove
- 1 cinnamon stick

- 6 to 7 ripe apricots (about 2 inches diameter), halved, pitted

Glaze

- $1/2$ cup fresh raspberries
- 1 tablespoon Kiona Vineyards Late Harvest Riesling
- 1 tablespoon sugar

- 1 Pâte Brisée tart shell (10 inches), baked, cooled (see **Basics**)
- 1 tablespoon sugar
- $1/2$ cup fresh raspberries
  Whipped cream
  Fresh mint sprigs

1. For poaching liquid: Bring to boil all ingredients in heavy skillet, large enough to hold apricot halves, over high heat. Immediately reduce heat and simmer 5 minutes.
2. Submerge apricot halves in poaching liquid, round side down, and poach until almost soft, 2 to 3 minutes. (Time will vary with ripeness of apricots; test with skewer.)
3. With slotted spoon, remove apricots from skillet and drain well on paper towels. Transfer to plate, cover and refrigerate until firm, 2 to 3 hours.
4. Meanwhile, bring poaching liquid to boil over high heat and reduce to $1/3$ cup. Set aside.
5. For glaze: Blend raspberries, wine and sugar in blender or food processor, fitted with steel knife, until smooth. Strain through fine-mesh sieve into small bowl, pressing on seeds with back of spoon to extract as much liquid as possible.
6. Brush bottom of prepared tart shell with glaze, then sprinkle with sugar.
7. Arrange chilled apricot halves, cut side down, in tart shell and decoratively dot with raspberries.
8. Brush tops of apricots and raspberries with reduced poaching liquid.
9. Cover tart and refrigerate until well chilled. To serve, remove tart from pan and cut into wedges. Top with dollop of whipped cream and garnish with fresh mint sprig.

Cook's Tip

Apricots must be completely covered by poaching liquid to cook evenly – if necessary, add a bit more wine.

Wine Selection

Kiona Vineyards
Late Harvest White Riesling

Mixed Nut Tart

Ray's Boathouse, along the shores of Shilshole Bay, is known for its picturesque, marine view, fresh Northwest seafood and the creative talents of Executive Chef Wayne Ludvigsen. Inspired from the pages of old cookbooks, chef Ludvigsen shares with us his wonderfully rich recipe for Mixed Nut Tart. Generous with Oregon hazelnuts from the Willamette Valley, this tantalizing final course is sure to please any sweet tooth. Ray's wine manager Jeff Prather suggests **Stewart Vineyards** Late Harvest Riesling to accompany chef Ludvigsen's lovely creation. The tart's rich, honey-nutty melange of flavors is highlighted by the wine's aromas of honey and apricots, while crisp underlying acidity prevents a cloying aftertaste on the palate.

8 to 10 servings

Filling

    8   tablespoons unsalted butter
   ¹/₂ cup lightly packed light brown sugar
   ¹/₄ cup honey
  1¹/₂ tablespoons granulated sugar
   ¹/₄ cup heavy cream
  1¹/₂ cups (6 ounces) toasted walnuts,
          chopped
   ³/₄ cup (4 ounces) toasted hazelnuts, husked,
          left whole
   ³/₄ cup (3 ounces) toasted, sliced almonds
    2   tablespoons bourbon

    1   Pâte Brisée tart shell (10 inches), baked,
          cooled (see **Basics**)

Topping

    2   ounces semisweet chocolate*, chopped
  1¹/₂ teaspoons unsalted butter
   ¹/₄ cup heavy cream

1. Position rack in center of oven and preheat to 350° F.
2. For filling: Melt butter with brown sugar, honey and granulated sugar in heavy medium saucepan over low heat, stirring to dissolve sugars.
3. Slowly bring mixture to boil over high heat and stir in cream, nuts (reserve a few for garnish) and bourbon.
4. Pour mixture into prepared tart shell, spreading evenly with spatula. Bake 15 minutes.
5. Transfer pan to wire rack and cool completely.
6. For topping: Melt chocolate and butter with cream in top of double boiler over gently simmering water, stirring until smooth.
7. Drizzle mixture over tart and decoratively garnish with reserved nuts. Cover and refrigerate until well chilled. To serve, remove tart from pan and cut into wedges.

* see **Special Ingredients**

Wine Selection

**Stewart Vineyards
Late Harvest Riesling**

Raspberry Walnut Tart

Juergen and Julia Grieb of **Cascade Mountain Cellars** own and operate their winery in the former Northern Pacific Railroad depot in downtown Ellensburg, Washington. Juergen "conducts" the winemaking end of the operation, while Julia handles the business side. She also finds time to develop tantalizing recipes to accompany her husband's wines, often with the help of her gourmet group. One of her delightfully simple, yet stunning, desserts is Raspberry Walnut Tart – just perfect to accompany any holiday dinner. Raspberries are nestled atop an invitingly sweet crust, topped with a rich custard filling, then baked to perfection. As the accompanying wine, try Juergen's méthode champenoise sparkling wine for a special holiday toast!

8 to 10 servings

Crust

    1 cup all-purpose flour
    8 tablespoons unsalted butter, softened
  $1/3$ cup powdered sugar

Filling

    1 container (20 ounces) frozen raspberries
         in syrup, thawed, drained, juices
         reserved (for topping)
    1 cup (4 ounces) chopped walnuts
    2 large eggs, room temperature
 $1^1/3$ cups sugar, divided
  $1/4$ cup all-purpose flour
    1 teaspoon vanilla extract
  $1/2$ teaspoon salt
  $1/2$ teaspoon baking powder
    2 tablespoons cornstarch
  $1/2$ cup water
    1 tablespoon fresh lemon juice
        Whipped cream
        Fresh raspberries (if available)

1. Position rack in center of oven and preheat to 350° F. Generously grease $8^1/2$-inch-diameter springform pan.
2. For crust: Combine all ingredients in medium bowl until well blended. Press firmly into bottom and halfway up sides of prepared pan.
3. Bake until light golden brown, 12 to 15 minutes. Transfer pan to wire rack and cool.
4. For filling: Arrange raspberries evenly over crust and sprinkle with walnuts. Set aside.
5. Using electric mixer, blend eggs, 1 cup sugar, flour, vanilla, salt and baking powder in large bowl until smooth.
6. Pour mixture over raspberries, spreading evenly with spatula. Bake until golden brown, about 25 minutes.
7. Transfer pan to wire rack and cool completely. Run small, sharp knife around sides of pan to loosen and remove tart. Transfer to serving plate and set aside.
8. Stir together cornstarch with water in small bowl. Set aside.
9. Stir together reserved raspberry juice, remaining sugar and lemon juice in heavy small saucepan over medium heat until sugar dissolves.
10. Stir in cornstarch mixture and cook until thickened. Cool slightly, then drizzle over tart. To serve, cut tart into wedges and top with dollop of whipped cream. Garnish with fresh raspberries.

Wine Selection
Cascade Mountain Cellars Brut

Cherry Marzipan Tart

Chateau Gallant of the Columbia Valley asked talented chef Erin Richards of Mangetout Catering in Seattle to create the perfect dessert for their delightful Riesling. Crafted in a classic Riesling style with 5% residual sugar, the wine is the perfect partner to Erin's delicious creation – Cherry Marzipan Tart. Fresh pitted Bing cherries, or a mixture of Bings and Rainiers, are nestled in a prebaked tart shell, covered with a rich marzipan custard, then baked to a light golden brown – sinfully simple! Pour a chilled glass of Chateau Gallant's rich and aromatic White Riesling and enjoy a great marriage of food and wine. The wine's aromas of apples and pears contrast the sweet cherry and almond in the tart, creating a unique medley of flavors.

8 servings

Pâte Brisée

1½ cups all-purpose flour
 4 tablespoons butter, cut into pieces, chilled
 1 tablespoon sugar
 1 large egg, room temperature
 2 tablespoons (about) ice water

Filling

 2 pounds Bing cherries or mixture of Bings and Rainiers, pitted
 5 ounces Marzipan*, room temperature, broken into pieces
 2 large eggs, room temperature
 2 large egg yolks, room temperature
½ cup heavy cream
¼ cup sugar

1. Position rack in center of oven and preheat to 400° F.
2. For pâte brisée: Mix flour, butter and sugar in bowl of food processor, fitted with steel knife, until mixture resembles coarse meal. Blend in egg, then enough water, drop by drop, to form ball. (Do not overwork.) Flatten into disk, wrap in plastic wrap and refrigerate at least 30 minutes.
3. Roll out dough on lightly floured surface to ⅛-inch-thick round. Transfer to lightly greased 11-inch tart pan with removable bottom. Fit and trim dough, as necessary. Pierce bottom of pastry with tines of fork.
4. Line pan with parchment paper or aluminum foil. Fill with raw rice or dried beans.
5. Bake 10 minutes. Remove parchment paper with rice. (Do not let any spill onto dough.) Continue to bake until bottom barely begins to color, 5 to 7 minutes longer.
6. Transfer pan to wire rack and cool. Reduce heat to 350° F.
7. For filling: Arrange cherries in tart shell and set aside.
8. Blend marzipan, whole eggs, egg yolks, cream and sugar in bowl of food processor, fitted with steel knife, until smooth.
9. Pour mixture over cherries and bake until set and top is starting to brown, about 40 minutes.
10. Transfer pan to wire rack and cool completely. Cover and refrigerate until well chilled. To serve, remove tart from pan and cut into wedges.

* See **Special Ingredients**

Cook's Tip

Northwest cherries are usually harvested around mid-June and are available for only a short while. The harvest is usually 21 days, so the later you wait to buy, the sweeter your cherries will be.

Wine Selection

**Chateau Gallant
White Riesling**

Huckleberry Tart

At the foot of Mount Hood in the Columbia River Gorge lies the Hood River Valley. This remarkable area is well-known for orchards of apples and pears, as well as for wild huckleberries that are harvested from the nearby mountain meadows. Chef Patrick Edwards of Hood River's **Stonehedge Inn** proudly shares his recipe for a favorite summertime dessert, Huckleberry Tart. Freshly picked wild huckleberries are neatly arranged in a flaky tart shell, topped with a delightfully rich and sumptuous custard, then baked to heavenly perfection. Served chilled, this lovely creation of simplicity is the perfect dessert to accompany the delectable White Riesling crafted by Bill Swain of nearby **Three Rivers Winery**.

8 to 10 servings

Sugar Pastry

12	tablespoons margarine, room temperature
$3/4$	cup sugar
$1/2$	teaspoon salt
$1^{1}/_{2}$	cups all–purpose flour
1	small egg, room temperature

Filling

2	cups fresh huckleberries, well rinsed, drained, picked over, patted dry
2	large eggs, room temperature
1	large egg yolk, room temperature
1	cup sugar
1	teaspoon vanilla extract

1. For sugar pastry: Using electric mixer, cream margarine, sugar and salt in large bowl. Slowly mix in flour, then beat in egg until just incorporated.
2. Press mixture firmly into bottom and up sides of lightly greased 12-inch tart pan with removable bottom. Cover and refrigerate 30 minutes.
3. Meanwhile, position rack in center of oven and preheat to 400° F.
4. Bake pastry until light golden brown, 10 to 12 minutes. Transfer to wire rack and cool.
5. For filling: Arrange huckleberries in prepared tart shell and set aside.
6. Using electric mixer, blend whole eggs, egg yolk, sugar and vanilla in large bowl until slightly thick and creamy, about 4 minutes. (The consistency should be that of light batter.)
7. Pour mixture over huckleberries and bake until set and top is golden brown, 10 to 12 minutes.
8. Transfer pan to wire rack and cool completely. Cover and refrigerate until well chilled. To serve, remove tart from pan and cut into wedges.

Wine Selection

Three Rivers Winery Riesling

Late Harvest Tarte Tatin

A cookbook on the cuisine of the Pacific Northwest is not complete unless we share our rendition of the famous French tarte, Tarte Tatin. This upside-down apple pie was created by the two Tatin sisters of Sologne, France, at the beginning of the century and has graced the pages of many American cookbooks. Washington's Golden Delicious is our apple of choice for just about everything – snacking, baking, cooking – and for our rendition of this time-honored favorite. **Zillah Oakes Winery** of Zillah, Washington, makes a delicious late harvest Riesling that brings out the flavor of the apples and hints at the combination of spices in the tarte. The apples are marinated in the wine creating a delightful play of unifying flavors and aromas.

6 servings

$^1/_2$ recipe Pâte Brisée (see **Basics**)
5 Golden Delicious apples
$^1/_2$ cup Zillah Oakes Late Harvest
    White Riesling
$^2/_3$ cup light brown sugar
2 tablespoons water
$1^1/_2$ tablespoons all-purpose flour
2 teaspoons cinnamon
    Dash nutmeg
3 tablespoons unsalted butter, melted,
    divided
    Vanilla ice cream (optional)
    Fresh mint sprigs

1. Roll out dough on lightly floured surface to $^1/_8$-inch thickness. Cut into 10-inch round and place on lightly greased baking sheet. Cover and refrigerate until needed.
2. Peel, core and quarter apples. Place in medium bowl and toss to coat with wine. Set aside.
3. Stir together sugar with water in heavy small saucepan over low heat until sugar dissolves. Increase heat and boil, without stirring, until syrup turns deep, golden brown, about 225° F. on candy thermometer. Do not burn. Immediately pour mixture over bottom of 9-inch-diameter, flameproof skillet and swirl to coat. Set aside.

4. Combine flour, cinnamon and nutmeg in plastic bag until well blended. Set aside.
5. Drain apple quarters well and lightly pat dry with paper towels. Place in plastic bag with flour mixture and shake well to coat.
6. Arrange half apple quarters, round side down, in concentric circle atop caramel in skillet. Top with remaining apple quarters, round side up, filling in all open spaces. (If necessary, cut quarters to fit.)
7. Drizzle with 2 tablespoons butter and cover snugly with buttered aluminum foil. Make several slits with sharp knife in foil to allow steam to escape.
8. Set over medium-low heat and cook until apple quarters are slightly softened, shaking pan occasionally, about 20 minutes. Remove pan from heat and let stand briefly.
9. Meanwhile position rack in center of oven and preheat to 375° F.
10. Remove foil from skillet and place pastry round atop apples. Tuck in edges and make several slits with sharp knife in pastry to allow steam to escape. Brush top with remaining butter.
11. Bake until apples are soft and top of pastry is golden brown, 40 to 45 minutes. Transfer skillet to wire rack and cool 5 minutes. To serve, loosen pastry from skillet with small, rubber spatula and invert onto serving dish. Cut into wedges and top with vanilla ice cream, if desired. Garnish with fresh mint sprigs.

Cook's Tip

Cutting your apples into smaller wedges is certainly advisable, if you feel they will fit more snugly in the pan – you be the judge.

Wine Selection

**Zillah Oakes
Late Harvest Riesling**

Poached Pears *with Raspberry Couli and Chocolate Sauce*

From the highly touted French restaurant **Le Tastevin** in Seattle, comes this picture-perfect presentation of Poached Pears with Raspberry Couli and Chocolate Sauce. To accompany this magnificent dessert, we highly recommend a glass of **The Hogue Cellars** Late Harvest White Riesling from the Markin Vineyard. The delicate pear takes center stage, while the fruity nuances of the luscious wine blend and harmonize to delight the palate. Don't pass up the opportunity to serve this lovely dessert as the grand finale to your next elegant dinner party!

4 servings

Raspberry Couli

> 1   cup fresh raspberries or blueberries, well rinsed, drained, picked over
> 1/4   cup vodka

Chocolate Sauce

> 6   ounces semisweet chocolate*, chopped
> 1/4   cup heavy cream
> 1/4   cup strongly brewed coffee

> 4   pears, preferably Bartlett
> 3   cups water (or more)
> 1   cup dry white wine
> 1   cup sugar
> 1   cinnamon stick
>   Zest of 1 orange
>   Fresh mint sprigs

1. For raspberry couli: Purée berries with vodka in blender or bowl of food processor, fitted with steel knife. Strain through fine-mesh sieve into small bowl, cover and set aside.
2. For chocolate sauce: Melt chocolate in top of double boiler over gently simmering water. Stir in cream with coffee until well blended. Set aside and keep warm.
3. Peel pears and place in bowl of acidulated water to keep from turning brown. Set aside.
4. Bring water, wine, sugar, cinnamon stick and orange zest to boil in deep, heavy large saucepan over high heat. Reduce heat to simmer.
5. Submerge pears in liquid, adding more water to cover, if necessary, and poach until they have little resistance when pierced with skewer, about 12 minutes.
6. With slotted spoon, remove pears from liquid and cool completely with ice.
7. Halve pears and remove centers. Fan-slice halves. To serve, pool raspberry sauce on half of plate and warm chocolate sauce on other half. Arrange 2 fan-sliced halves atop sauces and garnish with fresh mint sprig.

* see **Special Ingredients**

Cook's Tip

When in season, Bartlett pears are a must for this dramatic fall dessert – their delicate flavor is unsurpassed and they hold their shape beautifully when poached.

Wine Selection

**The Hogue Cellars
Late Harvest White Riesling**

Chocolate-Merlot Dipped Strawberries

The Pasco Basin, land made fertile by irrigation from the nearby Columbia River, is home to **Preston Wine Cellars** in Washington State. The Preston family began their grape growing and winemaking endeavor early-on in the history of Washington viticulture. Their longtime passion for the making of fine wines extends into the kitchen, where family members create recipes to accompany their broad selection of varietals. Their delightful recipe for Chocolate-Merlot Dipped Strawberries will enlighten you to the wonderful combination of chocolate with red wine. Luscious Northwest strawberries – picked at just the right moment – are dipped in a rich chocolate-Merlot combination, chilled briefly, then served with Preston's full-bodied Merlot. The fruity qualities of the wine highlight the strawberries, while the rich palate and soft tannins complement the chocolate. For the perfect ending to a white-wine dinner, present this lovely dessert on a large silver tray lavished with fresh flowers.

Makes 24

 24 large strawberries, preferably with stems
   attached
  8 ounces semisweet chocolate*, chopped
 $^1/_4$ cup Preston Wine Cellars Merlot

1. Rinse strawberries well under cold, running water and pat dry with paper towels. Set aside.
2. Line baking sheet with waxed paper and set aside.
3. Melt chocolate with wine in top of double boiler over gently simmering water, stirring until smooth. Remove from heat.
4. Holding 1 strawberry by stem, carefully dip bottom half into chocolate mixture, shaking excess chocolate back into pan.
5. Place strawberry, stem up, on prepared baking sheet. Repeat with remaining berries and chocolate.
6. Refrigerate until chocolate is set, about 30 minutes. Serve immediately.

* see **Special Ingredients**

Wine Selection

Preston Wine Cellars Merlot

Muscat Sabayon *with Fresh Northwest Berries*

Starting in June and ending in late November, the Northwest's ideal growing conditions set the stage for a parade of the most delicious berries you'll find anywhere. Sweet, luscious strawberries are followed by tasty raspberries, blueberries, blackberries and, last but not least, cranberries. Summer calls for light and refreshing desserts, and berries fill the bill as delightful tag-alongs to any backyard barbecue or informal dinner party. After dinner, whip up our tasty Muscat Sabayon as a topping for goblets of your favorite fresh berries. The sabayon takes on the orange and spice flavors found in **Livingstone Cellars** Muscat Canelli, and the wine is a perfect warm-weather-sip to accompany the dessert.

6 servings

Sabayon

  6 large egg yolks, room temperature
  1 cup Livingstone Cellars Muscat Canelli
$1/4$ cup sugar

  3 cups fresh Northwest berries of your choice, well rinsed, drained, picked over, patted dry
$1/4$ cup ($1 1/4$ ounces) hazelnuts, roasted, husked, coarsely chopped
    Fresh mint sprigs

1. For sabayon: Using electric mixer (with whisk attachment), whisk egg yolks, wine and sugar in top of double boiler over gently simmering water until slowly dissolving ribbon forms, when whisk is lifted, about 10 minutes.
2. Transfer mixture to large, stainless steel bowl set over ice water.
3. Using electric mixer (with clean, dry whisk), whisk mixture until chilled, 8 to 10 minutes. Set aside.
4. Divide berries among 6 stemmed goblets. Top with sabayon and sprinkle with hazelnuts. Garnish with fresh mint sprigs. Serve immediately.

Cook's Tip

Before your guests arrive, divide the berries among goblets, cover and chill. Serving time will be a snap!

Wine Selection

**Livingstone Cellars
Muscat Canelli**

Piña Colada Logs

Cookies? Well, not exactly – if you like piña coladas, you'll love the exotic, tropical flavors of our Piña Colada Logs. Coconut combines with the richness of chocolate and a hint of dark rum to create a whimsical dessert that brings a little sunshine to Northwest wine lovers! The complex flavors and aromas of these tasty after-dinner treats flatter the spicy nuances of the muscat grape, with its perfumed bouquet and delicate flavors. Of the several styles that are produced in the Northwest, we love **Bookwalter Winery** Muscat Blanc for this dessert. A superb, off-dry sipping wine, the Muscat Blanc offers just enough sweetness – balanced by crisp acidity – to work well with these tropical delights.

Makes about 24

2 cups powdered sugar
1 package (14 ounces) sweetened flaked coconut
8 tablespoons unsalted butter, melted
1 teaspoon vanilla extract
2 ounces semisweet chocolate*, chopped
1 teaspoon dark rum

1. Line baking sheet with waxed paper and set aside.
2. Using electric mixer, combine sugar, coconut, butter and vanilla in large mixing bowl until well blended.
3. Form mixture into $^3/_4$- by 3-inch-long logs.
4. Place logs on prepared baking sheet, cover and refrigerate until firm, about 3 hours.
5. Melt chocolate with rum in top of double boiler over simmering water, stirring until smooth. Remove from heat.
6. Dip both ends of logs in chocolate mixture, shaking excess chocolate back into pan.
7. Place logs back on prepared baking sheet and refrigerate until chocolate is set, about 30 minutes. Serve immediately or cover and refrigerate until serving time.

* See **Special Ingredients**

Wine Selection
Bookwalter Winery
Muscat Blanc

Hazelnut Cookies

Margy Buchanan of **Tyee Wine Cellars** in Corvallis, Oregon, cooks farm style food using the exceptional products of her region. One of her favorite after-dinner treats is Hazelnut Cookies, made with homegrown hazelnuts from the Buchanan family farm. After a long day of crush at the winery, these delightful cookies hit the spot when accompanied by winemaker Barney Watson's Gewürztraminer. The wine offers the classic Gewürz aromas of lychees with a background of apricots and spice, while the slight tannin bite on the finish complements the nutty flavor of the cookies.

Makes about 3 dozen

2	cups all-purpose flour
$1/2$	teaspoon salt
8	tablespoons unsalted butter, cut into pieces, room temperature
1	teaspoon vanilla extract
1	cup lightly packed dark brown sugar
1	medium egg, beaten to blend, room temperature
$2^{1}/_{2}$	tablespoons hazelnut liqueur, such as Frangelico
$3/4$	cup ($3^{3}/_{4}$ ounces) toasted hazelnuts, husked, finely chopped

1. Sift together flour with salt into medium bowl. Set aside.
2. Using electric mixer, cream butter with vanilla in large bowl until light and fluffy, about 3 minutes.
3. Mix in sugar until well blended.
4. Beat in egg with liqueur until well blended.
5. Mix in dry ingredients until beginning to gather together. (When dough is touched lightly with an unfloured finger, it should come away clean.)
6. Mix in hazelnuts just until incorporated.
7. Remove dough from bowl and flatten into disk. Wrap in plastic wrap and refrigerate 1 hour.
8. Position rack in center of oven and preheat to 350° F. Lightly grease 2 cookie sheets and set aside.
9. Roll out dough on lightly floured surface to $1/8$-inch thickness. Cut out cookies using $2^{1}/_{2}$-inch-round cookie cutter. Place on prepared cookie sheets 1-inch apart. (Gather scraps, reroll and cut out additional cookies.)
10. Bake cookies until light golden brown, about 10 minutes.
11. Transfer cookie sheets to wire rack and cool 10 minutes. Remove cookies with wide spatula and store in airtight container at room temperature or freeze up to 1 month.

Cook's Tip

For an added taste sensation, melt butterscotch morsels in the top of a double boiler over gently simmering water. Dip half of the cookie into the butterscotch and chill on foil-lined cookie sheet until set.

Wine Selection

**Tyee Wine Cellars
Gewürztraminer**

Lemon Squares

Northwest wines are prized for their crisp acidity and, when serving late harvest styles, this attribute makes seemingly impossible wine matches work like a charm. The rich aromas and flavors of **Chateau Ste. Michelle's** Late Harvest White Riesling combine with the wine's firm acid backbone to highlight the citrus qualities of our delightfully simple Lemon Squares. The fresh lemon aroma is complemented by a cornucopia of fruity nuances in the wine, while hints of honey and botrytis on the palate create a complex symphony of flavors. Make this popular dessert ahead and chill until serving time.

Makes 15

Crust

2$^1/_2$ cups all-purpose flour
$^2/_3$ cup powdered sugar
1$^1/_4$ cups unsalted butter, cut into pieces,
        slightly chilled

Filling

4 large eggs, room temperature
2$^1/_2$ cups sugar
5 tablespoons fresh lemon juice (about 2
        small lemons)
1$^1/_2$ tablespoons grated lemon zest
1$^1/_4$ teaspoons baking powder
        Powdered sugar

1. Position rack in lowest third of oven and preheat to 350° F. Lightly grease and flour bottom and sides of 13$^1/_2$- by 8$^3/_4$- by 1$^3/_4$-inch glass baking dish. Shake out excess flour and set aside.

2. For crust: Mix flour with powdered sugar in bowl of food processor, fitted with steel knife, using on/off turns. Evenly distribute butter atop mixture and cut in, using on/off turns, until mixture resembles coarse meal.

3. Press mixture firmly into bottom of prepared dish and bake until light golden brown, about 25 minutes.

4. Transfer dish to wire rack and cool completely.

5. For filling: Using electric mixer, blend eggs in large bowl until smooth, about 1 minute. Beat in sugar, lemon juice, lemon peel and baking powder until well blended, about 2 minutes.

6. Pour mixture over crust, spreading evenly with spatula. Bake until filling is just set and top is golden brown, 20 to 25 minutes.

7. Transfer dish to wire rack and cool completely. Cover and refrigerate until well chilled, about 4 hours. To serve, sift powdered sugar over top and cut into squares.

Wine Selection

**Chateau Ste. Michelle
Late Harvest White Riesling**

Honey Muscat Pound Cake

Tom and Hema Campbell of **Horizon's Edge Winery** produce a slightly sweet Muscat Canelli that offers intense orange and spice aromas and flavors. Try matching this delicious wine with our Honey Muscat Pound Cake. The dessert and wine combination complement each other so well that, once tried, one can simply not imagine having one without the other. Taste and sip slowly to appreciate the complexity of flavors at play. Enjoy!

10 to 12 servings

Cake

    3 cups cake flour *
1½ teaspoons baking soda
    1 cup yellow raisins
 ½ cup (2 ounces) chopped walnuts
 ½ cup Horizon's Edge Muscat Canelli
    3 cups sugar
    1 cup unsalted butter, cut into pieces, room temperature
    6 eggs, room temperature
    1 container (8 ounces) sour cream
1½ teaspoons vanilla extract
 ½ teaspoon ground cloves
 ½ teaspoon cinnamon
 ½ teaspoon ground cardamom
 ¼ teaspoon ground ginger
 ⅛ teaspoon freshly grated nutmeg

Honey Muscat Canelli Glaze

    1 cup sifted powdered sugar
    2 tablespoons Horizon's Edge Muscat Canelli
    2 tablespoons honey

1. Position rack in center of oven and preheat to 350° F. Butter and flour 2½-quart fluted tube pan. Shake out excess flour and set aside.
2. For cake: Sift together flour with baking soda into medium bowl. Set aside.
3. Combine raisins and walnuts with wine in small bowl. Let stand until needed.
4. Using electric mixer, cream sugar with butter in large bowl until light and fluffy, about 3 minutes. Beat in eggs, 1 at a time, then beat in remaining ingredients, scraping down bowl, as necessary.
5. Gently mix in dry ingredients, just until incorporated. Fold in raisin mixture.
6. Spoon batter into prepared pan, tapping on counter to release air bubbles. Bake until skewer inserted into middle of cake comes out clean, 70 to 75 minutes, covering with aluminum foil last 10 minutes of cooking time.
7. Uncover and transfer pan to wire rack. Cool 1 hour.
8. Meanwhile prepare glaze: Using electric mixer, blend all ingredients in medium bowl until smooth.
9. Invert cake onto cake plate and drizzle with glaze. Cut into slices and serve.

* see **Special Ingredients**

Cook's Tip

Before creaming butter, rinse bowl with hot water and dry well – butter always creams better in a warm bowl.

Wine Selection

**Horizon's Edge Winery
Muscat Canelli**

Ginger Peach Cheesecake

Northwest peaches come to market around mid-July and keep arriving through mid-September. Early Red Havens often start the parade of delicious varieties with Hale, Elberta and others following later on. These succulent tree-ripened peaches always make the best cobblers, pies, ice cream and fruit sauces and provide a flavorful, colorful topping for our intriguing Ginger Peach Cheesecake. **The Hogue Cellars** Late Harvest White Riesling is a stunning partner for this delightful dessert, echoing the peach flavors and offering hints of spice to complement the ginger. The light alcohol of the wine cuts the richness of the filling and the flavors marry perfectly.

8 servings

Gingersnap Crust

6$^1/_2$ ounces (about 1$^1/_4$ cups) ground ginger snaps
1 tablespoon sugar
2 tablespoons unsalted butter, melted

Filling

1$^1/_2$ pounds fresh cream cheese, room temperature
4 large eggs, room temperature
1 cup sugar
2 slices ($^1/_4$-inch-thick each) fresh ginger, minced
1 teaspoon vanilla extract
1 teaspoon ground cardamom

Sour Cream Topping

1 cup sour cream
1 tablespoon sugar
$^1/_2$ teaspoon vanilla extract
$^1/_2$ teaspoon ground ginger

Caramel

1 cup sugar
$^1/_2$ cup water

2 fresh peaches, peeled, pitted, thinly sliced, chilled

Fresh mint sprigs

1. Position rack in center of oven and preheat to 375° F. Line bottom of 8$^1/_2$-inch-diameter springform pan with parchment paper and lightly grease sides. Set aside.
2. For crust: Finely grind gingersnaps in bowl of food processor, fitted with steel knife, scraping down sides of work bowl, as necessary. Blend in sugar with butter, using several on/off turns.
3. Press mixture firmly into bottom and 1$^3/_4$ inches up sides of prepared pan. Refrigerate while preparing filling.
4. For filling: Using electric mixer, soften cream cheese in large bowl. Blend in remaining ingredients until smooth.
5. Pour mixture into prepared pan and place in baking pan, just large enough to accommodate it. Pour in hot water to come halfway up sides of pan.
6. Bake until cheesecake is set and top is light golden brown, about 40 minutes.
7. Meanwhile prepare topping: Blend together all ingredients in small bowl and set aside.
8. Remove cheesecake from oven (maintain oven temperature) and generously spread with topping. Return to oven, turn off heat and let stand 5 minutes.
9. Transfer pan to wire rack and cool completely. Cover and refrigerate until well chilled before final assembly.
10. For caramel: Stir together sugar with water in heavy medium saucepan over low heat until sugar dissolves. Increase heat and boil until mixture is rich, caramel color, about 12 minutes. Cool briefly.
11. Run small, sharp knife around sides of pan to loosen cheesecake and remove from pan. Set on serving dish.
12. Decoratively arrange peach slices in concentric circle atop cheesecake. Drizzle with caramel and garnish with fresh mint sprigs. Cut into wedges and serve.

Wine Selection

The Hogue Cellars
Late Harvest White Riesling

Lemon Meringue Pie

Little Miss Muffet sat on a tuffet . . . but she never dreamed that someday a sincere, but unconventional, winemaker from Oregon would create a tantalizing nectar from the whey she so fondly loved. Paul van der Veldt of **Shallon Winery** in Astoria, Oregon, does just that. Fond childhood memories of his mother Esther's cooking are inspiration and fuel for thought as he artfully creates some of the most unique wines ever to come out of the Northwest. His Lemon Meringue Pie Wine echoes the flavors of everyone's favorite childhood pie. Our rendition of this classic dessert, along with sips of van der Veldt's intriguing wine, demonstrate how wonderful a marriage of food and wine can be! Lemon desserts with their tart acidity usually turn off those in search of a wine match, but for a pleasant surprise, try the complementary flavors in this pairing.

6 to 8 servings

Filling

1³/₄ cups sugar
¹/₂ cup cornstarch
¹/₄ teaspoon salt
4 large egg yolks, beaten to blend, room temperature
1³/₄ cups water
2 tablespoons unsalted butter, softened
¹/₂ cup fresh lemon juice
Finely grated zest of 1 lemon

1 Pâte Brisée pie shell (9 inches), baked, cooled (see **Basics**)

Meringue

3 large egg whites, room temperature
¹/₄ teaspoon cream of tartar
6 tablespoons sugar
¹/₂ teaspoon vanilla extract

1. For filling: Combine sugar, cornstarch and salt in small bowl until well blended. Set aside.
2. Whisk together egg yolks with water in heavy large saucepan over medium heat.
3. Gradually whisk in dry ingredients. Cook until thick and bubbly, stirring constantly with wooden spoon, about 5 minutes.
4. Remove saucepan from heat and stir in butter, lemon juice and lemon zest.
5. Pour mixture into prepared pie shell, spreading evenly with spatula. Set aside and cool completely.
6. For meringue: Using electric mixer, beat egg whites with cream of tartar in large bowl until soft peaks form. Gradually beat in sugar, 1 tablespoon at a time, until stiff and glossy. Beat in vanilla.
7. Pipe or spread meringue atop pie. Brown lightly under broiler. Chill briefly, then cover and refrigerate until well chilled. Cut into wedges and serve.

Wine Selection

Shallon Winery
Lemon Meringue Pie Wine

Not-Just-For-Holidays Pumpkin Pie

Thanksgiving and Christmas dinners just aren't complete unless the grand finale is pumpkin pie, but don't wait for the holidays when you can round out any culinary extravaganza with our voluptuously rich version of this time-honored classic. The perfect accompaniment is **Columbia Winery's** Cellarmaster Reserve Johannisberg Riesling. This delicious wine offers fruity and spicy aromas that marry beautifully with the pie's enticing flavors of cinnamon, nutmeg, ginger and honey. Treat yourself to a dollop of whipped cream or go even further and indulge in a scoop of vanilla ice cream.

6 servings

Filling

2 large eggs, room temperature
2 cups fresh (or canned) pumpkin purée
1¼ cups lightly packed light brown sugar
¾ cup evaporated milk
¼ cup honey
2 tablespoons fresh orange juice
2 tablespoons dark rum
1½ teaspoons cinnamon
1½ teaspoons ground ginger
½ teaspoon freshly grated nutmeg
¼ teaspoon salt

1 Pâte Brisée pie shell (9 inches) unbaked, chilled (see **Basics**)
Whipped cream

1. Position rack in center of oven and preheat to 425° F.
2. For filling: Using electric mixer, blend together all ingredients in large bowl until smooth, about 2 minutes.
3. Pour into prepared pie shell and bake 15 minutes.
4. Reduce temperature to 350° F. and bake until knife inserted into center of pie comes out clean, 40 to 50 minutes.
5. Transfer pan to wire rack and cool completely. Cover and refrigerate until well chilled. To serve, cut into wedges and top with dollop of whipped cream.

Cook's Tip

Always check toward the end of cooking time to see that your crust isn't burning – if necessary, cover rim of pie with aluminum foil or aluminum crust-covers.

Wine Selection

**Columbia Winery
Cellarmaster Reserve
Johannisberg Riesling**

Oregon Blue Cheese Log *with Dried Fruits and Walnuts*

Ports traditionally are paired with dried fruits, nuts and blue-veined cheeses. Why not enjoy all three accompaniments with Whidbeys Port, the Northwest's first port-style wine? In our Oregon Blue Cheese Log with Dried Fruits and Walnuts, the ingredients combine to make a piquant spread that complements the rich flavors of the Cabernet Sauvignon-based port.

Whidbeys Greenbank Farm produces the famed Loganberry Liqueur as well as the above-mentioned Whidbeys Port. While the loganberries for Whidbeys Liqueur are grown at the farm, the grapes for Whidbeys Port come from Chateau Ste. Michelle's Cold Creek Vineyard in the Columbia Valley.

Makes one 2-pound Cheese Log

1 pound fresh cream cheese, cut into pieces, room temperature
6 ounces Oregon Blue cheese, crumbled, room temperature
1 package (6 ounces) Sun-Maid Fruit Bits, divided
1 cup (4 ounces) chopped walnuts, divided
3 tablespoons honey, divided
1 tablespoon Cognac or other brandy
Assorted crackers

1. Using electric mixer, blend cheeses in large bowl until smooth.
2. Beat in half fruit bits, half walnuts, 1 tablespoon honey and Cognac until just incorporated, scraping down bowl and paddle, as necessary.
3. Cover with plastic wrap and refrigerate until slightly firm, 1 to 2 hours.
4. Shape mixture into log of desired length and wrap in plastic wrap. Refrigerate 30 minutes.
5. Meanwhile, combine remaining fruit bits with remaining walnuts on waxed paper.
6. Roll log in mixture, pressing mixture firmly onto log.
7. Wrap log in plastic wrap and refrigerate at least 3 hours to let flavors blend. Soften slightly at room temperature before serving. To serve, place log on serving plate and drizzle with remaining honey. Accompany with assorted crackers.

Cook's Tip

If fresh cream cheese is not available, substitute 2 packages (8 ounces each) Philadelphia brand cream cheese.

Wine Selection
Whidbeys Port

Burnt Rum Crème

Gerard and JoAnn Bentryn grow wine-grapes on Bainbridge Island in Washington's Puget Sound. The cool, maritime climate is a far cry from the blazing heat of Eastern Washington's summer days, but is just right for ripening the Germanic varietals planted at **Bainbridge Island Winery**. A little-known winegrape, grown only at this site, is Sieger-rebe, a cross between Gewürztraminer and Madeleine Angevine. The Bentryns' efforts with this varietal have consistently produced stunning late harvest wines, rich with the flavors of honey and spice and scented with the herbaceous notes of botrytis cinerea. The combination of aromas and flavors calls for a dessert that can serve as a subtle background – sweet, but not too sweet, and flavorful in a complementary, friendly way. Try our Burnt Rum Crème for a delightful accompaniment that truly glorifies the wine.

6 servings

   1   pint heavy cream
   4   large egg yolks, room temperature
$^1/_2$ cup sugar
   1   tablespoon dark rum
   2   teaspoons vanilla extract
       Sugar

Wine Selection

**Bainbridge Island Winery
Late Harvest Siegerrebe**

---

1. Position rack in lowest third of oven and preheat to 350° F.
2. Scald cream in heavy medium saucepan over medium-high heat. Set aside.
3. Using electric mixer (with whisk attachment), whisk egg yolks with sugar in medium bowl until light and fluffy, about 3 minutes. Slowly whisk in cream, then rum with vanilla.
4. Strain mixture through fine-mesh sieve into six 1-cup custard cups, removing any foam with spoon.
5. Place cups in baking pan, just large enough to accommodate them. Pour in hot water to come halfway up sides of cups.
6. Bake custard until set around edges and soft in center, about 45 minutes.
7. Transfer cups to wire rack and cool. Cover and refrigerate until well chilled, 3 to 4 hours.
8. Sprinkle tops with sugar and brown lightly under broiler until sugar caramelizes. (Do not leave unattended, as sugar burns quickly). Cover and refrigerate until well chilled before serving.

Cook's Tip

Other delightful flavorings that work well with this easy dessert are Amaretto di Saronno, Frangelico and Grand Marnier.

Chocolate Espresso-Amaretto Mousse

Seattle, Washington, is a haven for espresso lovers and home to many regionally famous coffee companies. Seattleites live for their daily caffé lattés or other fancy coffee concoctions served at dozens of espresso bars throughout the city. Taking this delightful addiction one step further, we share our Chocolate Espresso-Amaretto Mousse. The flavors of chocolate, coffee and Amaretto di Saronno liqueur blend deliciously into a classic, rich mousse to create a light-as-a-feather fantasy. For those who prefer red wine with chocolate, we recommend **Henry Estate** Cabernet Sauvignon with this rich dessert. The flavors of the mousse each find a compelling match in this rich, oak-aged wine. If sweet-with-sweet is more your style, match the mousse with Henry Estate's distinctive Late Harvest Gewürztraminer.

8 to 10 servings

 1 pound semisweet chocolate*, chopped
 4 tablespoons unsalted butter, cut into
     pieces
 1 tablespoon freshly brewed espresso
 1/3 cup Amaretto di Saronno liqueur
 3 large eggs, separated, room temperature
 1/2 cup sugar
 2 cups heavy cream, chilled
     Whipped cream
     Toasted sliced almonds

1. Melt chocolate with butter in top of double boiler over gently simmering water, stirring until smooth.
2. Stir in espresso with Amaretto. Transfer mixture to medium bowl, set aside and cool.
3. Using hand-held electric mixer (with whisk attachment), whisk egg yolks in heavy medium saucepan over low heat until light and fluffy, about 3 minutes. Gently fold into chocolate mixture and set aside.
4. With electric mixer, beat egg whites in medium bowl, gradually adding sugar, until stiff, about 3 minutes. Gently fold into chocolate mixture and set aside.
5. Using electric mixer (with clean, dry beaters), beat cream in large bowl to soft peaks, about 3 minutes. Gently fold into chocolate mixture.
6. Spoon mousse into goblets and cover with plastic wrap. Refrigerate until set and well chilled. To serve, top with whipped cream and toasted almonds.

* see **Special Ingredients**

Wine Selection

**Henry Estate
Cabernet Sauvignon**

Chocolate Sin - *with Eau de Vie de Poire Crème Anglaise*

Stephen McCarthy, proprietor of **Clear Creek Distillery** in Portland, Oregon, creates Eau de Vie-style brandies using high quality Northwest fruit. His Eau de Vie de Poire (pear brandy), Calvados-style Apple Brandy, Framboise (raspberry brandy) and Grappa are the only authentic high-proof essences made in the Northwest and are highly sought after by connoisseurs across the country. We find the intensity of the Pear Brandy to be an exciting foil to our rich Chocolate Sin with Eau de Vie de Poire Crème Anglaise. As you partake of this sinful pleasure of excess, picture yourself in Paris at an earlier time, reveling in the joys of self-indulgence!

8 servings

Crème Anglaise

  5 large egg yolks, room temperature
 $^1/_4$ cup sugar
 $1^1/_2$ cups milk, scalded
  1 tablespoon Eau de Vie de Poire brandy
  1 teaspoon vanilla extract

Cake

  1 pound bittersweet or semisweet chocolate*, chopped
 10 tablespoons unsalted butter, cut into pieces, room temperature
  4 large eggs, separated, room temperature
  1 tablespoon sugar
  1 tablespoon sifted cake flour *

 Fresh raspberries
 Fresh mint sprigs

1. For crème anglaise: Using electric mixer, beat egg yolks in large bowl, gradually adding sugar, until mixture is pale, lemon-colored and forms ribbon, when beater is lifted, about 3 minutes.
2. Stir in milk and transfer mixture to heavy large saucepan atop stove over low heat. Cook until mixture coats back of spoon, stirring occasionally (with wooden spoon), about 5 minutes.
3. Remove mixture from heat and stir in brandy with vanilla. Strain through fine-mesh sieve into bowl set over ice and stir to cool. Cover surface completely with plastic wrap and refrigerate until needed. (Makes $2^1/_2$ cups.)
4. Position rack in center of oven and preheat to 350° F. Line bottom of 8-inch-diameter springform pan with parchment paper. Butter and flour bottom and sides, shaking out excess flour. Set aside.
5. For cake: Melt chocolate in top of double boiler over gently simmering water. Stir in butter, 1 piece at a time, until smooth. Remove from heat, set aside and cool.
6. Using electric mixer, beat egg yolks with sugar in large bowl until light and fluffy, about 3 minutes.
7. Stir in chocolate mixture, then gently fold in sifted cake flour. Set aside.
8. Using electric mixer (with clean, dry beaters), beat egg whites in medium bowl until stiff but not dry. Gently fold into chocolate mixture.
9. Spoon batter into prepared pan, spreading evenly with spatula. Bake until cake is moist in center, about 25 minutes.
10. Transfer pan to wire rack and cool completely in pan.
11. Run small, sharp knife around sides of pan to loosen and invert cake onto plate. Peel off parchment paper and cut into wedges. To serve, pool sauce on plates and arrange wedge of cake atop sauce. Decoratively garnish with fresh raspberries and fresh mint sprig.

* see **Special Ingredients**

Sommelier's Tip

If Eau de Vie de Poire is not available, we recommend Framboise (raspberry brandy), Grand Marnier (orange liqueur) or Kirsch (cherry brandy) – they all work beautifully with chocolate.

Wine Selection

**Clear Creek Distillery
Eau de Vie de Poire**

Chocolate Cassis Torte

Jeff and Bill Gordon of **Gordon Brothers Cellars** have won many awards for their rich and flavorful Merlot. While this outstanding wine is often matched with rich meats and hearty sauces, an intriguing alternative is to save the best for last and serve it with our Chocolate Cassis Torte! The fruity, berry-like qualities of their Washington Merlot complement the hints of cassis in this delicate dessert, while the soft tannins of the wine play off the walnuts and chocolate. Late harvest Rieslings are the dessert darlings of many Northwest wine aficionados, but the Gordon Brothers Merlot brings red-wine-only lovers back to the table for a second piece!

12 to 14 servings

Cake

    6   ounces semisweet chocolate*, chopped
    1   cup boiling water
    2   tablespoons crème de cassis liqueur
            (black currant)
    1   tablespoon strongly brewed coffee
    1   teaspoon vanilla extract
 2¼   cups cake flour *
 1½   teaspoons baking powder
  ½   teaspoon baking soda
  ½   teaspoon cinnamon
  ¼   teaspoon salt
   16   tablespoons unsalted butter, cut into
            pieces, room temperature
 1½   cups sugar
    3   large eggs, room temperature

Buttercream

8½   ounces sugar, divided
  ½   cup water
  ½   cup egg whites (about 4), room
            temperature
    2   cups (1 pound) unsalted butter, cut into
            pieces, room temperature
    6   ounces semisweet chocolate*, melted
    2   tablespoons crème de cassis liqueur
            (black currant)
    1   teaspoon vanilla extract

        Natural Currant Jam or Jelly, warmed
    2   cups (8 ounces) chopped walnuts

1. Position rack in center of oven and preheat to 350° F. Line bottom of 17¾- by 11¾- by ¾-inch jelly roll pan with parchment paper. Butter and flour bottom and sides, shaking out excess flour. Set aside.
2. For cake: Cover chocolate with boiling water in large mixing bowl, stirring until smooth. Stir in liqueur, coffee and vanilla. Set aside and cool.
3. Sift together cake flour, baking powder, baking soda, cinnamon and salt into medium bowl. Set aside.
4. Using electric mixer, cream butter with sugar in large bowl until light and fluffy, about 3 minutes.
5. Beat in eggs, 1 tablespoon at a time, scraping down bowl, as necessary.
6. Adjust machine to lowest setting and alternatively mix in chocolate mixture with dry ingredients until smooth.
7. Spoon batter into prepared pan, spreading evenly with spatula. Bake until center of cake springs back when lightly touched and pulls away from sides of pan, about 25 minutes.
8. Transfer pan to wire rack and cool completely.
9. For buttercream: Stir together 6 ounces sugar with water in heavy medium saucepan over medium-low heat until sugar dissolves. Increase heat and boil, without stirring, until candy thermometer, set in syrup, registers exactly 250° F., 4 to 5 minutes.
10. Meanwhile, using electric mixer, beat egg whites in large bowl until soft peaks form, adding remaining 2½ ounces sugar toward end.
11. When sugar syrup reaches exactly 250° F., gradually beat it into eggs whites until mixture cools to room temperature, about 20 minutes. (Never stop beating or mixture will curdle.)

12. Beat in butter, 1 piece at a time, then remaining ingredients.
13. To assemble, remove cake from pan and cut, crosswise, into 3 equal layers. Place 1 layer on cake plate and generously brush with warm jam. Spread buttercream over jam and top with second cake layer. Repeat as above.
14. Ice cake with remaining buttercream, reserving ³/₄ cup for decorating top. Press nuts firmly onto sides of cake.

15. Fill pastry bag, fitted with small star tip (no. 1), with remaining buttercream and pipe border around top edge of cake. Refrigerate 30 minutes to set. Cut into slices and serve.

* See **Special Ingredients**

Cook's Tip

Fresh strawberries dipped in white chocolate make a lovely garnish for this show-stopper!

Wine Selection
Gordon Brothers Merlot

Northwest Winemaking

As in other winegrowing regions, most Northwest wines are made from the grape species vitis vinifera – wine grapes. The grapes arrive at the winery in late September or early October from the vineyard.

The Crush

Grape clusters are dumped into the mechanical crusher/stemmer where rollers break the grape skins releasing juice and pulp for fermentation. Stems are removed by fast-rotating impellers that throw the berries off the stems then deposit the stems into a collector where they are later hauled to the vineyard for use as compost.

Pressing

White grapes (and red grapes destined to be white wine, blanc de noir) are pressed after minimal skin contact. The Willmes bladder press gently extracts the juice by inflating a neoprene balloon inside the mass of skins and pulp and pressing against a stainless steel wire cage. The juice trickles into a trough from where it is pumped into tanks.

Fermentation

Fermentation is carried out in stainless steel tanks, large wooden tanks or oak barrels. Whites and rosés are chilled in special refrigerated tanks for a cool fermentation. Red wines are fermented at higher temperatures on their skins to extract color and tannin. After fermentation in nearly complete, the skins are lightly pressed before discarding. Both white and red wines are often filtered before bottling.

Bottling

Modern, self-contained bottling lines are used at many wineries. Empty bottles are first sterilized and then are "sparged" with an inert gas like nitrogen or carbon dioxide. The bottle is then filled with wine and the cork is inserted. A decorative capsule is then stretched into place by a device called a "foil spinner." Finally the labels are applied to the bottles and they are placed into cases for shipment.

Hazelnut Cognac Custard Ice Cream

The marriage of ice cream and wine has never been touted as one made in heaven – we tend to disagree. The intense character of **Covey Run Winery** Late Harvest White Riesling offers just the flavors to complement the rich complexity of our Hazelnut Cognac Custard Ice Cream. Eat the ice cream slowly and savor each bite. Let your tongue warm up between tastes so that a sip of the wine releases the entire aromatic spectrum of the collaboration. The crisp acid of the wine cuts through the richness of the dessert, while the spicy aromas and flavors play nicely with the nutty, brandy undertones.

Makes about 1¹/₂ quarts

- 2 pints heavy cream
- ¹/₂ cup (2¹/₂ ounces) hazelnuts, roasted, husked, finely ground
- ²/₃ cup sugar
- 6 large egg yolks, room temperature
- 2 large eggs, room temperature
- 2¹/₂ tablespoons Kahlúa liqueur
- 2¹/₂ tablespoons crème de cacao liqueur
- 4 tablespoons Cognac or other brandy
- 1 teaspoon vanilla extract

1. Scald cream in heavy medium saucepan over medium-high heat.
2. Remove saucepan from heat and stir in hazelnuts. Cover and let steep 30 minutes.
3. Strain cream through fine-mesh sieve into clean saucepan, pressing on hazelnuts with back of spoon to extract maximum flavor. Discard hazelnuts and briefly reheat cream. Set aside and keep warm.
4. Using electric mixer (with whisk attachment), whisk sugar, egg yolks and whole eggs in large bowl until light and fluffy, about 3 minutes. Slowly whisk in cream.
5. Strain mixture through fine-mesh sieve into heavy medium saucepan over low heat.
6. Using wooden spoon, stir until mixture just coats back of spoon, 5 to 7 minutes.
7. Stir in remaining ingredients.
8. Transfer mixture to ice cream maker and freeze, according to manufacturer's instructions. Transfer to container, cover and freeze overnight before serving.

Wine Selection

**Covey Run Winery
Late Harvest White Riesling**

Plum Wine Granité

Northwest plums are at their "sweet peak" around July and August and combine beautifully with **Mount Baker Vineyards** Royal Crimson Plum Wine to produce our Plum Wine Granité. A light, fat-free mixture of shaved ice with a distinctive flavor, this refreshing ending to an evening leaves one in total ecstacy. To sip with the granité, we highly recommend Mount Baker Vineyards Gewürztraminer, redolent of freshly grated nutmeg, cinnamon and cloves. Eat slowly to savor this most impressive final course and, for a dramatic presentation, serve in your finest stemmed goblets – enjoy!

Makes about 1 quart

> 2 pounds very ripe plums
> 1/2 cup Mount Baker Vineyards Royal Crimson Plum Wine
> 1 tablespoon minced crystallized ginger *
> 1 tablespoon fresh lemon juice
> 1 egg white, room temperature
> Mount Baker Vineyards Gewürztraminer
> Fresh mint sprigs

Wine Selection

Mount Baker Vineyards Gewürztraminer

1. Blanch plums in large pot of boiling water over high heat about 30 seconds. With slotted spoon, remove and cool slightly. Peel and pit, discarding peels and pits.
2. Purée pulp in bowl of food processor, fitted with steel knife.
3. Strain through fine-mesh sieve into metal bowl, pressing on solids with back of spoon to extract as much liquid as possible.
4. Stir in plum wine, ginger and lemon juice. Cover and partially freeze about 2 hours.
5. Using electric mixer, beat egg white to soft peaks and set aside.
6. Using electric mixer (with clean, dry beaters), beat partially frozen plum mixture until frothy, 2 to 3 minutes. Gently fold in beaten egg white.
7. Pour mixture into metal bowl, cover and freeze overnight. To serve, scoop into chilled goblets and drizzle with Mount Baker Vineyards Gewürztraminer. Garnish with fresh mint sprig.

* see **Special Ingredients**

Sommelier's Tip

The limited production of Mount Baker Vineyards delicious plum wine makes it hard to find – even in Washington State. The wine is patterned after the many well-made Japanese plum wines which are in wide distribution throughout the U.S. Failing to find the Mount Baker version, substitute Japanese plum wine, available at most Oriental markets.

Basics

Some of our basic recipes are used more than once in the book, so we have grouped them together for your convenience in this special section.

1. Béchamel Sauce
2. Crème Fraîche
3. Dark Chicken Stock
4. Fish Stock
5. Oven-Dried Tomatoes
6. Pâte Brisée
7. Pesto
8. Shellfish Broth
9. Spicy Tomato Sauce
10. Veal Stock

Béchamel Sauce

(Basic White Sauce)

Makes 3³/₄ cups

5 cups milk
10 tablespoons unsalted butter
10 tablespoons Wondra flour
Salt and freshly ground white pepper

1. Bring milk almost to boiling point in heavy large saucepan over high heat. Set aside and keep warm.
2. Melt butter in heavy large skillet over medium-high heat. When it foams, immediately stir in flour and let bubble 1 to 2 minutes. Do not burn. Adjust heat, as necessary.
3. Stir in warm milk until smooth and cook several minutes. Season with salt and white pepper. Use as directed. (If not using immediately, rub surface of sauce with unsalted butter to prevent skin from forming.)

Cook's Tip

We prefer the light, silky results Wondra flour gives, but all-purpose flour may be substituted, if desired.

Crème Fraîche

Makes about 1 cup

1 cup heavy cream
2 tablespoons cultured buttermilk, room temperature

1. Heat cream in heavy small saucepan over low heat to lukewarm.
2. Stir in buttermilk.
3. Transfer mixture to glass jar and cover loosely with plastic wrap. Let stand at room temperature until fairly thick or overnight.
4. Cover tightly and refrigerate at least 4 hours before using. (Crème fraîche will keep several days in refrigerator; tangy flavor continues to develop.)

Dark Chicken Stock

Makes 3 quarts

6 to 7 pounds chicken bones, preferably backs, wings, necks with some meat
2 celery stalks, coarsely chopped
1 medium onion, coarsely chopped with skin
1 medium leek, cleaned, coarsely chopped
1 medium carrot, peeled, coarsely chopped
2 cups dry white wine, divided
8 quarts cold water
Bouquet garni (4 sprigs fresh Italian flat-leaf parsley, 4 sprigs fresh thyme, 1 sprig fresh rosemary, 1 bay leaf – all tied in cheesecloth)
6 white peppercorns, slightly crushed
2 garlic cloves, bruised
2 whole cloves

1. Position rack in lowest third of oven and preheat to 350° F.
2. Rinse bones well and pat dry with paper towels.
3. Arrange in large, shallow roasting pan and roast until starting to brown, about 45 minutes.
4. Top with celery, onion, leek and carrot. Roast 30 minutes longer.

5. With slotted spoon, transfer bones with vegetables to colander and drain well. Place in large stockpot.
6. Degrease roasting pan and set over high heat atop stove. Deglaze with 1/2 cup wine, scraping up all browned bits.
7. Add mixture to stockpot with remaining wine and water. Bring to boil over high heat and skim foam from surface.
8. Immediately reduce heat and add remaining ingredients. Gently simmer about 3 hours, skimming foam and fat occasionally. (Do not stir or stock will become cloudy.)
9. Strain stock through fine-mesh sieve into clean pot and reduce to 3 quarts. Degrease. (Stock may be refrigerated several days. Always boil before using. May be conveniently frozen in 1-cup portions or further reduced.)

Cook's Tip

Light chicken stock may be prepared from the above recipe. Simply omit the onion skin and combine all ingredients in a stockpot. Simmer about 2 hours then proceed with step #9.

Fish Stock

Makes about 2 quarts

2 pounds firm-fleshed fish heads and bones
1 medium onion, coarsely chopped
1 carrot, peeled, coarsely chopped
1 celery stalk, coarsely chopped
  Bouquet garni (3 sprigs fresh Italian flat-
    leaf parsley, 2 sprigs fresh thyme,
    1 bay leaf – all tied in cheesecloth)
2 quarts cold water
1 cup dry white wine
  Salt

1. Combine fish trimmings, onion, carrot, celery and bouquet garni in stockpot.
2. Cover with water and wine. Season with salt and bring to boil over medium-high heat. Skim foam from surface.
3. Immediately reduce heat and gently simmer 30 minutes.

4. Strain stock through fine-mesh sieve into clean pot. (Stock may be refrigerated a day or two. Always boil before using. May be conveniently frozen in 1-cup portions or further reduced.)

Cook's Tip

Halibut and ling cod trimmings are our choice for making fish stock – they produce a mild, neutral stock and usually yours for the asking at local grocery stores and markets (freebies).

Oven-Dried Tomatoes

Makes about 12 ounces

6 pounds Italian plum tomatoes
1 tablespoon salt
3 sprigs fresh rosemary
6 garlic cloves, peeled, crushed
3 cups extra-virgin olive oil (or to cover)

1. Preheat oven between 150° F. and 200° F. Lightly grease 2 baking sheets and set aside.
2. Wash tomatoes and pat dry with paper towels. Slice lengthwise and remove core with seeds.
3. Lay tomatoes, cut side up, on prepared baking sheets and lightly sprinkle with salt.
4. Place in oven until dehydrated, about 8 hours. (Check frequently the last few hours, as some tomatoes complete the drying process faster than others. They are completely dry when no moisture or juice is visible, appearing almost hardened.)
5. Pack loosely in glass jar (with rosemary and garlic), just large enough to accommodate them with oil.
6. Cover completely with oil and secure top. Store in cool, dark place at least 1 month to let flavors blend.

Pâte Brisée

(Tart Shell and Pie Crust Dough)

Makes 1 single crust (8 to 11 inches)

1¼   cups all-purpose flour
½   teaspoon salt
½   teaspoon sugar
8   tablespoons unsalted butter, cut into
      pieces, chilled
3 to 4 tablespoons ice water

1. Mix flour, salt and sugar in bowl of food
   processor, fitted with steel knife, using 2 to
   3 on/off turns.
2. Evenly distribute butter atop mixture and
   cut in, using on/off turns, until mixture
   resembles coarse meal.
3. With machine running, blend in ice water,
   drop by drop, through feed tube, just until
   dough holds together. (Do not overwork.)
4. Turn dough out onto plastic wrap and
   gather into ball. Flatten into disk and wrap
   in plastic wrap. Refrigerate at least 30
   minutes before using. (Can be prepared 1
   day ahead.)
5. Roll out dough on lightly floured surface to
   ⅛-inch thickness. Transfer to lightly
   greased tart pan (of desired size) or pie
   plate. Fit and trim. Pierce bottom of pastry
   with tines of fork ½-inch apart. Cover and
   refrigerate 30 minutes.
6. Meanwhile position rack in center of oven
   and preheat to 400° F.
7. Line pastry with parchment paper or
   aluminum foil. Fill with dried beans or
   aluminum weights.
8. Bake 15 minutes (7 to 10 minutes for
   partially baked).
9. Remove beans with foil. Continue to bake
   until golden brown, 10 to 15 minutes longer
   (7 to 10 minutes longer for partially baked).
10. Transfer to wire rack and cool before filling.

Pesto

Makes about 1½ cups

2   cups loose-packed fresh basil leaves (no
      thick stems), well rinsed, patted dry
½   cup fruity olive oil, such as Antinori
½   cup (2 ounces) freshly grated Parmesan
      cheese
2   tablespoons freshly grated Romano
      cheese
2   tablespoons toasted pine nuts
3   garlic cloves, minced
2   sprigs fresh Italian flat-leaf parsley
      Salt and freshly ground black pepper to
      taste

Blend above ingredients in bowl of food
processor, fitted with steel knife, until smooth.

Cook's Tip

Authentic Parmigiano Reggiano from Italy is always
best for this Italian favorite, but Argentine
Reggianito makes a wonderful Parmesan-style
substitute, for less than half the price. Shop for it
at specialty cheese shops or Italian groceries. In
the Seattle area, try Delaurenti.

Shellfish Broth or Stock

Makes 1½ quarts

5   tablespoons olive oil, divided
1   pound shellfish shells, cleaned
1   tablespoon Cognac or other brandy
2   shallots, coarsely chopped with skin
2   garlic cloves, bruised
1   carrot, peeled, coarsely chopped
1   celery stalk, coarsely chopped
½   cup dry white wine or vermouth
1   teaspoon tomato paste
2   quarts cold water (about)
      Bouquet garni (3 sprigs fresh Italian flat-
      leaf parsley, 2 sprigs fresh thyme,
      1 bay leaf – all tied in cheesecloth)

1. Heat 3 tablespoons oil in large Dutch oven over medium heat. Add shells and sauté 3 to 4 minutes.
2. Pour over Cognac and ignite. Set Dutch oven aside.
3. Heat remaining 2 tablespoons oil in heavy medium skillet over medium heat. Add shallots with garlic. Sauté until soft and translucent, about 3 minutes.
4. Add carrot with celery. Cook until slightly softened, stirring occasionally, about 5 minutes.
5. Stir in wine with tomato paste. Pour mixture over shells (in Dutch oven) and return to high heat.
6. Stir in remaining ingredients and bring to boil. Immediately reduce heat and gently simmer about 1 hour.
7. Strain stock through fine-mesh sieve into clean pot and reduce to 1$\frac{1}{2}$ quarts. (Stock may be refrigerated for a day or two. Always boil before using. May be conveniently frozen in 1-cup portions.)

Cook's Tip

Keep a 2 to 3-quart Tupperware container in your freezer and reserve shrimp shells when you have them. When you get about 1 pound of shells (5 to 6 pounds of shrimp yields about 1 pound shells), make stock and freeze it. This way, stock-making isn't such a chore. (Reduce to ice-cube size for ideal freezing.)

Spicy Tomato Sauce

Makes about 3 quarts

- 6 tablespoons olive oil, divided
- 2 large onions, chopped
- 7 medium garlic cloves, minced
- 2 medium red bell peppers, stemmed, seeded, deribbed, diced
- 2 serrano chilies, stemmed, seeded, deribbed, finely diced
- 4 pounds very ripe tomatoes, cored, seeded, finely chopped
- 5 cups water
- 1 can (6 ounces) tomato paste
- $\frac{1}{2}$ cup dry red wine
- $\frac{1}{2}$ cup Veal Stock (see **Basics**)
- 4 tablespoons chopped fresh oregano
- 2 tablespoons chopped fresh basil
- 2 tablespoons chopped fresh Italian flat-leaf parsley
- 2 tablespoons soy sauce
- 2 tablespoons chopped Oven-Dried Tomatoes with 2 tablespoons oil (see **Basics**)
- 1 tablespoon sugar
- 1 tablespoon Pernod
- 1 tablespoon balsamic vinegar *
- 1 tablespoon chopped fresh thyme
- 1 tablespoon chopped fresh chervil
- 1 tablespoon chopped fresh rosemary
- 1 tablespoon chopped fresh marjoram
- 1$\frac{1}{2}$ teaspoons chopped fresh savory
- $\frac{1}{2}$ teaspoon red pepper flakes
- 1 large bay leaf
  Salt and freshly ground black pepper to taste

1. Heat 4 tablespoons oil in large Dutch oven over medium heat.
2. Add onions with garlic. Cook until onions start to brown, stirring occasionally, about 25 minutes. Add remaining oil last half of cooking time.
3. Stir in red bell peppers with chilies. Cook until slightly softened, stirring occasionally, about 5 minutes.
4. Stir in remaining ingredients and gently simmer about 2 hours. Remove bay leaf before serving.

* see **Special Ingredients**

Cook's Tips

Fresh tomatoes may be substituted by 2 cans (28 ounces each) Italia brand, peeled crushed tomatoes.

All fresh herbs may be substituted by $\frac{1}{3}$ the dried amount.

Veal Stock

Makes 3 quarts

6 to 7 pounds veal bones, preferably shank, knuckle, joint bones with some meat
2 celery stalks, coarsely chopped
1 large onion, coarsely chopped with skin
1 medium leek, cleaned, coarsely chopped
1 medium carrot, peeled, coarsely chopped
2 cups dry white wine, divided
8 quarts cold water
Bouquet garni (4 sprigs fresh Italian flat-leaf parsley, 4 sprigs fresh thyme, 1 sprig fresh rosemary, 1 bay leaf – all tied in cheesecloth)
10 black peppercorns, slightly crushed
2 garlic cloves, bruised
2 dried Chinese black mushrooms * (optional)
1 small tomato, chopped (optional)

1. Position rack in lowest third of oven and preheat to 400° F.
2. Wipe bones well with paper towels.
3. Arrange in large, shallow roasting pan and roast until starting to brown, about 1 hour.
4. Top with celery, onion, leek and carrot. Roast 45 minutes longer.
5. With slotted spoon, transfer bones with vegetables to colander and drain well. Place in large stockpot.
6. Degrease roasting pan and set over high heat atop stove. Deglaze with ¹/₂ cup wine, scraping up all browned bits.
7. Add mixture to stockpot with remaining wine and water. Bring to boil over high heat and skim foam from surface.
8. Immediately reduce heat and add remaining ingredients. Gently simmer 6 to 8 hours, skimming foam and fat occasionally. (Do not stir or stock will become cloudy.)
9. Strain stock through fine-mesh sieve into clean pot and reduce to 3 quarts. Degrease. (Stock may be refrigerated several days. Always boil before using. May be conveniently frozen in 1-cup portions or further reduced to demi-glace. (1 cup stock reduces to about ¹/₄ cup demi-glace.)

* see **Special Ingredients**

Cook's Tip

The above stock may be prepared with game bones, feathered or furred. Simply add 5 bruised juniper berries. Also, try it with lamb bones for a wonderful, rich stock.

Basic Ingredients

Butter – We use unsalted butter in most of our preparations – favorites are Darigold and Tillamook. For those watching the "Big C," we have found <u>I Can't Believe It's Not Butter</u> to be excellent for cooking and especially wonderful for sauce-making. Available at most supermarkets.

Cognac – Enriching a sauce or stock with your best Cognac is great, but it's not necessary. Select a good quality brandy from the liquor store and keep it on hand as your cooking brandy. We use Korbel brand – about $8 a bottle.

Garlic – Gone are the days when 8 cloves of garlic equaled 1 teaspoon. Garlic cloves now come in so many different sizes, it's entirely up to the cook what size to use. When we call for garlic cloves, we refer to an average size clove – one average head of garlic weighs about 2 ounces and yields 12 to 15 cloves – the rest is up to you!

Heavy Cream – When a recipe calls for heavy cream, we mean just that – look out diets! Shop your favorite creamery for the real stuff or feel free to use the supermarket type labeled whipping cream – this way, you won't feel so guilty.

Herbs – We cannot stress the importance of using fresh herbs in all of your preparations, but realize there are times when it is not possible. Most, if not all, of our recipes call for fresh herbs. Feel free to substitute dried, when necessary. Use about $\frac{1}{3}$ to $\frac{1}{2}$ of the amount of fresh called for in the recipe.

Lemon Juice – Squeeze your own, it tastes so much better. Don't cheat and buy that convenient little plastic lemon, no matter how tempting. One average size lemon yields 2 to 3 tablespoons.

Oil – The oil you select to cook with is certainly your choice. We use Puritan, made from canola oil, a vegetable oil low in saturated fat.

Olive Oil – We use pure olive oil in preparations calling for olive oil – a mild one like Sasso or Bertolli from Italy is excellent. For salads and marinades, a stronger taste may be desired and we recommend extra-virgin olive oil – a fruity one like Antinori or Badia a Coltibuno from Italy is excellent. Experiment with the many brands available today and be your own judge. Bertolli also has a great olive oil spray.

Onions – We use yellow onions in most of our preparations. They are mild tasting onions that store beautifully. Here's a handy guideline – 1 large onion is about 12 ounces, 1 medium is about 8 ounces and 1 small is about 6 ounces. Walla Walla Sweets are a real treat in late June, so take advantage of this regional specialty. We use them in everything! To keep them past the season, simply wrap snugly in newspaper and store in a cool, dark place. They should last from 3 to 4 weeks – but who can resist eating them before that?

Pasta – Making fresh pasta is so much fun and so much better tasting. If you have never done it, try it. So many supermarkets and specialty food stores carry good brands today, so try them and decide on your favorite. When we don't have time to make it fresh, we always purchase it at Seattle's Pasta and Company in the University Village. Many brands of dried are good too – we prefer De Cecco. Available at most supermarkets and specialty food stores.

Pepper – There is nothing in the world like freshly ground black pepper. We buy the whole black peppercorns and grind about $\frac{1}{4}$ cup at a time, to always have on hand for cooking. We also buy white peppercorns and do the same for light dishes that require no color. No kitchen should be without a spice grinder!

Basic Ingredients, continued

Powdered Sugar – Often referred to as confectioner's sugar. We use C & H brand and always keep it on hand.

Salt – The only salt we use is Morton's Lite-Salt. We always wait to the end of cooking to add salt or let the individual salt his own serving. Many cooks prefer kosher salt as it adheres to foods nicely. Available at some supermarkets and specialty food stores.

Shallots – Borrowed from French cuisine, this pungent relative of the onion is indispensable in our kitchen – it adds flavor to just about any dish. Buy only a few at a time and store in a dark, cool place. Available at most supermarkets.

Tomatoes – There's nothing like fresh Northwest tomatoes in the summer, but when big, juicy, flavorful ones are not available, we highly recommend the canned variety – they will be much better than the tasteless ones available. We have given recommendations in several recipes for our favorites – Italia and Contadina brands are always good. To seed or not to seed is up to you. To seed fresh tomatoes, simply slice the tomato vertically and shake out the seeds.

Special Ingredients

Anchovy Paste – A paste of puréed anchovies with oil and salt. More convenient and economical than opening a whole can of anchovies, when a recipe calls for a small amount of anchovy flavor. Available in tubes at most supermarkets and specialty food stores.

Arborio Rice – An imported, Italian short-grain rice widely used in risotto and Spanish paella. Available at Italian markets and specialty food stores. We prefer Irisi Classici or Alcazaba brand.

Balsamic Vinegar – A highly aromatic wine vinegar produced in Moderna, Italy, possessing a pungent, sweet-sour taste. Available at Italian markets, specialty food stores and some supermarkets.

Black Bean Garlic Sauce – A sauce of fermented, salted, black soybeans enlivened with garlic. Usually imported from China in cans or jars and available at Asian markets. We prefer Sun-Luck brand.

Bread Flour – A flour with a high gluten content (that gives an elastic quality to the dough), which produces bread with more volume. Available at supermarkets. We prefer Gold Medal Better for Bread Flour.

Cake Flour – A flour high in starch and low in protein, which produces very light and tender cakes. It blends easily into batters and absorbs and retains moisture while baking. Available at most supermarkets. We prefer Softasilk by Betty Crocker.

Chanterelle – A wild, trumpet-shaped mushroom with a characteristically fruity and slightly peppery, nutlike taste. Abundant during the fall. Available at some supermarkets, specialty food stores and Seattle's Pike Place Market, when in season. Also sold dried in packages. To rehydrate, simply cover with hot water and let stand until soft. Squeeze out excess moisture and snip off tough stems. Rinse well before using.

Chilies – There are so many varieties of chilies available in the Northwest today – all members of the Capsicum family. The hottest are usually the smallest, so take caution when handling them. The alkaloid component, capsaicin, is the substance that makes chilies hot and is highly concentrated in the placental membranes and seeds. Always wear rubber gloves when seeding a fresh chili. Many varieties are available at most supermarkets, Asian markets and Latin American markets, when in season. During the off-season they are imported. We use the serrano chili in our recipes. Also available dried in packages. To rehydrate, simply cover with hot water and let stand until soft.

Chinese Black Mushrooms – Mushrooms of the shiitake variety usually sold dried in packages (by size). Available at Asian markets and specialty food stores. To rehydrate, simply cover with hot water and let stand until soft. Squeeze out excess moisture and snip off tough stems. Rinse well before using.

Chocolate – For all of our chocolate creations, we suggest Lindt or Tobler chocolate. Available at specialty food stores.

Chorizo – A spicy, garlic-flavored Spanish sausage made with pork and hot peppers. Sold fresh, or dried and smoked. Usually encased in narrow casings, but also sold in bulk in some markets. Available at Spanish markets and specialty food stores.

Clarified Butter – That part of butter obtained by melting whole butter and spooning off the foamy, white substance that has risen to the top and discarding the milky solids that remain in the bottom of the pan. It enables you to cook at higher temperatures. 8 tablespoons (1 stick or 1/2 cup) of butter yields about 1/3 cup clarified butter.

Coconut Cream – The rich, solid milk found at the top of a can of coconut milk. If a recipe calls for coconut cream, simply scoop out the top, solid portion. Each 14-ounce can of coconut milk contains 3 to 4 ounces of coconut cream.

Coconut Milk – The liquid produced when freshly grated coconut is soaked in water or milk for a designated length of time, then strained. This milk has a sweet fragrance and gives body and flavor to dishes. Widely used in many Southeast Asian cuisines, it is available in cans at Asian markets, specialty food stores and some supermarkets. We prefer the Chaokoh brand. If a recipe calls for coconut milk, vigorously shake the can to thoroughly mix.

Feta Cheese – A fresh Greek cheese usually made from goat's or sheep's milk, with a sharp, salty taste. Available at Greek markets, specialty food stores and supermarkets.

Fish Sauce – A thin, translucent liquid drained from salted fish and shellfish, which is fermented in wooden barrels. Possesses a pungent odor which mellows when cooked. Widely used in many Southeast Asian cuisines. Available in bottles at Asian markets and specialty food stores.

Grape Leaves – Leaves from grape vines originally planted in the Mediterranean region, but now grown locally. Available in jars, packed in brine, at specialty food stores and some supermarkets. Leaves bought in jars should be soaked briefly in hot water and rinsed well before using. Fresh leaves should be steamed or poached briefly to soften before using.

Grape Vine Cuttings – These dried branches left over from yearly grape pruning make an excellent addition to the grill for smoking various meats and fish. Short segments (6 to 8 inches) should be soaked in water about 1 hour prior to placement on hot coals. You can probably get as many cuttings as you want for free if you visit the wine country around pruning time – November to February.

Greek-Style Olives – There are several types of Greek olives available at Greek markets and specialty food stores. We prefer the black-purple, brine-cured Kalamata olive for its great flavor.

Green Onion Brushes – A decorative garnish used in many Asian cuisines. To make a green onion brush, simply slice off the root end and top 3 inches. (You will have a 3 to 4-inch piece.) Slice, all the way around the root end, 1-inch of the way up. Place in ice water until ends start to curl, about 1 hour.

Hog Casings – Sausages are stuffed into various sizes of casings and most often these casings are the intestines of hogs. Packed in salt, they keep indefinitely. Available at local butcher shops. Always buy more than your recipe calls for, as they often burst or have a hole or two in them.

Hoisin Sauce – A spicy-fruity sauce made from fermented wheat or soybean bases widely used in Chinese cuisine. Available in cans at Asian markets and specialty food stores. We prefer the Koon Chun brand. Store indefinitely in a cool place.

Jasmine Rice – The wonderfully aromatic long-grain rice of Thailand, often called Mali or fragrant rice. Available in various size bags at Asian markets and specialty food stores. We buy the 10-pound bag for about $7.00 – Golden Anchor brand.

Kosher Salt – Salt with larger crystals which adheres better to foods. Preferred to regular salt by many professionals in the culinary field. Available in some supermarkets and specialty food stores.

Lumpfish Roe – The salted eggs of the lumpfish are referred to as caviar, but technically only the eggs of the sturgeon can be called caviar. Available in small jars, the red or black roe can be found at some supermarkets and specialty food stores. Romanoff brand seems to be the most widely used. Rinse well before using and always keep refrigerated.

Marzipan – A mixture of sugar, almonds and egg whites also called almond paste. Widely used in dessert preparations. Available at some supermarkets and specialty food stores.

Minced Crystallized Ginger – Pieces of ginger with a sugary coating that are eaten as a confection and widely used in desserts. Available by Spice Islands in 2 ounce jars or in bulk at local spice shops. In Seattle, try the spice shop at the Pike Place Market.

Montrachet – Undoubtedly the best of the French goat cheeses (chèvre). Creamy and pungent with a moderate goat flavor. Available at specialty food stores and cheese shops. In Seattle, we shop at The Wedge in The University Village or Brie and Bordeaux for our cheeses.

Morel – Not a true mushroom, but certainly treated as one. This wild, spring delicacy is identifiable by its brown, sponge-like cap, pitted with hollows in which the spores are produced. Available at some supermarkets, specialty food stores and Seattle's Pike Place Market, when in season. Also sold dried in packages. To rehydrate, simply cover with hot water and let stand until soft. May be necessary to cut open with a sharp knife and rinse out excess sand. Squeeze out excess moisture and snip off tough stems. Rinse well before using.

Muslim Curry Paste – A Thai curry paste originating in India. Sweet Indian spices such as cinnamon and nutmeg are included in this paste. Available at Asian markets.

Oriental Sesame Oil – Oil extracted from the seed capsules of the sesame plant. Lends a wonderfully nutty flavor to any dish and widely used in Asian cuisines. Available at Asian markets and some supermarkets.

Oyster Mushrooms – A wild, smoky-gray mushroom with a silky texture and, some say, an oyster-like flavor. The entire mushroom is edible. Available at Asian markets, some supermarkets and most specialty food stores.

Parmesan Cheese – Authentic Parmigiano Reggiano is a granular-type cow's milk cheese imported from Italy to the U.S. when it is about 2 years old. Sweet and nutty, this cheese is government controlled and produced only in the region around Parma, Italy. Wonderful grated and the only cheese to top off your pasta! Available at specialty food stores and cheese shops at about $16.00 per pound. (Try the Argentine Reggianito for about $6.00 per pound – a great buy for the taste. We prefer Milkaut brand.) In Seattle we shop The Wedge at The University Village and Brie and Bordeaux for our cheeses.

Phyllo Pastry Sheets – Ultra-thin sheets of pastry dough widely used in appetizer and dessert preparations. Available frozen at some supermarkets and most specialty food stores. Often spelled Fillo. We prefer Apollo or Pepperidge Farm brands.

Prosciutto – An uncooked, unsmoked ham, air-cured near Parma, Italy. Imported to the U.S. and sold for about $18.00 per pound. Usually eaten in paper-thin slices. Available at Italian markets, specialty food stores and some supermarkets in the deli department. (Try the domestic Boar's Head brand for about $13.00 a pound. It's a little less salty and a nice substitute. Available at above places.)

Puff Pastry Shells – Unbaked pastry shells made from puff pastry widely used in many elegant preparations. Available frozen at some supermarkets and specialty food stores. We prefer Pepperidge Farm brand.

Raspberry Vinegar – A white wine vinegar flavored with red raspberries widely used in salads and cooking. Available at specialty food stores and some supermarkets. Locally, The Country Store and Farm on Vashon Island produces a delightful one that we use. It's made from fresh Northwest fruit and herbs from Vashon Island farms.

Rice Noodles – Flat, ribbon-like noodles widely used in many Oriental and Southeast Asian cuisines. Comes in various widths and often called rice sticks. Sold dried in packages and available at Asian markets and some specialty food stores. To rehydrate, simply cover with hot water and let stand until soft. We prefer Kim Tar brand. About 85-cents for a 16-ounce package.

Rice Vinegar – Vinegar made from fermented rice, available in a range of flavors. Widely used in many Asian cuisines. Available at Asian markets a specialty food stores.

Salad Burnet Vinegar – Vinegar flavored with the herb salad burnet. The herb has a distinctive cucumber flavor with beautiful foliage. Available at some specialty markets.

Saffron – The dried stamens (stigmas) of the crocus flower, native to the Far East and considered the world's most expensive spice. Indispensable in dishes such as Spanish paella and French bouillabaisse. Lends a pungently aromatic flavor and slight bitter taste to many dishes. Available at Spanish markets, specialty food stores and, in Seattle, at the spice shop at the Pike Place Market.

Shiitake – An eastern tree fungus from oak logs and shii trees originating in Japan. Lends a smoky flavor and spongy texture to many Oriental dishes. Widely grown in the United States today and available year 'round at Asian markets. Also sold dried in packages. To rehydrate, simply cover with hot water and let stand until soft. Squeeze out excess moisture and snip off tough stems. Rinse well before using.

Shredded Picked Radish – An ingredient widely used in Thai cuisine, usually sold in packages. Lends an interesting flavor and texture to many dishes. Wa Sang in Seattle's International District is the only place we have ever found it locally. About 65 cents for a 1-ounce package.

Sriracha Sauce – A sauce similar to our Tabasco sauce but thicker and hotter. Made with the tiny little peppers of Thailand called prik kee noo and widely used in their cuisine. Available at Asian markets and some specialty food stores.

Straw Mushrooms – Small, conical, silky-textured mushrooms grown on wet rice, straw beds in China. Imported to the United States in cans and also sold dried in packages. Available at Asian markets, specialty food stores and some supermarkets. We prefer the Longevity brand.

Szechwan Red Peppers – Small red peppers native to the tropical Americas. Used in Oriental and Southeast Asian cuisines. Available at Asian markets and specialty food stores.

Tamarind Water – The tamarind tree is a majestic tree grown in Southeast Asia that produces a fruit much like a big bean pod. It is the pulp that is highly prized for its sour taste, lending a distinctive flavor to many Asian dishes, especially Thai. Sold in compressed packages at most Asian markets and some specialty food stores. To obtain tamarind water, simply soak 1 part tamarind pulp in 4 parts warm water about 15 minutes. Press liquid through a fine-mesh sieve and discard solids. **Tamarind concentrate** is also available at The Souk, an Indian grocery at the Pike Place Market in Seattle. Use 1 part concentrate to 3 parts water – soften in microwave.

Tarragon Vinegar – One of the most popular flavored vinegars with an anise flavor. Available at specialty food stores and some supermarkets.

Thai Basil – Often called holy basil or red basil, this aromatic herb gives a wonderful aniseed, sharp flavor to many Southeast Asian dishes. Available at some Asian markets and well worth seeking out. We always find this delightful herb at Uwajimaya in the International District in Seattle.

Tofu – Pressed soybean curd with a bland taste but high in protein. Absorbs the flavors of a dish beautifully and is available in various degrees of firmness. Widely used in many Oriental and Southeast Asian cuisines. Available at Asian markets, specialty food stores and most supermarkets.

Wild Mushrooms – we refer to chanterelles, morels, shiitakes and oyster mushrooms as wild mushrooms in the recipes – refer to individual listings. One pound fresh wild mushrooms is equivalent to about 4 ounces dried.

Won Ton Wrappers – Squares of fresh noodle dough widely used in Chinese cuisine. Available at Asian markets, specialty food stores and most supermarkets.

Ingredients through the Seasons

Many Northwest cooks prefer to create their menus based on what particular food is available fresh, rather than preserved or frozen. This "shopping by the seasons" is a wonderful way to put the finest, most flavorful cuisine on your table. Fresh foods available by the season are presented below for Northwest shoppers.

Spring – March through May
Asparagus, rhubarb, Pacific shrimp, Pacific halibut, local lamb.

Summer – June through August
Summer vegetables, especially: Walla Walla sweet onions, vine ripened tomatoes, peppers, fresh herbs. Summer Fruits, especially: apricots, cherries, peaches, plums, strawberries, raspberries and blackberries. Salmon and scallops

Fall – September through November
Fall vegetables, peppers, squash, pumpkins, wild mushrooms like Chanterelles. Fall fruits, apples, late peaches. Hazelnuts and walnuts. Dungeness crab, clams, oysters. Gamebirds.

Winter – December through February
Time for hearty soups and stews. Seafood, especially: Dungeness crab, oysters, clams.

Washington Wine Country

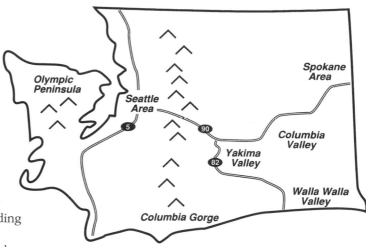

Winemaking in Washington State dates back to the late 1930s when production began at St. Charles Winery on Stretch Island and at the Grandview facility of what is now Chateau Ste. Michelle. These first wines were made from either concord grapes or hybrids and had little resemblance to the current French vinifera wines available today. The making of fine vinifera wines was to wait until the late 1960s.

In 1967 two companies began making wine from vitis vinifera plantings in the Yakima Valley. Ste. Michelle Vineyards (later to become Chateau Ste. Michelle) was expanding their brand name from the Pommerelle and Nawico labels whose fortified wines were made from predominantly Concord varieties. The Associated Vintners was a group of University of Washington professors led by Lloyd Woodburne who bonded a winery in Woodburne's garage in Kirkland. Their previous home winemaking efforts had been praised and they decided to go commercial.

Research by Dr. Walter Clore and others encouraged further grape planting in the Yakima Valley, and by 1976 the Washington wine industry celebrated its birth with an article in *Time* magazine featuring pioneer grape grower and winemaker Mike Wallace of Hinzerling Vineyards.

The late 1970s and early 1980s saw a dramatic increase in acreage of wine grapes as well as in the number of bonded wineries. Expansion came first to the Yakima and Columbia Valleys, then to the peripheral urban areas of the state. It seems that folks discovered that grapes from the vineyards of Eastern Washington could be trucked to Seattle, Spokane and even to Sequim to make wine!

Touring

If you are interested in visiting the wine country of Washington, you should obtain a copy of *Touring the Washington Wine Country* from the Washington Wine Commission, P.O. Box 61217, Seattle 98121. This pocket guide offers detailed traveling instructions to each facility as well as information about wines and tasting room hours of operation. (The guide was created for the WWC by your humble co-author, Chuck Hill.)

For this book, we have treated the state as eight separate wine touring areas, described on the following pages. You'll find general information on the wineries in each area as well as other points of interest and suggestions for dining out based on our personal experiences. The maps provided give general information about the location of each winery. More exact directions should be obtained from the Wine Commission booklet or by calling the individual wineries.

Picnicking in the wine country is a popular spring and summer activity and many wineries offer tables, shady lawns and other amenities for your convenience. If you're traveling with children, this gives the kids a chance to unwind and let off a little steam. Many wineries also offer deli-type items for sale such as cheese, salami, bread and crackers.

Traveling distances should be noted carefully with an accurate highway map so you don't find yourself driving back from Eastern Washington or Spokane in the middle of the night and dog-tired. The roads in the far reaches of Washington State stretch long and far, and you should plan your itinerary to allow enough time for safe travel.

As you find yourself in the car merrily traveling from winery to winery, please have the common sense to designate one of your party as a non-drinking participant. Even though each winery is only allowed to offer small samples of four wines, these can add up quickly, especially in areas where many tasting rooms are located close together. This designated driver program has been very successful in helping keep cars on the road and passengers and pedestrians out of harm's way.

Note: At the end of this section is a roster of Northwest wineries with exact addresses and phone numbers. Anytime you're planning a tour, give a call to the wineries you wish to visit to confirm that someone will be there to receive you. Many smaller vintners have odd hours of operation and take days off if the tourist traffic is light.

As the commercial and cultural hub of the Pacific Northwest, Seattle is naturally a center for wine lovers and wine sellers alike. The many fine wine shops and specialty grocery stores in Seattle offer many limited bottlings available only at a few locations as well as broad selections of everyday wines at attractive prices.

Additionally, Seattle offers some of the Northwest's finest dining opportunities as well as the finest overnight accommodations. Whether you're looking for the elegance of **Fullers** at the Seattle Sheraton, **The Hunt Club** at the Sorrento, or for more informal dining at **Ray's Boathouse** or the **Anthony's HomePorts**, you'll no doubt enjoy the freshest Northwest ingredients creatively prepared and presented. On the east side of Lake Washington, near the winery enclave of Woodinville, check out Peter Dow's **Cafe Juanita** and Ray's **Yarrow Bay Grill** (both in Kirkland) or **Pacifica Restaurant** on the Woodinville-Redmond Road.

Opportunities to visit producing wineries abound in the Seattle area but be aware that almost all of the grapes for these facilities come from Eastern Washington. Some wineries prefer to have just a tasting room with a small aging cellar, while others actually produce thousands of gallons of wine on premise. Either way you'll have an opportunity to taste their wares and ask questions.

Staton Hills Winery has a tasting room in the Pike Place Market that is a delightful sidelight to this center of fresh produce, creative crafts and local color. Ballard's **Whittlesey Mark** winery is open only by appointment and the **E. B. Foote Winery** in the south end also keeps abbreviated hours.

East of Lake Washington almost a dozen wineries offer tourists the chance to observe the winemaking process and taste some recent releases. Near downtown Kirkland are **Covey Run Winery** at Moss Bay (next to Hale's Ale Brewery), **Cavatappi Winery** (located at Cafe Juanita) and **Cascade Estates Winery** near Totem Lake shopping center.

Further northeast, the Woodinville wine scene is dominated by **Chateau Ste. Michelle** and **Columbia Winery**. Both facilities offer extensive touring opportunities and the chance to picnic outside when you're finished in the winery.

On north toward downtown Woodinville, you'll find Lou and Sandy Facelli greeting visitors at **Facelli Winery**, tucked into a business park just off the main road. In the town of Woodinville, **French Creek Cellars** continues to create unusual wines with an avid local following. Just down the road, Bruce Crabtree's **Salmon Bay Winery** offers

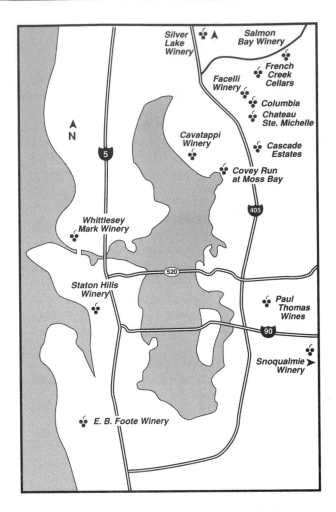

Northwest varietals crafted to accompany foods.

A round trip through town and back south on 140th N.E. leads to Hollywood Corner where you may sample **Tagaris** wines at Mits Edward's Wine Rack. Quite a collection of gifts for cooks and wine lovers is an added draw.

North of Woodinville in Bothell, **Silver Lake Winery** produces both varietal grape wines and a line of sparkling ciders made from apples, pears and other fruits. **Paul Thomas Winery** is open Fridays and Saturdays near downtown Bellevue, while on the Interstate 90 corridor you'll find **Snoqualmie Winery** perched on a bluff overlooking Mount Si and the Cascade foothills. Bring a picnic lunch to enjoy with the view.

Olympic Peninsula Wine Touring

The Olympic Peninsula is one of North America's last areas where pristine, old-growth forest shelters wildlife in quiet seclusion. Wineries in the wilderness? Not quite. The perimeter of the Olympic Peninsula borders on Puget Sound and the Strait of Juan de Fuca, scenic areas that attract retirees and weekend recreationalists. These semi-permanent residents and tourists from the big cities make for a natural clientele seeking locally made products. With one notable exception, the four wineries in this area use grapes imported from Eastern Washington to make their wine.

Aside from the fun of taking a ride on a Washington State ferry to get there, the Olympic Peninsula offers many activities for both young and old. The town of Port Townsend has dozens of restored Victorian homes (many converted to B & Bs) and the many local beaches give the kids a place to run off some of their pent-up energy. The town of Dungeness will no doubt inspire admirers of the namesake crab, while the beauty of the Olympic National Forest can be appreciated by driving up to Hurricane Ridge near Port Angeles.

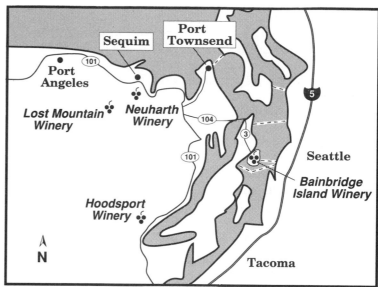

Closest to Seattle, and technically not on the Olympic Peninsula, **Bainbridge Island Winery** is Washington's only winery that uses only Western Washington fruit for its entire production. Locally grown Müller-Thurgau and Siegerrebe complement the more familiar Chardonnay as well as the winery's annual production of strawberry wine made from locally harvested berries. Their vineyard at the winery is posted with interpretive signs that educate visitors about the cyclical work that keeps the vineyard operating throughout the year.

Up on the Peninsula proper, the town of Sequim (pronounced skwim) is home to two wineries. Gene Neuharth retired from grape growing in the Central Valley of California to the Olympic Peninsula. Oddly enough, he felt compelled to convert a 60 year old cedar barn to rustic **Neuharth Winery** and to start making wine from Eastern Washington grapes. He makes the drive to the Columbia Valley each year to pick up grapes at harvest time.

In the deep forest above the Sequim/Dungeness area you'll find Romeo Conca quietly making wine at **Lost Mountain Winery**. A retired chemical engineer whose Italian upbringing instilled wine-

making as a way of life, Romeo enjoys a wonderfully peaceful environment with wildlife of all kinds visiting his winery/home in the Olympic Mountain foothills.

On the southeast side of the Olympic Peninsula the wilderness comes nearly to the edge of Hood Canal, an arm of Puget Sound famous for quality seafood and water recreation. **Hoodsport Winery**, located just across Highway 101 from Hood Canal, was once a fruit and berry winery selling sweet and off-dry wines to local residents and tourists. Times have changed and now the Patterson family makes mostly varietal grape wines from fruit harvested in the Yakima Valley. A regionally famous raspberry wine continues to be popular for dessert and has even been incorporated into a decadently rich chocolate/raspberry truffle available at the winery.

Just a ferry ride away from Port Angeles is Victoria, British Columbia, capital of that province and one of the Northwest's most charming cities. A few miles west of town is **Sooke Harbour House**, a restaurant and B & B whose reputation is international for the most innovative cuisine prepared from ultra-fresh local ingredients.

The greater Puget Sound area includes a lot of real estate from the Canadian border to the Skookumchuck Valley south of Olympia. Almost all of the wineries in this region use grapes from Eastern Washington for at least part of their production.

In the South Sound area, Vince de Bellis and his wife Anne operate a locally famous dinner house named Alice's Restaurant. Vince's **Johnson Creek Winery,** on the same site, provides varietal wines for the restaurant and for local distribution. In the foothills above the Puyallup (pew al up) River Valley **Manfred Vierthaler Winery** continues to be successful at selling his unusual selection of wines made mostly from California grapes.

Vashon Island Winery, owned by William and Karen Gerrior, produces Cabernet Sauvignon, Chardonnay and Semillon. Nearby **Coolen Wine Cellars** on the Kitsap Peninsula offers wines made without the addition of sulfites. The varietal blends are currently from both California and Eastern Washington grapes, although a small vineyard of Müller-Thurgau is planted on the property.

North of the greater Seattle area, near the town of Snohomish, Alex Golitzin crafts world-class Cabernet Sauvignon at **Quilceda Creek Vintners**. His career as a chemical engineer is certainly an appropriate credential to bring to winemaking, but many chemical engineers cum winemakers have failed to show the artistic insight necessary to create the exquisitely balanced, long-lived reds that have brought international fame to Alex's doorstep.

Doug McCrea, owner of **McCrea Cellars,** similarly limits his varietal offerings. A refreshing and complex Chardonnay is complemented by Mariah (a delightfully fruity Grenache) that has won him a following among fanciers of Rhone-style reds.

Charles Dawsey saw a niche for sulfite-free wines when the BATF passed a law requiring sulfite labeling, and his successes with small scale production of this genre led to the bonding of **Fidalgo Island Winery** at his home in Anacortes.

East of Bellingham, on the Mount Baker Highway, is **Mount Baker Vineyards**. An extensive vineyard at the winery features varietals selected by owner Dr. Albert Stratton who researched the Nooksack Valley microclimate with experimental plantings during the 1970s and 1980s. Chardonnay, Gewürztraminer, Müller-Thurgau, Madeleine Angevine and Royal Crimson Plum Wine are complemented by small quantities of Cabernet Sauvignon and other varietals.

Out on Whidbey Island, the loganberry harvest from **Whidbeys Greenbank Farm** is used to create

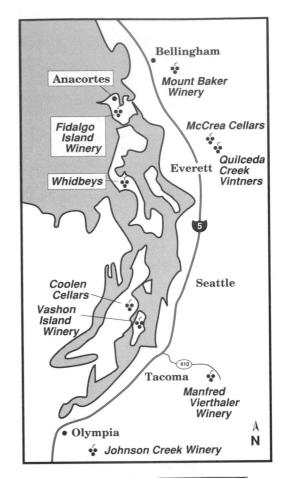

Whidbeys Loganberry liqueur, a sweet liqueur that may be sipped, mixed into coolers or used as a flavoring ingredient in dessert recipes. Owned by Stimson Lane Wine & Spirits, Whidbeys also makes a Cabernet Sauvignon Port wine.

Elegant dining opportunities in the far-flung reaches of the greater Puget Sound area are few, but Doug Charles' **Oyster Creek Inn** on Chuckanut Drive near Bellingham offers a magnificent food and wine experience.

Southwest Washington & Columbia Gorge Wine Touring

Southwest Washington and the Columbia River Gorge are home to several notable wineries and restaurants. While these areas are not known as popular destinations for wine tourists, per se, they take advantage of tourists traveling by for other purposes. The Columbia Gorge, for example, has become the mecca for wind surfers from all over the world with local wineries and restaurants providing a less exhilarating, but enjoyable, break from the action. Dining out in Hood River is not comparable to the Northwest's larger population centers with two exceptions, The Stonehedge Inn and The Columbia Gorge Hotel. **The Stonehedge Inn** is a family-owned dinner house featuring fresh local ingredients and a reliable wine list that includes many local bottlings. The **Columbia Gorge Hotel** is a local landmark with an elegant dining room serving lunch and dinner as well as their expansive country breakfast.

In the Columbia Gorge, only a short toll bridge stands between Washington and Oregon, and wineries on both sides of the river take advantage of a favorable climate to produce fine varietal wines.

In Washington, **Mont Elise Vineyards** holds tenure as the first winery operation in the area. Begun in 1975 by the Charles Henderson family, Mont Elise is well known for their quality varietals including Gewürztraminer, Pinot Noir, Gamay and others. In the picturesque town of Bingen, the winery is open daily during the summer tourist season. Perched on the steep hills overlooking the Gorge is the **Charles Hooper Family Winery** above the town of White Salmon. Boasting a dramatic, terraced vineyard and a fabulous view across the Gorge to Mount Hood, the winery offers several tasty varietals of the Germanic style.

On the Oregon side of the Columbia River, Cliff Blanchette's **Hood River Vineyards** has been making varietal and fruit wines for almost a decade on a hillside overlooking the area's famed orchards of apples and pears. Well known for production of a red Zinfandel from local grapes, Cliff also makes Chardonnay, Riesling, Cabernet Sauvignon and other wines. Bill Swain began **Three Rivers Winery** in 1986 after a training career in the California wine industry working for Charles Krug and Cresta Blanca. While Bill is most interested in the future of Pinot Noir from his nearby vineyard, he has a selection of flavorful varietals available at the tasting room including White Riesling, Chardonnay, Gewürztraminer and Rose of Pinot Noir.

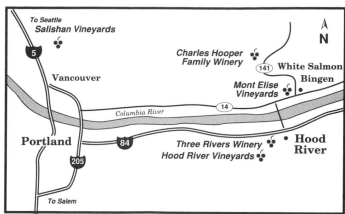

Salishan Vineyards in La Center is geographically a stand-alone operation, more associated with Oregon's Willamette Valley than the Washington wine industry. Joan and Lincoln Wolverton have labored for 15 years to carve out a reputation for fine Pinot Noir vinted from estate-grown grapes. Their research into the Lewis River Valley microclimate in the early 1970s has paid handsome dividends with many awards for their fine quality wines.

Discussion of Southwest Washington would not be complete without mentioning two famous dining spots on the coast near Long Beach. **The Shoalwater Restaurant** is located adjacent to the Shelburne Inn and offers exquisite meals and a wide selection of wines. It is not uncommon for visitors to travel from Seattle to enjoy a fine dinner at The Shoalwater and a night's rest at the Shelburne Inn. Equally famed for remarkably delectable cuisine from local ingredients is **The Ark** restaurant at Nahcotta on Willapa Bay. Owners Nancy Main and Jimella Lucas have created a wide following with both their fine foods served at the restaurant and with the annual Garlic Festival which draws hundreds of Northwesterners to this corner of the state.

If you're in the Long Beach area, be sure to take the short trip across the bridge to Astoria, Oregon, to visit Paul van der Veldt at **Shallon Winery**.

The west end of the Yakima Valley is populated with more wineries than the average wine tourist can visit in one day, so it's a good idea to plan a weekend (or longer!) to visit this area.

Most visitors begin their tour in Yakima and head east to Wapato to visit **Staton Hills Winery** just off I-82. The Statons have provided picnic tables and a lovely lawn for picnics or just a relaxing glass of wine.

Not far down the highway is the bustling wine-metropolis of Zillah, where a half-dozen wineries await your inspection. **Covey Run Winery** is the largest of these facilities with a large tasting room, gift shop and viewing area looking down into the winery. Not as large, but with just as warm a welcome, are five other nearby wineries. Gail and Shirley Puryear greet guests at their **Bonair Winery** with Shirley documenting the visits of wine lovers from faraway with a world map on the tasting room wall. Tom and Hema Campbell of **Horizon's Edge Winery** pour wines for eager tasters in their unique loft tasting room with a view of Mount Adams. **Hyatt Vineyards** with their trademark windmill is the winery project of longtime valley grape growers, Leland and Lynda Hyatt.

The **Portteus Vineyards** winery is a more recent addition to the Zillah wine scene with Paul Portteus crafting Cabernet, Chardonnay, Semillon and Zinfandel (first commercial quantity available 1993). Travel back to the freeway to visit **Zillah Oakes Winery** owned by Covey Run but concentrating on a slightly different line of varietals.

Not far down I-82 you can take Exit 58 to head north to **Eaton Hill Winery** or south to **Stewart Vineyards**. George and Martha Stewart have been growing grapes in Sunnyside and on the Wahluke Slope since the late 1970s and have been making wine on Cherry Hill in Granger since 1983. The winery is in the middle of a cherry orchard where you can enjoy the blossoms in April and the cherries in June! Eaton Hill Winery is at the site of the old Rinehold Cannery Homestead B & B, and owners Ed and Joann Stear welcome visitors to this remarkable 80-year-old building.

The large town of Sunnyside (by valley standards) offers two visits for wine lovers. On the western edge of town on Lincoln Avenue, is **Cascade Estates Winery** making wine in the old Darigold plant. This operation has sights on selling wine to Europe and other off-shore markets. On the eastern side of Sunnyside the Tucker family has

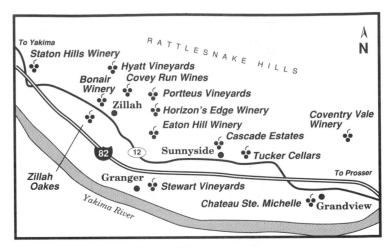

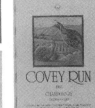

been farming in the valley for several generations and added **Tucker Cellars** winery to their produce market in 1982. Try their pickled vegetables and fluffy popcorn while you sip the latest releases. The fresh produce next door makes a delectable, edible souvenir of your trip to the Yakima Valley!

Another few miles down the road is the town of Grandview, named for the splendid, clear weather views of Mt. Rainier and Mt. Adams. Here you'll find **Chateau Ste. Michelle's** red wine facility, the valley's oldest continuous operating winery. Visit at harvest time to see vats of rich Cabernet and Merlot bubbling away and to watch the fascinating pump-over operation.

The fine dining opportunities in the Yakima Valley are limited, but several places deserve mention. A few miles outside of Yakima, Will Massett's **Birchfield Manor** offers the finest multicourse meal east of the Cascades with a remarkable wine selection and attentive staff. Downtown, **The Greystone** is a place to gather for a pre-prandial glass of wine and a delightful dinner of selected regional specialties. Across the street from The Greystone is the new **Grant's Ale Pub** where regulars meet each evening for a pint of Bert Grant's ales and a game of darts. The brewery itself is open by appointment.

This end of the Yakima Valley offers almost as many visits for wine lovers as the west end, so plan another weekend journey to fully discover the remarkable wines of this area. The town of Prosser is the center for winemaking here with the wineries near Benton City often considering themselves a part of the Tri-Cities area group.

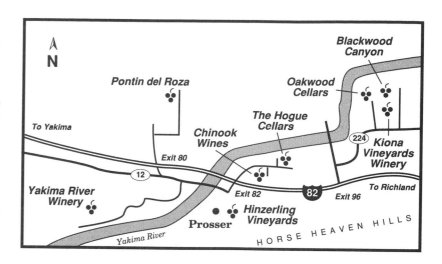

Mike Wallace of **Hinzerling Vineyards** was a pioneer in the commercial planting of vinifera wine grapes in Prosser, putting his first vines in the ground in 1972. After a disastrous freeze in the winter of 1973, he harvested his first commercial-size crop in 1976. Hinzerling Vineyards winery made a name with their intense Cabernet and offers tastes at the winery tasting room in Prosser.

The Hogue Cellars is just one part of a family operation that includes vast agricultural holdings throughout the Yakima Valley. Hop growing for brewing beer, mint growing for gum flavoring and large fields of asparagus, beans and other crops are just part of the story. The most recent chapter is the making of fine wine at their winery just off Interstate 82. Winemaker Rob Griffin oversees the production of Cabernet, Merlot, Chardonnay and other varietals.

Near the large Hogue Cellars facility is Kay Simon and Clay Mackey's **Chinook Wines**. The little house that serves as a tasting room is a quaint reminder of an earlier time, and your hosts offer you a picnic site under the spreading oak tree out back. The wines are made in small quantities and have been widely acclaimed for their ability to complement Northwest foods.

Out on North River Road, west of downtown Prosser, is **Yakima River Winery**. John and Louise Rauner welcome guests to sample in the tasting room and feature special tasting programs during the Thanksgiving weekend and April Barrel Tasting weekend. John is one of the Northwest's only producers of vintage port.

North of Prosser, the Pontin family has been farming along the Roza Canal for many years. In honor of the area, they named their winery **Pontin del Roza**. Young Scott Pontin crafts several varietals in the small winery on Hinzerling Road.

About 20 miles east of Prosser is Benton City, a small hamlet along the Yakima River where several well-known wineries have settled to pursue grape growing and winemaking. The most widely distrib-

uted is **Kiona Vineyards**, an operation that began as a project of two Richland engineers and has grown to include several family members from both sides. The Williams family operates the tasting room and oversees the vineyard operation at the foot of Red Mountain. The Jim Holmes family in Richland holds down the winemaking duties. Delectable late harvest Riesling, rich Cabernet Sauvignon and spicy Lemberger are among the specialties.

Not far from Kiona, **Blackwood Canyon Winery** is the ongoing dream of M. Taylor Moore. Mike Moore creates unique wines from grapes harvested throughout the valley and is an engaging conversationalist on the subject of grape growing and winemaking. Enjoy a sampling of his latest creations by stopping by his winery on Sunset Road.

Down the hill from Kiona and Blackwood Canyon is **Oakwood Cellars** in Benton City. Bob Skelton and Evelyn McLain operate this small facility and are eager hosts to visiting wine tourists.

To most travelers, the vast Columbia Valley is best known for dramatic vistas of desolate sagebrush punctuated by the occasional "circle farm" irrigated out of the desert with water from the Columbia River. Since most visitors are "just passing through" on their way between Seattle and Spokane, much of the remarkable beauty of the area remains hidden from the highway view.

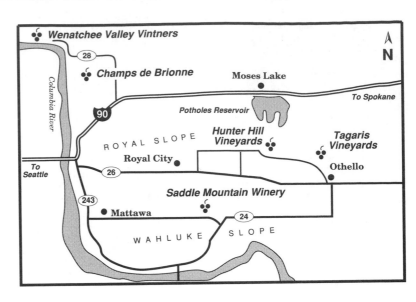

While wine touring in the northern Columbia Valley offers plenty of desert landscapes, there are also some delightful surprises in store. First-time visitors to the area are often amazed at the size of the region and at the proliferation of orchards and farms where the usual topsoil is dry, sandy dust. It is the irrigation projects made possible by several dams on the Columbia River that have brought the desert into bloom during the last 50 years.

Grapes were among the last crops to be planted in this area and the prime growing areas were among the last to be served by irrigation. Today, hundreds of acres of vinifera vines cover vast tracts on Evergreen Ridge, on the Wahluke Slope and on the Royal Slope.

The few wineries that have made this area their home are out to please visitors who travel a long distance to visit. Starting at Wenatchee you'll find Mike and Debbie Hansen tucked in among apple orchards with their **Wenatchee Valley Vintners**. Trained in agriculture and a former employee of the apple juice industry, Mike grows grapes at the winery site above the Columbia River in East Wenatchee and also at his father's larger vineyard in the Yakima Valley.

Further south and perched above the Columbia near Quincy, **Champs de Brionne** established one of the first vineyards in this area. The fantastic view from their property prompted the owners to build an amphitheater overlooking the canyon and soon they were booking impressive jazz and rock concerts into the venue. The likes of Chuck Berry, Bob Dylan, Ray Charles and others have all performed at this remarkable site. Enjoy a sip of wine while admiring the view from the tasting room.

On the Wahluke Slope near Mattawa stands **Saddle Mountain Winery** where the monolithic facility dominates the surrounding landscape. One of Washington's largest and most modern wineries, Saddle Mountain offers a wide selection of very

affordable wines. The self-guided tour and tasting room with a view of the working winery make for an enjoyable visit.

Northeast of the Wahluke Slope is the Royal Slope, home to **Hunter Hill Vineyards**. This winery is named for its proximity to the Potholes Wildlife Refuge where sportsmen hunt waterfowl during the annual fall migration. The winery offers an interesting side trip when "bluebird weather" has the ducks and geese flying out of range.

Further east, near the town of Othello, is the headquarters for the Taggares' family large agricultural operation. Owners of vast concord vineyards in the Yakima Valley, the family recently expanded their wine grape vineyards near Othello and bonded **Tagaris Winery**. The wines are made at another Washington location but are available for sale throughout the Northwest.

A winery not shown on the map, but very convenient to travelers is **Cascade Mountain Cellars** located in downtown Ellensburg. Juergen and Julie Grieb spruced up the old Ellensburg train depot and they now "conduct" winery tours and wine tastings at this special location.

Columbia Valley Wine Touring – South

The southern part of the Columbia Valley is also referred to as the Pasco Basin, an area of lowland bordering the broad bend in the Columbia River as it turns west toward the Pacific Ocean. Several wineries have set up shop in the vicinity not only to take advantage of local grape sources but to sell their wines to the population centers of Richland, Pasco and Kennewick. Also, the area is blessed with a long, warm summer that attracts many tourists from the state's wet side.

The Richland/Kennewick area is home to two wineries, **Seth Ryan** and **Badger Mountain Vineyards**. Both operations are relatively new and are open by appointment only.

Close by in Pasco you'll find several interesting stops just north of town off Highway 395. The **Quarry Lake** winery is owned by the Balcom family of Balcom and Moe farms. This agricultural operation is one of the largest in the state and produces wine grapes, concord grapes and a variety of other row crops. Right next door is **Bookwalter Winery** where Jerry and Jean Bookwalter craft delectable wines and offer tours of their unusual facility. You'll find a genuine, warm welcome at both of these wineries, with the owners often on hand to chat about their wines.

A few miles up the highway is **Preston Wine Cellars**, one of the area's original winery operations begun in the early 1970s. Owners Bill and Joann Preston have instilled the winemaking spirit in their offspring with son Brent Preston handling the winemaking and daughter Cathy Preston Mouncer taking care of public relations and marketing. Their second floor tasting room offers expansive views of the vineyard and surrounding countryside.

Alongside the Snake River confluence with the Columbia, Dave and Mary Gallant planted a vineyard and bonded **Chateau Gallant** winery. The winery is open for visitors just off Highway 182.

Gordon Brothers Cellars is the winery operation of Jeff and Bill Gordon who operate a large farm and vineyard near Levey Park on the Snake River. In addition to providing grapes to many other wineries, the Gordons have crafted some fine Merlots, Cabernets and Chardonnays for release under their own label.

Along the Columbia River, south of Prosser, is the area's largest and most impressive winery facility. **Columbia Crest** winery is part of the

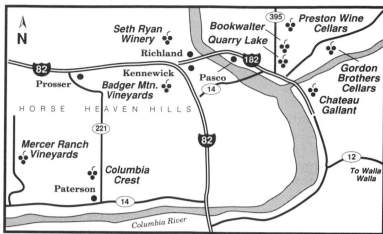

Stimson Lane Wine & Spirits group (parent company of Chateau Ste. Michelle) and offers just about everything a wine tourist could ask for. From the imported tapestries and antique furniture in the lobby to the ultra-modern winery spreading over nine acres, everything is first rate and very impressive. Outside, a courtyard picnic area, duck pond and rose garden complete the perfect picture.

West of Columbia Crest and a little farther up from the river is **Mercer Ranch Vineyards**. While the facility is not as impressive, the history of the family more than makes up for the lack of glamor. The Mercer family has been raising sheep in this part of the state for almost 100 years and also planted some of the first Cabernet vineyards in the early 1970s. Enjoy a chat with Don and Lynda Mercer over a glass of their trademark Limberger.

Fine dining choices in the Pasco area are limited. The dining rooms at the local Red Lion and Thunderbird motels are good, but for an ethnic dining experience try **The Emerald of Siam** in Richland. Owner Ravadi Quinn offers excellent Thai cuisine along with a good selection of local wines.

Spokane Area Wine Touring

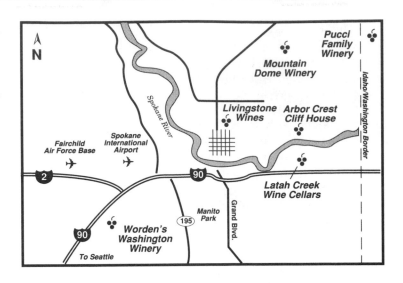

As Washington's second largest city and the commercial hub of Eastern Washington, Spokane is an important market for regional wineries. With the close proximity to the vineyards of the Columbia Valley and Yakima Valley, several winemakers decided to locate in this beautiful city and bring in the grapes to make their wine.

Spokane offers much to the spring and summer visitor including the annual Lilac Festival. This special weekend celebrating the city's namesake flower culminates in the famous Bloomsday Run, a 12K running event where more than 50,000 participants wind up and down the hills of Spokane for fun and exercise. Spokane is also famous for its beautiful golf courses, and many visitors come for this reason alone.

Certainly the wineries here are another point of interest that should not be missed. One of the most unique facilities in Washington is Arbor Crest Cliff House, home to **Arbor Crest Winery**. Perched 450 feet above the Spokane River near the east end of town, this mansion and expansive grounds date back to 1924 and have been restored to accommodate the winery's business offices and tasting room. The view of the Spokane area from the gazebo is breathtaking. A working winery on the site is in the plans, but for now the wine is made in a former fruit warehouse closer to downtown Spokane.

Also in the east end of town is **Latah Creek Wine Cellars** owned by Mike and Ellena Conway. Mike Conway began his Washington winemaking career at Hogue Cellars, crafting some of their first award-winning wines from Chenin Blanc and Riesling. Founding his own facility in 1982, he continues to make the state's best Chenin and also has impressed wine lovers with his Merlot, Cabernet and Chardonnay. A pet wine labeled Spokane Blush is also made from Merlot. Latah Creek's labels feature wildlife art by Floyd Broadbent.

Worden's Washington Winery is the area's oldest facility, located in a quiet pine forest on the city's western edge. A rustic log cabin houses the tasting room and winery office, while a larger building out back holds the tanks and equipment for winemaking. An annual grape stomp is held at the winery during early October.

A newcomer to the Spokane wine scene is **Steven T. Livingstone Wines** located in a former bakery building near downtown. A creative entrepreneur who counts winemaking as only one of his interests, Livingstone has garnered much praise with

his first releases. Grapes for his winemaking efforts come from the highly regarded Red Mountain area in the Yakima Valley.

Though no wine has been released from **Mountain Dome Winery**, several vintages of méthode champenoise sparkling wine are aging at the facility awaiting the owner's approval for release. Michael Manz crafts his wines from a cuvée of Chardonnay and Pinot Noir. First release is scheduled for 1992.

As a major urban center, Spokane has a number of fine dining opportunities to please the discriminating palate. **Patsy Clark's** is a luxuriously restored mansion with fine cuisine and a good selection of Northwest wines. **Ankeny's** atop the Ridpath Hotel is another good choice, as is **Milford's Fish House and Oyster Bar**.

If you don't mind a short drive for an interesting day trip, head over to Sandpoint, Idaho, to visit the many shops and eateries along the Pend Orielle River. A visit to **Pucci Winery** is right on your way.

In the quiet southeast corner of Washington State you'll find a relaxed pace of life, friendly people and some of the nation's best Cabernet Sauvignon and Merlot. Using grapes from local vineyards and also from nearby Columbia Valley sources, the wineries of Walla Walla have won great praise for the intensity, structure and overall enjoyability of their wines.

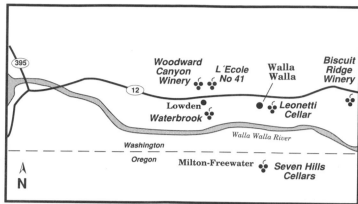

For tourists seeking to meet the winemakers behind these great wines, the area has a great Hot Air Balloon Stampede each May that coincides with the wineries' open house weekend. Come out to see the beautiful balloons soar above the wheat fields and fill in the afternoons with visits to local vintners who are normally open by appointment only. If you choose to visit later in the summer, don't miss the opportunity to pick up a bag of Walla Walla sweet onions at one of the roadside stands.

Woodward Canyon Winery is the life's passion of winemaker Rick Small and his wife Darcey. Crafting award-winning Cabernet, Chardonnay and two blended wines under the name of Charbonneau (red and white), Rick is a dedicated perfectionist who always strives to get the absolute best wine from each vintage. The unpretentious winery is across the highway from the local grain elevator, giving a hint to yet another of the area's important agricultural products.

Gary and Nancy Figgins are the proprietors of **Leonetti Cellar** just east of downtown Walla Walla. Winemaker Gary began his career as a part-time venture but now has retired from his non-wine job to devote his full energies into making Cabernet Sauvignon and Merlot. Preferring to stick to these two red varieties, Gary creates many different lots from each vintage that ultimately are combined to produce regular and reserve bottlings of great style and character.

Waterbrook Winery is the area's largest producer and has also gained a reputation for excellent Cabernet Sauvignon, Merlot, Chardonnay and Sauvignon Blanc. Their widest following has been for their regular and reserve bottlings of Chardonnay which offer the toasty, vanilla nuances of barrel fermentation and oak aging. Waterbrook has expanded hours of operation to accommodate visitors during the summer months.

L´Ecole No 41 was the labor of love of Baker and Jean Ferguson, two of the area's notable citizens who turned an old schoolhouse into one of Washington's most unique wineries. As a retirement

project, the winery held their attention for many years, but is now operated by their daughter and son-in-law, Megan and Marty Clubb. The Fergusons still contribute suggestions but are spending more time traveling and relaxing.

Eleven miles east of Walla Walla, the town of Dixie is home to **Biscuit Ridge Winery** where owner Jack Durham is busy growing and producing Pinot Noir and Gewürztraminer. A moderate microclimate in the area tends to favor these early ripening varietals. The wines are produced in a dry style with crisp acidity to accompany food.

On the Oregon side of the border, local vineyard owners Herb Hendricks and Jim McClellan have created their own label with **Seven Hills Cellars**. Jim's son, Casey McClellan, has proven a dependable winemaker having crafted Cabernet, Chardonnay and Sauvignon Blanc, as well as an award-winning Merlot.

For the gourmet visitor, a 30-mile drive is necessary to achieve culinary delight at Bruce Hiebert's **Patit Creek Restaurant** in Dayton. In the Northwest tradition, Hiebert uses fresh, local ingredients and creates delicious meals to please both local residents and visitors alike.

Oregonians point with pride to their state's tough stand on environmental issues, and this has carried into the wine industry with stringent labeling laws concerning wine origin and other issues. The center of winegrowing in Oregon is the Willamette River Valley stretching from Portland south to Eugene. This broad, fertile valley offers the advantages of warm winters free from killing freezes and a mild growing season that stretches from June through October. The climate here is perfect for Burgundian grape varieties like Pinot Noir and Chardonnay. The southern part of Oregon boasts several viticultural areas which are among the state's fastest growing.

Portland is the cultural and commerce center of Oregon and offers the largest market for all of the state's wineries. Fine dining and upscale accommodations are pluses for the visitor as well as nearby wine touring opportunites. Several wineries are in the immediate area and several more are just an hour away, near Forest Grove.

South of Portland, the Yamhill County wine country stretches from Newberg to McMinnville and offers literally dozens of wineries both large and small. The winemaking centers of Newberg, Dundee and McMinnville each have their own personality and offer the down-home style of accommodations and dining. The residents here are fiercely proud of their region for both its winemaking reputation and the unspoiled nature of the surrounding countryside.

The Eola Hills area northwest of Salem is quickly gaining a reputation for quality wines equal to those of Yamhill County. While several wineries are located deep in the hills, taking advantage of warm microclimates on southwest slopes, others are located nearer the valley floor near Rickreall, Dallas and Airlie. Oregon's capital of Salem is a nearby haven for fine meals and accommodations.

The southern Willamette Valley growing area is centered around the college towns of Corvallis (Oregon State University) and Eugene (University of Oregon). The populations of these academic centers support the local winemakers by buying their wines at the many fine local restaurants. The growing areas stretch from the valley floor up into the foothills of the Oregon Coast Range.

Southern Oregon's Umpqua River Valley and Rogue River Valley offer winegrowing climates that are slightly different than the Willamette Valley to the north. Warm summers allow the cultivation of Cabernet Sauvignon and Sauvignon Blanc as well as

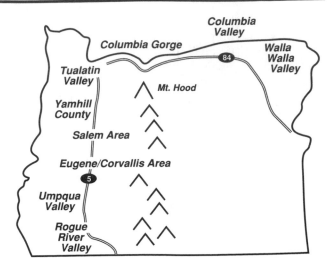

the cool weather varieties of Pinot Noir and Chardonnay. Cold winters have been known to cause freezing problems due to the high elevation of some vineyards. This area is internationally known for its fine fishing opportunities, and the Shakespearean Festival at Ashland is world-renowned.

Small pockets of winemaking activity dot other areas of the state including **Shallon Winery** at Astoria and **Nehalem Bay Winery** on the Oregon Coast. In the Molalla River Valley east of I-5 are **St. Josef's Weinkeller**, **Marquam Hill Vineyards** and **Saga Vineyards**. Other small wine operations spring up seemingly overnight so keep your eyes open for additional visiting opportunities.

As mentioned earlier in our wine touring section, carloads of wine country visitors should appoint a designated driver to refrain from wine sampling. The many stops possible, especially in Yamhill County on holiday weekends, could easily lead to dangerous overconsumption for drivers. Oregon's weather often leads to damp and slippery roads so extra caution should be observed.

The Northwest Wineries Roster, found on pages 155 - 157, will provide exact addresses and phone numbers for each winery. Plan to call ahead to check on the wineries' operating hours. An informative brochure with maps to each winery is available from The Oregon Wine Advisory Board, 1200 N.W. Front Ave., Suite 230, Portland, OR 97209.

Portland and Tualatin Valley Wine Touring

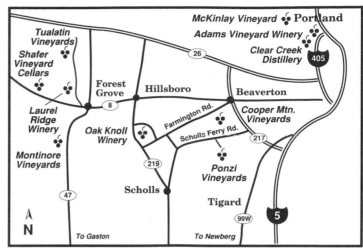

Unlike Seattle, Portland has producing vineyards as well as working wineries within a few minutes' drive of downtown. As a complement to Portland's fine hotels, restaurants and cultural activities, the local vineyard areas near Beaverton, Hillsboro and Forest Grove provide quick access to true wine country ambiance. Before leaving town for the vineyards, be aware that several facilities are right downtown. **Adams Vineyard Winery**, **McKinlay Vineyards** and **Clear Creek Distillery** all welcome visitors by prior appointment.

Peter and Carol Adams craft Pinot Noir and Chardonnay from grapes harvested at their vineyard in Yamhill County. **Adams Vineyard** wines have proved to be among the most ageable of Oregon Pinot Noirs.

Clear Creek Distillery is the project of Stephen McCarthy. His love for eau de vie brandies led to the creation of his mini-distillery producing a variety of spirits from pears, apples, raspberries and grapes.

Just south of Portland in the outskirts of Beaverton-Hillsboro are **Ponzi Vineyards**, **Cooper Mountain Vineyards** and **Oak Knoll Winery**. Dick and Nancy Ponzi are among Oregon's wine-growing pioneers, having planted their vineyard in 1970 with their first wines released in 1975. The Ponzis are now equally famed for quality Northwest microbrews crafted at their **Bridgeport Brewery** in downtown Portland.

Cooper Mountain Vineyards, owned by Bob and Corrine Gross, is a major supplier of grapes to several area wineries and recently added a winery of its own. The vineyard is located on the slopes of an extinct volcano and has a reputation for fine quality Pinot Noir, Chardonnay and Pinot Gris.

Oak Knoll Winery, another of Oregon's wine-growing pioneers, has been a moving force in the state's wine industry since the early 1970s. In addition to crafting award-winning varietals and fruit and berry wines, the Vuylsteke family hosts the Bacchus Goes Bluegrass festival each May.

An hour west of Portland, Forest Grove offers wineries both old and new with one facility boasting a winemaking history back to the 19th century. **Laurel Ridge** winery is located on the site of the original Reuter's Hill Vineyard planted by Ernest Reuter in the 1890s. The winery operated until prohibition when the entire local wine industry closed down. Revived in 1966, the property is now home to Laurel Ridge producing a line of sparkling and still wines.

Just over the hill, **Tualatin Vineyards** and **Shafer Vineyard Cellars** are both long-time area grape growers and winemakers. Bill Fuller at Tualatin has been a moving force in the Oregon wine industry for almost 20 years, producing estate-bottled wines from his 85 acre vineyard. Watch for Tualatin's Thanksgiving weekend art show and sale featuring live music, wine tasting and other holiday festivities. South of Forest Grove, **Montinore Vineyards** is a new facility that has quickly become one of Oregon's largest. Under the direction of Jeff Lamy, over 400 acres of vineyards are under cultivation. Wine production is increasing annually in an impressive winery facility constructed in 1989.

While fine wines are crafted throughout the area, it is downtown Portland that offers the absolute finest in gourmet cuisine. **The Heathman**, **Atwater's** and **Genoa** are all excellent choices for fine dining with expansive wine selections and impeccable service. For an intimate luncheon, look up **Table for Two**, Nancy Briggs and Juanita Crampton's delightful one-table eatery featuring unique cuisine and fine wines from around the state.

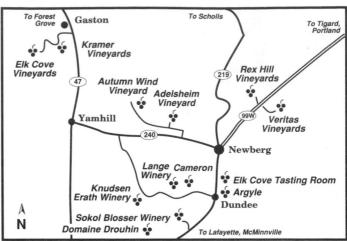

The North Yamhill County wine touring area includes the towns of Newberg and Dundee as well as the area west of the valley in the foothills of the Oregon Coast Range. Several vineyards in the Chehalem Mountains northwest of Newberg have become well known for excellent Pinot Noir and Chardonnay as have those in the Red Hills above Dundee. A very tight concentration of fine quality wineries is touring heaven for wine lovers.

North of Newberg, **Rex Hill Vineyards** and **Veritas Vineyards** wineries are located just seconds off Highway 99W, and both facilities are geared to provide an educational visit for those interested in the workings of both winery and vineyard. The wines from these two facilities are favorites among Northwest chefs and are recommended with several recipes throughout our book.

On the southwest slope of the Chehalem Mountains, **Adelsheim Vineyards** has pioneered the growing of Pinot Noir since the mid-1970s. David Adelsheim's Elizabeth's Reserve Pinot is consistently recommended as one of the state's finest wines to accompany fine food. Recently, other interested parties have selected nearby sites to grow this varietal and one other, **Autumn Wind Vineyards**, bonded their winery here in 1988.

In the foothills of the Oregon Coast Range near Gaston, Joe and Pat Campbell forged **Elk Cove Vineyards** into one of the area's most respected producers. Their vineyard-designated Pinot Noirs have won national acclaim along with late harvest wines and Chardonnay. A newcomer to this area is **Kramer Vineyards**, owned by Keith and Trudy Kramer. Their production of homegrown fruit and berry wines expanded to varietal grape wines in 1989 with the maturation of their vineyard.

The cluster of wineries around the town of Dundee includes some of the most notable names in the state. Along Worden Hill Road are the facilities of **Cameron Winery**, **Lange Winery** and **Knudsen Erath**. Dick Erath, another pioneer winemaker in Oregon, has been one of the state's largest producers for many years. John Paul of Cameron is a relative newcomer to Oregon but has quickly established a reputation for Pinot Noir and Chardonnay using grapes from his partner's Abbey Ridge Vineyard just up the hill. Don and Wendy Lange were the latest to bond a winery here and offer Pinot Noir, Chardonnay and Pinot Gris.

The **Sokol Blosser Winery** facility south of "downtown" Dundee has been an area landmark since its opening in 1988. Their striking visitor center offers views of the vineyard and valley below as well as tastes of Sokol Blosser wines and an extensive selection of gifts and goodies.

Argyle sparkling wine facility owned by Australian Brian Croser is located in the old Dundee Nut Farm building in Dundee. No tours or tasting, but the wine is available for sale at local stores and restaurants. **Domaine Drouhin Oregon** has planted vines in the Red Hills area and made some wine from purchased grapes. Look forward to their first release in 1991.

If you're planning to spend the evening in Yamhill County, check out the dining opportunities in McMinnville farther south. If you are looking for overnight accommodations in the area, Newberg's **Secluded Bed & Breakfast** is your best bet.

The southern Yamhill tour includes several facilities in or near McMinnville as well as those just north and south of town. This picturesque agricultural community is a popular weekend jaunt for Portland residents as well as a point of interest for visitors from around the country. Each summer the International Pinot Noir Celebration draws attendees from around the world to taste and discuss this most important Oregon varietal.

In the north end of the region, **Chateau Benoit** near Lafayette has been the area's largest producer of sparkling wine. Their méthode champenoise Benoit Brut was the sparkling wine that inspired other wine-makers to utilize Oregon fruit for this bubbly alternative.

In downtown McMinnville you'll find **The Eyrie Vineyards**, **Arterberry Winery** and **Panther Creek Wine Cellars**. These wineries are among the state's most respected producers of Pinot Noir, each crafting the varietal in a slightly different style. David Lett is considered to be THE pioneer grape grower for Oregon Pinot Noir. His vineyard in the hills above Dundee was planted in 1966 and from it have come wines that have challenged the best Pinots made anywhere in the world. His small winery in McMinnville is open during the Thanksgiving holiday weekend.

Arterberry Winery is right next door to The Eyrie and came to fame in a slightly different way. Fred Arterberry, Jr. began by making sparkling apple cider that evolved into a champagne-style sparkling wine and finally still wines from Pinot Noir, Chardonnay and Riesling. Nearby **Panther Creek Wine Cellars** specializes in making full-bodied, intense Pinot Noir. Winemaker Ken Wright has strong feelings about the style of wine he wants to make and many Pinot lovers applaud his election to use extended skin contact and warm fermentation temperatures.

Just south of downtown McMinnville, **Yamhill Valley Vineyards** is an impressive facility (great for a picnic) that offers some unique wines like their Elder Blossom Riesling. This aromatic wine is scented with extract of elder blossoms, creating a bouquet similar to that found in some late harvest wines. The winery also crafts quality Pinot Noir, Chardonnay and other varietals.

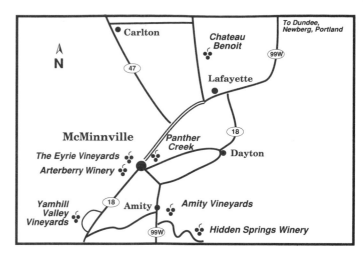

The north end of the Eola Hills is home to **Amity Vineyards** and **Hidden Springs Winery**. Amity's Myron Redford is well known for his fine quality Winemaker's Reserve Pinot Noir and for his efforts in promoting Oregon's wine industry both at home and abroad. The winery has recently expanded and improved their visitor facilities. Hidden Springs is located in a renovated fruit warehouse in the picturesque Eola Hills. Adjacent orchards were removed to make room for grape vines.

Dining in McMinnville offers several attractive alternatives. Most famous of any Oregon wine country restaurant is **Nick's Italian Cafe** in downtown McMinnville. Nick Peirano offers innovative Italian cuisine utilizing the best and freshest of local ingredients. Also in McMinnville, try **Roger's Seafood Restaurant**. For McMinnville accommodations, both the **Mattey House B & B** and **Steiger House B & B** take pride in serving wine country visitors in style and comfort.

The Eola Hills growing area has recently seen a surge in popularity with those seeking quality Pinot Noir grapes and also those seeking to acquire land for future vineyards. Land sales to California interests are becoming regular, if not commonplace, occurences in Oregon, and currently the Eola Hills is the hot location.

The best-known producer in this area is **Bethel Heights Vineyard** just off Zena Road. Brothers Ted and Terry Casteel, and their spouses, Pat Dudley and Marilyn Webb, take an enthusiastic interest in the winery and vineyard and are producing some of the best food-styled wines in Oregon. The production of their vineyard is large and you'll find Bethel Heights grapes in the blends of many area wines.

Just east of Bethel Heights, **Pellier Mirassou Winery** brings a relative of the California Mirassous to Oregon to grow Pinot Noir instead of Cabernet. Mitch and Bev Mirassou welcome visitors to their operation daily. A little farther up Spring Valley Road is **Witness Tree Vineyard** where airline pilot Douglas Gentzkow has begun his winemaking venture with assistance from winemaker Rick Nunes.

Russ and Mary Raney are the proprietors of **Evesham Wood Vineyard** in association with Tom Robbins of Redhawk Vineyard just off Wallace Road in West Salem. The Raneys named their winery after a location in England they visited on their honeymoon in 1984. Wines produced include Pinot Noir and Chardonnay.

Schwarzenberg Vineyards is near the junction of Highways 22 and 99W, perched on a hill over-looking the Basket Slough Wildlife Refuge. Helmut and Helga Schwarz planted their vineyard in 1981 with the first wines released in 1987. Just north on Highway 99W, Wayne Flynn is now working with winemaker Rich Cushman to craft sparkling wine at **Flynn Vineyards**. Construction of a winery and tasting room are underway.

Two winery operations in downtown Salem deserve mention. **Honeywood Winery** has been in business since the 1930s, making fruit and berry wines for the pleasure of the local wine lovers with a sweet tooth. Recent production of grape wines of Pinot Noir and Chardonnay reflects the change in local consuming habits. A sparkling new venture in Salem is **St. Innocent Winery**. While owner Mark

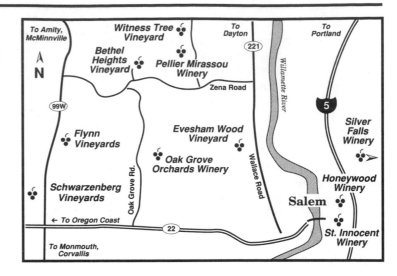

Vlossak is aging his sparkling, méthode champe-noise wine on the lees, he is selling Pinot Noir and Chardonnay through local outlets.

The fine dining scene in Salem has had its ups and downs over the years with many residents preferring to drive to McMinnville to visit Nick's for a premium food and wine experience. Hans d'Allessio's **Inn at Orchard Heights** is a bright spot for local diners however, as is **The Terrarium.** If you're seeking picnic fare, try **Sally's Market Basket** deli near downtown. For a pleasant over-night stay, look up the **State House B & B** near Willamette University.

The southern part of Polk County and the area south of Salem along Interstate 5 offer many wine touring opportunities. Grapes are grown on-site at many of these properties, providing a chance to observe vineyard practices or even the fall grape harvest if your visit is timely.

Just off I-5 near the Enchanted Village amusement park is the new **Willamette Valley Vineyards**, Oregon's first consumer-owned winery. Through a stock offering during 1989 the corporation raised $1.5 million and constructed a state of the art winery and visitor center. Winemaker for the venture is talented veteran Bob McRitchie.

Across the freeway and a little farther south, a winding route leads to **Ankeny Vineyard**. This rustic facility is located on one of Oregon's oldest homesteads with the barn on the property dating to 1847. The massive 16-inch fir beams are joined with mortise and tenons, while smaller members are held with wooden pegs. Owner Joe Olexa invites visitors to enjoy their picnic lunch under the spreading oak tree next to the tasting room.

A few miles west across the valley, along Highway 99W, you'll find **Ellendale Winery's** tasting room and **Eola Hills Wine Cellars** in the town of Rickreall. Ellendale's owner/winemaker Robert Hudson crafts both varietal and fruit wines and has recently expanded to sparkling wine production. His fruit wine blend labeled "Woolly Booger" sports a label with a caricature of a grizzly-faced '49er caterpillar – ask the staff for the story behind this amusing wine.

Tom Huggins' **Eola Hills Wine Cellars** is just up the highway and offers a grassy picnic area, wine tasting and a view into the working winery. Grapes for the winery come from Huggins' Oak Grove Vineyard in the Eola Hills about 5 miles northeast of the winery. Current production includes Pinot Noir, Chardonnay, Chenin Blanc and other varietals.

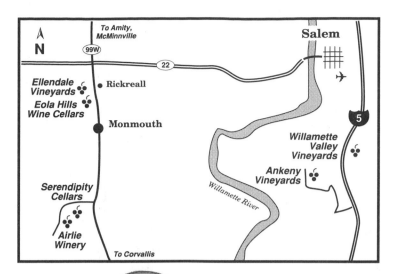

The final two stops in this region are **Serendipity Cellars** and **Airlie Winery**. Located just a stone's throw apart on Dunn Forest Road southwest of Monmouth, these two facilities offer distinctly different approaches to attract tourists. Larry and Alice Preedy of Airlie Winery offer a blue grass festival each Memorial Day weekend to liven up the area with foot-stompin' music to accompany wine tasting. The Longshore family of Serendipity Cellars host several summer events of which their Scottish Festival and August Star-Gazing parties are the most popular.

Corvallis and Eugene Area Wine Touring

The southern Willamette Valley has long been an agricultural center for many of Oregon's well-known crops. Dairy farming, orchards of nuts and fruits, and now vineyards have all contributed to the economic well-being of the region. The college towns of Corvallis and Eugene inject an air of academia and intellectual interest into the fast-growing local wine industry.

Spring Hill Cellars near Albany is one of the area's newest operations. Owners Mike McLain and Gary Budd produce small quantities of Pinot Noir, Chardonnay and Riesling for local distribution.

Southwest of Corvallis, two family-operated wineries cultivate grapes near the rolling foothills of Oregon's Coast Range. Dave and Margy Buchanan teamed up with OSU viticultural researcher Barney Watson and his wife Nola Mosier to form **Tyee Wine Cellars**. Vines planted on the Buchanan's Century Farm provide Pinot Noir, Pinot Gris and Gewürztraminer for the winery's enological efforts.

Nearby **Bellfountain Cellars** is the project of Jeanne and Robert Mommsen. Their production includes a majority of Pinot Noir, although Chardonnay, Sauvignon Blanc, Riesling and Gewürztraminer are also made.

In the Eugene area, several wineries have been growing grapes and making wine for a decade or longer. Dan Jepson's **Alpine Vineyards** is located in a bowl-shaped site that provides warm temperatures for ripening grapes more reliably than more exposed locations. Pinot Noir, Chardonnay and Riesling, as well as a small annual bottling of Cabernet, have all contributed to Alpine's reputation for fine wines. Close to the highway in Monroe, **Broadley Vineyards** concentrates on a hearty style of Pinot Noir as well as Chardonnay.

Two facilities west of Eugene have extensive vineyards and large production volumes. **Forgeron Vineyards** near Elmira is the area's oldest operator and produces almost 20,000 gallons a year of Pinot Noir, Chardonnay, Cabernet Sauvignon, Riesling and other varieties.

Hinman Vineyards southwest of Eugene makes wine from grapes harvested at two vineyards. The estate vineyard at the winery is a large operation in its own right, but the large Boardman Farms in Eastern Oregon's portion of the Columbia Valley appellation provides an even larger amount of fruit. The production includes Chardonnay, Riesling, Pinot Noir and White Pinot Noir.

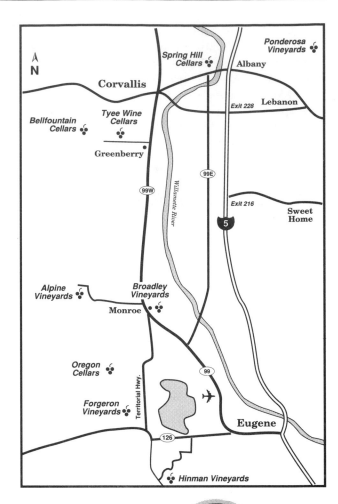

Wining and dining opportunities are better in Eugene than in Oregon's capital city of Salem. Many fine restaurants cater to the faculty of the University of Oregon and to the broad base of support staff and students. For a fine French meal you can always count on **L 'Auberge**, while for less formal lunches or dinners visit **Cafe Central** or **Leah's Wine Company**.

Umpqua Valley Wine Touring

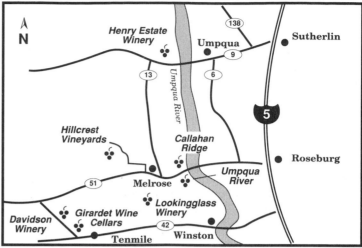

When Richard Sommer came to the Roseburg area in 1961, he had firm convictions about the suitability of the climate and soils of the region for grape growing. His first efforts were successful, but slightly ahead of their time. Today, a half-dozen wineries are prospering in the Umpqua River basin.

Sommer's **Hillcrest Vineyard** is one of these, located on the western edge of town with a large, well-established vineyard and rustic winery. His belief that most wines are released too young results in his bottlings arriving at market about a year later than most wines from the same vintage. The increase in complexity and character is noticeable. Hillcrest's flagship wine has been Riesling with several wine styles made depending on the vintage. Late harvest versions are very long lived and are among the best available in the Northwest.

Just north of Roseburg, **Henry Estate** winery has become the area's largest producer bottling over 10,000 cases annually. Three generations of the Henry family participate in the winery's operation and produce Pinot Noir, Chardonnay, Cabernet Sauvignon, Riesling, Gewürztraminer and other varietals. Recent additions to the winery have increased production and improved facilities for visitors.

Callahan Ridge Winery is the domain of Richard Mansfield, a strong-spirited individualist who crafts a wide selection of varietals. His personal favorite is Riesling, a variety he studied in depth during his winemaking training in Germany. The rustic, barn-like winery and tasting room are an interesting visit just west of the Garden Valley shopping center.

Swiss-born Philippe Girardet and his wife Bonnie are transplanted academicians who came from California in the 1970s to pursue a more natural lifestyle. Their **Girardet Vineyards** southwest of Roseburg has provided a healthful way of life and a feeling of working with the land to create a natural and traditional product. Their Chardonnay, Pinot Noir and other varietals are joined by Philippe's blended wines Vin Blanc and Vin Rouge that have gained a wide following.

Just west of Girardet is **Davidson Winery**, the reincarnation of Bjelland Vineyard. Guy and Sandra Davidson came north from San Francisco to pursue their dream of owning a winery. Purchase of more modern equipment and additional storage tanks has increased production level and improved quality. The former Bjelland facility was known for a mix of varietals and fruit and berry wines. The Davidsons plan to concentrate on the traditional grape wines of Pinot Noir and Chardonnay.

Recent winemaking newcomers to the Roseburg area include **Lookingglass Winery** near Winston and **Umpqua River Winery** in Roseburg near Callahan Ridge Winery.

Rogue River Valley and Southern Oregon Wine Touring

The towns of Grants Pass, Cave Junction, Jacksonville and Ashland have become an unlikely circular wine route through Southern Oregon. All these places are well known for other activities but now share quality Oregon wine production as a common bond.

Rogue River Vineyards in Grants Pass is the most unusual of the area's wineries. In addition to blending sparkling wine coolers from wine and fruit juice, the winery's wood shop crafts wine racks, planters and even wooden store displays for California's Fetzer winery.

The area around Cave Junction has become the most promising of Southern Oregon's wine sub-regions. The Illinois Valley, as it is called, is home to three successful wineries. **Siskiyou Vineyards** holds tenure as the oldest of the three, producing Cabernet Sauvignon, Pinot Noir, Chardonnay and other varietals from their vineyard planted in 1974. Nearby **Foris Vineyards** is the project of Ted and Meri Gerber and produces Pinot Noir, Muscat and Chardonnay from their estate vineyard and from purchased grapes. The estate vineyard is planted on a rocky area of mine tailings from a 19th century gold mine operation. Ted Gerber believes the extra effort required of the vines to seek nutrients in this gravelly soil produces better grapes.

The Illinois Valley's largest venture into grape growing and winemaking is **Bridgeview Vineyards**. Their impressive 74 acre vineyard is completely surrounded by 8 foot high chain link fence to keep the deer out and is planted with site selection for particular varietals in mind. Winemaker Laurent Montelieu has proven his talent at utilizing the fruit of the vineyard to produce award-winning Pinot Noir, Gewürztraminer, Chardonnay and other varietals.

On the way to Jacksonville from Cave Junction is **Valley View Vineyards** near the town of Ruch. The Wisnovsky family has operated this winery since 1972 and concentrates on Cabernet Sauvignon, Merlot and Chardonnay. Their microclimate along the Applegate River provides the heat necessary to ripen these warm-weather varietals. Their winery tasting room is augmented by an additional outlet in Jacksonville.

Ashland's two wineries are new but their dedicated owners are committed to quality in both grape growing and winemaking. **Weisinger's Vineyard** operates their Chalet-style winery on the south edge of town offering tastes of their most recent bottlings. **Ashland Vineyards**, owned by

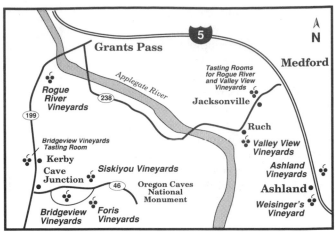

Bill Knowles, is across the freeway and adjacent to the Ashland airport. This is appropriate since Knowles and his son Mark are both commercial pilots. Mark serves as winemaker for the operation crafting a broad selection of varietals.

The best dining in Southern Oregon is in Ashland where the throngs attending the Shakespeare Festival demand fine cuisine to accompany their weekend visits to the theater. Make your reservations early for the three best: **Chateaulin**, **Winchester Inn** and **Change of Heart**. Closer to the heart of the wine country, the **Jacksonville Inn** is a combination B & B and restaurant that caters to the tourists visiting Oregon's gold rush town. An excellent place to dine, but somewhat crowded on weekends and during the summer season.

Idaho Wine Touring

The fertile valley along the Snake River in southern Idaho is a well-known agricultural area with rich soils and ample water for producing a wide range of crops. Apples, pears, sugar beets and potatoes have been the dependable commodities for over 100 years but recently have yielded some acreage to wine grapes.

Although other Idaho winery operations are up and coming, **Ste. Chapelle Vineyards** dominates the Idaho wine scene with its huge production and commitment to quality. Talented winemaker Mimi Mook has continued the award-winning tradition of Ste. Chapelle by crafting quality Cabernet Sauvignon, Chardonnay, Riesling and other varietals, as well as a broad line of Charmat process and méthode champenoise sparkling wines. Grapes for the operation come from the Symms family's 190 acres of prime vineyard nearby and also from selected Washington vineyards.

In the same area as Ste. Chapelle are **Weston Winery**, **Pintler Cellars** and **Hell's Canyon Winery**. Cheyne Weston is the owner and winemaker at his namesake winery and produces Chardonnay, Cabernet Sauvignon, Riesling and Sauvignon Blanc. His attractive labels featuring scenes of outdoor life in Idaho are designed by his brother, Jeff.

Brad and Stacy Pintler are the husband and wife team behind **Pintler Cellars**. Foregoing many of the typical varietals found in Idaho vineyards, they are concentrating mostly on Cabernet Sauvignon and Semillon. Although their other varietals have been well-received it is these two Bordeaux varieties that hold the fascination of the owners. The vineyard is located near the Snake River at Marsing.

Another winemaker that has situated in the Snake River area is Steve Robertson. His **Hell's Canyon Winery** has released several wines that have been well-received on the international market. The five acre vineyard at his home produces grapes for his varietal bottlings of Cabernet Sauvignon and Chardonnay.

Indian Creek Winery near Kuna competes with Oregon wineries for the making of quality Pinot Noir. Retired Air Force officer Bill Stowe has a fondness for that varietal and his dedication has been rewarded with several medals. His 18 acre vineyard is not in the same area as the larger Idaho operations, but his success with the cultivation of Pinot Noir, Chardonnay and Riesling has been encouraging.

Further east at Hagerman, Jamie and Susan Martin operate **Rose Creek Vineyards** in one of the most beautiful areas of the Snake River Canyon.

The sunset-hued rimrock canyon walls are the theme for their label and a major point of interest to tourists who travel through the area. Many of the visitors stop by the winery in downtown Hagerman to taste some wine and visit with the Martins. Jamie's winemaking efforts include Cabernet Sauvignon, Chardonnay, Riesling and Pinot Noir (made from Oregon grapes). Their wines have been widely praised as being excellent accompaniments to food.

Just across the Washington-Idaho border from Pullman is the town of Moscow, home to **Camas Winery**. The hobby of Stuart and Susan Scott, their production includes several varietal releases and the whimsical Hog Heaven Red and Hog Heaven White. The name comes from the belief that hogs enjoy digging up the local camas roots (a staple starch for early native Americans) and the abundance of the plant in the area led early settlers to call it Hog Heaven. A fun pair of wines with an amusing label.

In Idaho's panhandle near Sand Point, Skip and Nancy Pucci are the owners of **Pucci Winery**. Trained in the Italian family tradition of winemaking, Skip ferments all the wines in barrel. His wines are available at the winery or at local restaurants.

Northwest Microbreweries

The Pacific Northwest has established itself as one of the centers for "craft brewing" in the United States. The small producers here create small batches of ales, stouts, porters and lagers to quench the thirst of local residents and a little extra to ship to limited out-of-the-Northwest markets. The size of most of these operations was accurately summed-up by the tour guide at Seattle's Red Hook Brewery as he stated "Budweiser makes more beer every hour than we brew in a year." A startling fact, but true.

The first of the commercial sized operations to take hold in the Northwest were the Red Hook Brewery in Seattle and Yakima Brewing and Malting in Yakima. The latter firm is better known by the name of the owner and most successful product, Grant's Ale.

The **Red Hook Brewery** operation began in a small building in Ballard creating a copper colored ale (Red Hook) and a porter-style dark ale (Black Hook). Red Hook seemed to have a mind of its own in that every fourth or fifth batch came out with a distinct banana aroma. Ordering a "banana-beer" at many Seattle pubs was clearly understood. The problems with Red Hook Ale have been solved and, wisely, the company renamed the product ESB. Today the brewery is in larger quarters and offers Ballard Bitter, ESB, Black Hook, Wheat Hook and Winter Hook Christmas Ale. Stop by The Trolley-man Pub at Red Hook's new location in Fremont for a tour and a sampling of their latest brews.

Bert Grant's **Yakima Brewing** became famous for their draft product Grant's Scottish Ale. Though other ales have been introduced, non have achieved the success of the original. The best of the rest are Imperial Russian Stout, India Pale Ale (IPA) and White Bear (wheat beer). We prefer the draft product every time to the bottled versions. Bert Grant recently opened a larger and more pleasing brewpub in the retired Yakima Railway Station. Join the locals for a game of traditional darts or just a pint of cask-conditioned ale.

Another of the microbrew pioneers was Mike Hale of **Hale's Ales** in Colville, Washington. Mike was studying brewing techniques in England when he heard of the openings of Grant's and Red Hook. He immediately returned home to begin his business of crafting fine pale ale and other British-type varieties. His current offerings are Pale Ale, Special Bitter and Celebration Porter. A demonstration brewery is located on Central Avenue in Kirkland.

Portland has been a center for brewing for over one hundred years with the Weinhard brewery and other smaller operations. The Ponzi family of Oregon winemaking fame established **Bridgeport Brewing Company** in downtown Portland in 1984. Their Bridgeport Golden Ale (pale ale) and Bridge-port Ale (amber ale) were among the first products offered and continue to be popular. Two later products, their Blue Heron Bitter and Bridgeport Stout are among our current favorites. Seasonal ales have also been popular with fans of this brewery. Winterbrew strong ale, Spring Draught copper ale and Summer Wheat are very appealing with each season. The Bridgeport pub in downtown Portland does a rousing business and offers a glass wall into the brewery for viewing the beermaking activity.

To serve the wind surfers in the Columbia Gorge, the **Hood River Brewery** was begun in 1987. Located in the renovated Diamond Fruit Cannery overlooking the river, HRB produces Full Sail Pale Ale, Full Sail Amber Ale, Main Sail Brown Ale and Top Sail Porter. The view across the river from the brew pub is marvelous. These brews are great accompaniments to food.

One of the most recent breweries to open was the **Pike Place Brewery** in Seattle. A joint venture between Charles Finkel and John Farias, the brewery produces limited quantities of Pale Ale and XXXXX Stout for the Seattle market. Both are good beers to accompany hearty fare.

Many other breweries and brewpubs have opened their doors in the Northwest since Bert Grant and Paul Shipman (Red Hook) took the first daring steps in 1982. We've listed our favorites and invite you to try the ones nearest your home or any you might find on your travels. Cheers!

Oregon Wineries

Adams Vineyard Winery
1922 N.W. Pettygrove St.
Portland, OR 97209
503-294-0606

Adelsheim Vineyards
22150 N.E. Quarter Mile Lane
Newberg, OR 97132
503-538-3652

Airlie Winery
15305 Dunn Forest Road
Monmouth, OR 97361
503-838-6013

Alpine Vineyards
25904 Green Peak Rd.
Monroe, OR 97456
503-424-5851

Amity Vineyards
18150 Amity Vineyards Rd. S.E.
Amity, OR 97101
503-835-2362

Ankeny Vineyards
2565 Riverside Road South
Salem, OR 97306
503-362-2508

Argyle
691 Highway 99W
Dundee, OR 97115
503-538-8520

Arterberry Wine Cellars
905 East 10th St.
McMinnville, OR 97128
503-472-1587

Ashland Vineyards
2775 East Main St.
Ashland, OR 97520
503-488-0088

Autumn Wind Vineyard
15225 North Valley Rd.
Newberg, OR 97132
503-538-6931

Bellfountain Cellars
25041 Llewllyn Road
Corvallis, OR 97333
503-929-3162

Bethel Heights Vineyard
6060 Bethel Heights Rd. N.W.
Salem, OR 97304
503-581-2262

Bridgeview Vineyard
4210 Holland Loop Road
Cave Junction, OR 97523
503-592-4688

Broadley Vineyards
265 South 5th
Monroe, OR 97456
503-847-5934

Callahan Ridge Winery
340 Busenbark Lane
Roseburg, OR 97470
503-673-7901

Cameron Winery
8200 Worden Hill Road
Dundee, OR 97115
503-538-0336

Chateau Benoit
6580 N.E. Mineral Springs Rd.
Carlton, OR 97111
503-864-2991

Clear Creek Distillery
1430 N.E. 23rd Ave.
Portland, OR 97210
503-248-9470

Cooper Mountain Vineyard
Rt. 3, Box 1036
Beaverton, OR 97007
503-649-0027

Davidson Winery
2637 Reston Road
Roseburg, OR 97470
503-679-6950

Domaine Drouhin Oregon
P.O. Box 700
Dundee, OR 97115
503-864-2700

Elk Cove Vineyards
27751 N.W. Olson Rd.
Gaston, OR 97119
503-985-7760

Ellendale Vineyards
300 Reuben Boise Rd.
Dallas, OR 97338
503-623-5617

Eola Hills Wine Cellars
501 S. Pacific Hwy. W.
Rickreall, OR 97371
503-623-2405

Evesham Woods
2995 Michigan City Ave.
West Salem, OR 97304
503-371-8478

The Eyrie Vineyards
935 East 10th St.
McMinnville, OR 97128
503-472-6315

Flynn Vineyards
2095 Cadle Road
Rickreall, OR 97371
503-623-6505

Forgeron Vineyards
89697 Sheffler Road
Elmira, OR 97437
503-935-1117

Foris Vineyards
654 Kendall Road
Cave Junction, OR 97523
503-592-3752

Girardet Wine Cellars
895 Reston Rd.
Roseburg, OR 97470
503-679-7252

Henry Estate Winery
687 Hubbard Creek Road
Umpqua, OR 97486
503-459-5120

Hidden Springs
9360 S.E. Eola Hills Rd.
Amity, OR 97101
503-835-2782

Hillcrest Vineyards
240 Vineyard Lane
Roseburg, OR 97470
503-673-3709

Hinman Vineyards
27012 Briggs Hill Road
Eugene, OR 97405
503-345-1945

Honeywood Winery
1350 Hines St. S.E.
Salem, OR 97302
503-362-4111

Hood River Vineyards
4693 Westwood Drive
Hood River, OR 97031
503-386-3772

Knudsen Erath
17000 N.E. Knudsen Lane
Dundee, OR 97115
503-538-3318

Kramer Vineyards
26830 N. W. Olson Road
Gaston, OR 97119
503-662-4545

Lange Winery
18380 N.E. Buena Vista
Dundee, OR 97115
503-538-6476

Laurel Ridge Winery
Rt. 1, Box 255, David Hill Road
Forest Grove, OR 97116
503-359-5436

Lookingglass Winery
6561 Lookingglass Road
Roseburg, OR 97470
503-679-8198

Marquam Hill Vineyards
35803 S. Hwy. 213
Molalla, OR 97038
503-829-6677

McKinlay Vineyard
10610 N.W. St. Helens Road
Portland, OR 97231
503-285-3896

Mirassou Cellars
6785 Spring Valley Rd. N.W.
Salem, OR 97304
503-371-3001

Montinore Vineyards
P.O. Box 560 - Dilley Road
Forest Grove, OR 97116
503-359-5012

Mt. Hood Winery
Government Camp Road
Mt. Hood, OR 97041
503-272-0209

Nehalem Bay Wine Co.
34965 Hwy. 53
Nehalem Bay, OR 97131
503-368-5300

Oak Grove Orchards
6090 Crowley Road
Rickreall, OR 97371
503-364-7052

Oak Knoll Winery
29700 S.W. Burkhalter Road
Hillsboro, OR 97123
503-648-8198

Oregon Cellars Winery
9289 Templeton
Cheshire, OR 97419
503-998-1786

Panther Creek Cellars
1501 E. 14th St.
McMinnville, OR 97128
503-472-8080

Ponderosa Vineyards
39538 Griggs Drive
Lebanon, OR 97355
503-259-3845

Ponzi Vineyards
Route 1, Box 842
Beaverton, OR 97007
503-628-1227

Rex Hill Winery
30835 N. Hwy. 99W
Newberg, OR 97132
503-538-0666

Rogue River Vineyards
3145 Helms Rd.
Grants Pass, OR 97527
503-476-1051

Saga Vineyards
30815 South Wall St.
Colton, OR 97017
503-824-4600

St. Innocent Winery
2701-22nd St. S.E.
Salem, OR 97302
503-378-1526

St. Josef's Weinkeller
28836 S. Barlow Rd.
Canby, OR 97013
503-651-3190

Schwarzenberg Vineyards
11975 Smithfield Road
Dallas, OR 97338
503-623-6420

Serendipity Cellars
15275 Dunn Forest Rd.
Monmouth, OR 97361
503-838-4284

Seven Hills Cellars
235 East Broadway
Milton Freewater, OR 97862
509-529-3943

Shafer Vineyard Cellars
Star Route, Box 269
Forest Grove, OR 97116
503-357-6604

Shallon Winery
1598 Duane St.
Astoria, OR 97103
503-325-5978

Silver Falls Winery
4972 Cascade Hwy. S.E.
Sublimity, OR 97385
503-769-9463

Siskiyou Vineyards
6220 Oregon Caves Hwy.
Cave Junction, OR 97523
503-592-3727

Sokol Blosser
5000 Sokol Blosser Ln.
Dundee, OR 97115
503-864-2282

Spring Hill Cellars
2920 N.W. Scenic Dr.
Albany, OR 97321
503-928-1009

*Continued
Next Page*

Oregon Wineries *continued*

Tempest Vineyards
9342 N.E. Hancock Drive
Portland, OR 97220
503-538-2733

Three Rivers Winery
275 Country Club Rd.
Hood River, OR 97031
503-386-5453

Tualatin Vineyards
Rt. 1, Box 339
Forest Grove, OR 97116
503-357-5005

Tyee Wine Cellars
26335 Greenberry Road
Corvallis, OR 97333
503-753-8754

Umpqua River Vineyards
451 Hess
Roseburg, OR 97470
503-673-1975

Valley View Vineyards
1000 Applegate Rd.
Jacksonville, OR 97530
503-899-8468

Veritas Vineyards
31190 N.E. Veritas Ln.
Newberg, OR 97132
503-538-1470

Wasson Brothers Winery
41901 Highway 26
Sandy, OR 97055
503-668-3124

Weisinger's Vineyard
3150 Siskiyou Blvd.
Ashland, OR 97520
503-488-5989

Willamette Valley Vineyards
8800 Enchanted Way S.E.
Turner, OR 97392
503-588-9463

Witness Tree Vineyard
7111 Spring Valley Road N.W.
Salem, OR 97304
503-585-7874

Yamhill Valley Vineyards
16250 S.W. Oldsville Rd.
McMinnville, OR 97128
503-843-3100

Washington Wineries

Arbor Crest Winery
N. 4705 Fruithill Road
Spokane, WA 99207
509-927-9894

Badger Mountain Vineyard
110 Jurupa
Kennewick, WA 99337
509-627-4986

Bainbridge Island Winery
682 Hwy. 305 NE
Bainbridge Island, WA 98110
206-842-9463

Barnard Griffin Winery
1707 West 8th Place
Kennewick, WA 99336

Biscuit Ridge Winery
Rt. 1, Box 132
Waitsburg, WA 99361
509-529-4986

Blackwood Canyon
Rt. 2, Box 2169H
Benton City, WA 99320
509-588-6249

Bonair Winery
500 South Bonair Rd.
Zillah, WA 98953
509-829-6027

Bookwalter Winery
2708 Commercial Ave.
Pasco, WA 99301
509-547-8571

Cascade Estates Winery
111 East Lincoln Ave.
Sunnyside, WA 98944
509-839-9463

Cascade Mountain Cellars
606 W. Third
Ellensburg, WA 98926
509-925-2998

Cavatappi Winery
9702 N.E. 120th Place
Kirkland, WA 98034
206-823-6533

Champs de Brionne
98 Road West N.W.
Quincy, WA 98848
509-785-6685

Chateau Gallant
S. 1355 Gallant Rd.
Pasco, WA 99301
509-545-9570

Chateau Ste. Michelle
One Stimson Lane
Woodinville, WA 98072
206-488-1133

Chinook Wines
Wine Country Road
Prosser, WA 99350
509-786-2725

Columbia Crest Winery
P.O. Box 231
Paterson, WA 99345
509-875-2061

Columbia Winery
14030 N.E. 145th
Woodinville, WA 98072
206-488-2776

Coolen Wine Cellars
5759 Banner Road S.E.
Port Orchard, WA 98366
206-871-0567

Coventry Vale
P.O. Box 249
Grandview, WA 98930
509-882-4100

Covey Run Winery
1500 Vintage Rd.
Zillah, WA 98953
509-829-6235

Covey Run at Moss Bay
107 Central Way
Kirkland , WA 98033
206-828-3848

E. B. Foote Winery
9354-4th Ave. S.
Seattle, WA 98126
206-763-9928

Eaton Hill Winery
530 Gurley Road
Granger, WA 98932
509-854-2508

Facelli Winery
16120-Woodinville-Redmond
Road N.E., Suite 1
Woodinville, WA 98072
206-488-1020

Fidalgo Island Winery
5303 Doon Way
Anacortes, WA 98221
206-293-4342

French Creek Cellars
17721-132nd Ave. N.E.
Woodinville, WA 98072
206-486-1900

Gordon Brothers Cellars
531 Levey Road
Pasco, WA 99301
509-547-6224

Hinzerling Vineyards
1520 Sheridan
Prosser, WA 99350
509-786-2163

The Hogue Cellars
Wine Country Road
Prosser, WA 99350
509-786-4557

Hoodsport Winery
N. 23501 Highway 101
Hoodsport, WA 98548
206-877-9894

Hooper Family Winery
196 Spring Creek Road
Husum, WA 98623
509-493-2324

Horizon's Edge Winery
4530 E. Zillah Drive
Zillah, WA 98953
509-829-6401

Hunter Hill Vineyards
2752 W. McMannaman Rd.
Othello, WA 99344
509-346-2607

Hyatt Vineyards
2020 Gilbert Road
Zillah, WA 98953
509-829-6333

Johnson Creek Winery
19248 Johnson Creek Rd. S.E.
Tenino, WA 98589
206-264-2100

Kiona Vineyards Winery
Rt. 2, Box 2169E
Benton City, WA 99320
509-588-6716

L'Ecole No 41
41 Lowden School Rd.
Lowden, WA 99360
509-525-0940

Latah Creek Wine Cellars
E. 13030 Indiana
Spokane, WA 99216
509-926-0164

Leonetti Cellar
1321 School Ave.
Walla Walla, WA 99362
509-525-1428

Livingstone Cellars
East 14 Mission
Spokane, WA 99202
509-328-5069

Lost Mountain Winery
730 Lost Mountain Road
Sequim, WA 98382
206-683-5229

McCrea Cellars
12707 - 18th St. S.E.
Lake Stevens, WA 98258
206-334-5248

Mercer Ranch Vineyards
522 Alderdale Rd.
Prosser, WA 99350
509-894-4741

Mont Elise Vineyards
315 W. Steuben
Bingen, WA 98605
509-493-3001

Mount Baker Winery
4298 Mount Baker Hwy.
Deming, WA 98244
206-592-2300

Mountain Dome Winery
Rt. 2, Box 199M
Spokane, WA 99207
509-922-7408

Neuharth Winery
148 Still Road
Sequim, WA 98382
206-683-9652

Oakwood Cellars
Rt. 2, Box 2321
Benton City, WA 99320
509-588-5332

Washington Wineries *continued*

Pacific Crest Wine Cellars
1326 - 6th St.
Marysville, WA 98270
206-653-3925

Pontin del Roza
Rt. 4, Box 4735
Prosser, WA 99350
509-786-4449

Portteus Vineyards
5201 Highland Drive
Zillah, WA 98953
509-829-6970

Preston Wine Cellars
502 E. Vineyard Dr.
Pasco, WA 99301
509-545-1990

Quarry Lake Vintners
2520 Commercial Ave.
Pasco, WA 99301
509-547-7307

Quilceda Creek Vintners
5226 Machias Road
Snohomish, WA 98290
206-568-2389

Saddle Mountain Winery
2340 Winery Rd.
Mattawa, WA 99344
509-932-4943

Salishan Vineyards
Rt. 2, Box 8
La Center, WA 98629
206-263-2713

Salmon Bay Winery
13416-NE 177th Place
Woodinville, WA 98072
206-483-9463

Seth Ryan Winery
681 South 40th'
West Richland, WA 99352
509-375-0486

Silver Lake Winery
17616 15th Ave. S.E.
Bothell, WA 98012
206-485-2437

Snoqualmie Winery
1000 Winery Rd.
Snoqualmie, WA 98065
206-888-4000

Staton Hills - Wapato
71 Gangl Road
Wapato, WA 98951
509-877-2112

Staton Hills - Seattle
1910 Post Alley
Seattle, WA 98101
206-443-8084

Stewart Vineyards
1711 Cherry Hill Road
Sunnyside, WA 98944
509-854-1882

Tagaris Vineyards
1016 South Broadway
Othello, WA 99344
509-488-3321

Paul Thomas Wines
1717 - 136th Pl NE
Bellevue, WA 98005
206-747-1008

Tucker Cellars
Rt. 1, Box 1696
Sunnyside, WA 98944
509-837-8701

Vashon Winery
12629 S.W. Cemetery Road
Vashon Island, WA 98070
206-463-9092

Manfred Vierthaler Winery
17136 Hwy. 410 E.
Sumner, WA 98390
206-863-1633

Waterbrook Winery
Rt. 1, Box 46 - McDonald Road
Lowden, WA 99360
509-522-1918

Wenatchee Valley Vineyards
1111 S. Vansickle
East Wenatchee, WA 98802
509-884-8235

Whidbeys Greenbank Farm
Hwy. 525 at Wonn Road
Whidbey Island, WA 98253
206-678-7700

Whittlesey Mark Winery
5318 22nd Ave. N.W.
Seattle, WA 98117
206-328-5619

Woodward Canyon
Rt. 1, Box 387
Lowden, WA 99360
509-525-4129

Worden Winery
7217 W. 45th
Spokane, WA 99202
509-455-7835

Yakima River Winery
Rt. 1, Box 1657
Prosser, WA 99350
509-786-2805

Zillah Oakes Winery
Exit 52, Interstate 82
Zillah, WA 98953
509-829-6235

Idaho Wineries

Camas Winery
521 North Moore St.
Moscow, ID 83843
208-882-0214

Hell's Canyon Winery
18835 Symms Road
Caldwell, ID 83605
208-336-2277

Indian Creek Winery
1000 N. McDermott Rd.
Kuna, ID 83634
208-922-4791

Pintler Winery
13750 Surrey Lane
Nampa, ID 83686
208-467-1200

Pucci Winery
1055 Garfield Bay Rd.
Sandpoint, ID 83864
208-263-5807

Rose Creek Vineyards
111 West Hagerman
Hagerman, ID 83332
208-837-4413

Ste. Chapelle Vineyards
14068 Sunnyslope Road
Caldwell, ID 83605
208-888-9463

Weston Winery
16316 Orchard Ave.
Caldwell, ID 83605
208-459-2631

Index by Recipe Name

Index by Winery and Recipe Contributor